Contours of
AFRICAN
AMERICAN
POLITICS

Contours of
AFRICAN
AMERICAN
POLITICS

Volume III
Into the Future: The Demise of
African American Politics?

Edited by
Georgia A. Persons

Transaction Publishers
New Brunswick (U.S.A.) and London (U.K.)

Library of Congress Catalog Number: 2012007989
ISBN: 978-1-4128-5170-1
Printed in the United States of America

Library of Congress Cataloging-in-Publication Data

Contours of African American politics / Georgia A. Persons, editor.
    v. cm.
    An anthology of articles drawn from prior issues of the National Political Science Review.
        Contents: v. 1. Race and representation in American politics -- v. 2. Black politics and the dynamics of social change -- v. 3. Into the future: the demise of African American politics?
        ISBN 978-1-4128-4775-9 (v. 1) -- ISBN 978-1-4128-4776-6 (v. 2) -- ISBN 978-1-4128-5170-1 (v. 3) 1. African Americans--Politics and government. 2. United States--Race relations--Political aspects.
        I. Persons, Georgia Anne. II. National political science review.
E185.615.C664 2012
323.1196'073--dc23

                                                                  2012007989

Volume III
Into the Future: The Demise of the African-American Ethnic Moment?

Contents

Race and Ethnicity in Comparative Perspective, Volume 7; pp. 3-19

*Symposium: Race and Ethnicity
in Comparative Perspective*

Politics and Social Change: The Demise of the African-American Ethnic Moment?

Georgia A. Persons
Georgia Institute of Technology

T his essay is driven by two sets of interwoven and interrelated concerns regarding both the theory and practice of that which we call black politics. The first set of concerns is best characterized by what one might euphemistically call "the malaise of black politics." This euphemism refers to the fact that both the study and practice of black politics in America has reached a state of seeming inertia. There is very little which is new in terms of theory building or engaging analyses on the part of scholars. In analyzing the practice of black politics, scholars are increasingly inclined to speak disparagingly and despairingly of a politics without meaning or strategic logic. We see a persistence and preponderance of studies which describe and analyze the racially tinged dynamics of electoral contests in which blacks figure prominently as candidates or as major voting blocs. Most of these studies are directed toward answering questions about the changing or unchanging tendencies of whites to, with a few exceptions, offer only limited support for black candidates or only limited support for black issues and concerns.

Some studies of electoral dynamics specifically focus on deracialization strategies, defined as the eschewing of issues and tactics that are explicitly designed to mobilize black voter support beyond expressions of racial solidarity based on the symbolism of black candidates in favor of an issue set and campaign tactics designed to appeal to white voters by embracing issues that tend towards neutrality in racial impact and which can be projected as embracing the greater interests of all voters independent of race. Such studies follow the same line of inquiry as the general set referred to above. Careful analysis of deracialization cases always return to questions of the issue set on which such campaigns are mounted and the relevance of these campaigns in supporting a purposive politics of black advancement.

In the main, studies limited to explicating racial dynamics in electoral contests have long ceased to inform, particularly in terms of theory building, and only offer the negligible contribution which keenly observant laypersons might assert without the benefit of presumably sophisticated analysis: that in spite of three decades of exposure to large numbers of black candidates, and in spite of adjustments in issues and tactics on the part of black candidates, that is, the adoption of strategies of deracialization, white voters, in the main, do not vote for black candidates in large numbers when there is a choice of a white candidate to support. This singular finding holds whether the unit of analysis is a mayoral race, a contest for governor, a campaign for Congress, the state legislature, city council, or school board. In the main, black electoral successes are by far disproportionately attributable to solid black voter support.

A major dimension of the malaise of black politics is evidenced by the fact that analysts of black politics, especially black analysts, endlessly lament what they see as the lack of purpose in black politics in actual practice. At the core of the lament is a recognition and assertion that black politics has lost its zeal and purpose, and yet the black predicament persists as one of social inequality for all blacks, significant economic disparities for most blacks, and economically dire straits for a disproportionate number of blacks. The once promising momentum provided by a highly charged socio-political movement and the expectations of a responsive environment in major policy-making bodies of the national government have eroded into memory and history. Indeed, the current lament is reinforced and made more poignant by analyses of the high tide of black politics, that is, the civil rights movement and its successor movement, the electoral-based "new black politics." Such analyses are nearly consistent in suggesting that the legacies of this extended mobilization are significantly disappointing and very much wanting. The most recent and noted analysis of this type is that by Robert C. Smith in his latest book which bears the very provocative title of We Have No Leaders (Smith, 1996).

Yet despite this lament and the recognition of a decided and seemingly irreversible change in the nature, thrust, and direction of black politics, analysts of black politics generally have not responded with a conceptual framework which takes account of this change. Yet major questions are raised by this situation. How do we understand this state of affairs? What does this situation convey about the limits of social and political change, and how might the lessons of this situation inform the practice of black politics in the future?

A second major set of concerns which drive the thrust of this essay has to do with how to merge effectively an informative and engaging discussion of the African-American predicament of race in the United States with considerations of ethnicity in comparative perspective. Any analytical or expository exploration of race and ethnicity in comparative perspective encounters both awkwardness and significant difficulties when considering the U.S. context and the situation of blacks in America. There is an almost universal tendency to say and think "race" when considering the situation of blacks in the United States. This is reasonable given the omnibus, though bogus, category of race that has been applied to peoples around the world and the continuing legacies of slavery that significantly define the black predicament in the United States. In the international context, when examining or explaining intergroup conflict, which appears to be defined by differences of basic group identity, analysts and lay persons alike are inclined to label such conflicts as ethnic-based conflicts, frequently so even when such conflicts also parallel demarcations along lines of skin color, or what we call race. In the United States one rarely hears use of the concept of ethnicity anymore though the concept was liberally applied to conflicts in the late 1800s and around the turn of the century. In the current period one sees liberal use of the concept of "minority group conflict" in reference to conflicts between blacks and other minorities, and use of the term racial conflict for conflicts between groups which are lumped together as blacks and whites. In the United States, the issue of race has, in the main, easily dwarfed issues of ethnicity for the past 100 years.

Yet from the perspective of scholarship and theory, important questions emerge in joint considerations of race and ethnicity. One compelling question that immediately arises is how does the situation of African Americans and the U.S. race problem fit within a comparative framework? How might the conceptual lens of ethnicity inform the African-American predicament? By predicament I refer to the persistent oppression of blacks as an identifiable group in American society and the persistent failure of varied strategic efforts to satisfactorily ameliorate or resolve that predicament. In terms of the practice of black politics, are there insights from the experiences and analyses of ethnicity as a social and political phenomenon which might inform the development of strategic considerations in the struggle for full social and political equality for African Americans?

The objectives of this essay are not to provide definitive answers to the questions raised to this point or other questions raised herein. Rather the objectives are more modest. A primary objective is to provoke reflection on the status and thrust of African-American politics by viewing them through the conceptual and analytical lens of ethnicity. Implicit, and sometimes explicit, in this discussion is the assertion that the conceptual framework of ethnicity elicits insights—especially those of a developmental perspective—which are not provided by the traditional analytical framework of race. A second objective of this essay is to provoke scholarly and practical discourse about African-American politics from a fresh, and perhaps controversial, perspective which might in turn lead to consideration of some of the issues raised and implied herein in a more structured research agenda. A considerable portion of this essay is devoted to the scholarly explication of the concept of identity, a discussion which is likely to be quite familiar to comparativists but less familiar to scholars of American politics. The focus then shifts to a discussion of the ethnic experience in America as a means of rounding out an analytical canvas against which to contemplate the evolving status of blacks in the United States and the state of black politics. In a sense the essay ends where it begins, by raising questions about what the current state of practical politics and scholarly considerations in African-American politics portend for the future of black America. In this regard the essay is admittedly incomplete, a condition imposed in part by the very nature of the questions raised herein.

How might we begin an analysis that facilitates consideration of the racial situation in the United States through the conceptual lens of ethnicity? First, we must consider that within the context of a global or comparative scanning of intergroup conflicts, which can be characterized as ethnic conflict or ethno-racial conflict, the African-American situation is merely one of a large set of ethnic-based conflicts that have been played out in varying degrees of hostility and abject inhumanity across space and over the span of history, and which persist to the present time. Indeed such conflicts are a constant, over time and across space. Although the specific groups involved vary from place to place and time to time, the phenomenon of ethnic or ethno-racial conflict appears a constant of the global human condition. In other words, that which we call a problem of race in America is but a variant of global, ethno-political conflict.

A crystallization of the argument which is posited here as evolving theory and which provides the context for considering the remainder of this essay may be stated as follows: Is there in effect an identifiable and relatively brief period in the socio-political history of an oppressed ethnic group when the group is able to utilize its ethnic identity as a primary resource to achieve optimum mobilization, reap maximum possible benefits from the host political system, after which the group experiences a phased demobilization when both the strengths and benefits of ethnic identity wane and eventually disappear? In other words, is there an "ethnic moment" in the life of oppressed ethnic groups when the group experiences some indeterminate level of successful political and social mobilization and empowerment after which the significance of ethnic identity in determining the political behavior of the group wanes and the strength of and attachment to the ethnic bond dissipates? The obvious follow-up questions are: Have we experienced the apogee of the African-American ethnic moment in the United States and might we now be well into experiencing the demise of the African-American ethnic moment? If so, what are the implications of this kind of socio-political life-cycle for the theory and practice of black politics?

Understanding the Ethnic Phenomenon

At any point in time there exists numerous open conflicts around the world which are fueled by ethnic differences. Death tolls mount in numbers which stagger and numb the mind. Like a migrating viral strain, the phenomenon of ethnic conflict occurs in what are seemingly random patterns in different settings across space, and appear endlessly over the span of time. As Harold Isaacs so poignantly described it, "Ishmael and Isaac clash and part in panic and retreat to their caves" (Isaacs, 1975: 3). From time to time analysts have calculated both the number of open ethnic conflicts and their accompanying death tolls. Some 7.5 million deaths have been attributed to ethnic conflicts between the end of World War II and 1968 in some two dozen conflicts (Isaacs, 1975: 3–4). More recently Ted Gurr identified some 233 groups worldwide who were, in 1990, experiencing either economic or political discrimination, or both, and who were potential candidates for open, warlike ethnic conflict or, who were already engaged in such conflicts. Other tallies have gone as high as 435 depending on the categorization scheme utilized and the time in which the tallies were taken (Gurr, 1993).

One might expect that a phenomenon of such universality and such serious consequences might be fully understood except that a review of the literature does not point to this conclusion. It is rather the case that the best scholarly explanations of the phenomenon of ethnicity are at once complementary, contradictory, and also confusing.

In regard to scholarship on ethnicity, analysts generally set forth two major explanations of its origins. The primordialist perspective views ethnicity as a basic group identity: "basic in that fundamental human attributes are passed down from one generation to another" (Isaacs, 1975). These "assumed givens of social existence" include blood and kinship connections, broadly shared ancestral ties, shared religion, language, historical experiences, common social mores, similar and distinguishing physical characteristics (Geertz, 1973; Isaacs, 1975).

According to this perspective, one is born into an identity which is not only significant but is frequently so intense as to appear immutable over time and across space. According to this view, ethnicity derives from a cultural interpretation of descent (Keyes, 1982) and though the strength of this bond varies widely from person to person and from society to society, these bonds are seen as emanating from an affinity that is more "natural and even spiritual" than other social bonds, such as social class, for example (Geertz, 1973; Stack, 1986). Ethnicity is seen as a basic individual and group identity which may wax and wane in intensity but yet remain as a persistent or permanent part of the individual attachment and group existence (Stack, 1986: 9).

The primordialist perspective embraces a strong socio-psychological dimension which bonds the individual to the group and which answers the profoundly fundamental question of "Who am I?" According to this view, ethnicity also serves as a basis for distinguishing the group at the level of "we" and differentiating the group from "the other." It is this latter manifestation of the meaning and significance of ethnicity as identity which forms the basis of irrational appeals and fuels the oppressive and genocidal tendencies ever present in human history.

While the primordialist perspective acknowledges changes in the relative intensity of ethnic identity over time and across space and different circumstances, it is the rigidity of the primordialist perspective in its focus on the persistence of ethnic identity which forms the basis of major challenges by the structuralist or instrumentalist perspective. In brief, the structuralist/instrumentalist perspective holds that ethnic identity is socially constructed without the necessity or prerequisite of deep cultural ties, and derives from objective intergroup differences in the distribution of economic resources and political authority. From this perspective, ethnicity is situational and is greatly influenced and determined by social contexts in which rights, opportunities, and the distribution of other resources are determined differentially by the rules of the game which prevail in a given social setting. Ethnicity then is one of many social identities such as social class upon which individuals may form bonds. Both ethnicity and social class, it is argued, are identities that are structurally determined, and thus are not only situational but also transitory. Ethnicity in this view is seen as a form of social identity which individuals adopt in the pursuit of self-interests and collective group interests and is defined in relation to distinct stimuli (Nagel and Olzak, 1982; Rothchild, 1981).

The structuralist/instrumentalist perspective holds that much of ethnic identity and resulting ethnic mobilizations stem from processes of modernization which bring different groups together in sustained, competitive interactions. In these situations, ethnicity emerges not as a natural tendency, but as a practical tendency which serves a particular social function directed towards advancing individual self-interest and collective group interests. Challengers argue that structuralist interpretations of ethnicity are embedded in the larger worldview of liberalism, which holds that "as mankind moved from a primitive, tribal stage of social organization to an advanced state of modernity undergirded by advanced industrialization, capitalist political economy, and the forces of globalization, such premodern and atavistic ties as ethnicity would recede in salience and even disappear" (Stack, 1986: 6; Smith, A., 1981). But as has been pointed out "the enlightenment project" has failed; postmodern society is not at all free of supposedly premodern and atavistic ties such as ethnicity.

The primordialist and structuralist perspectives stand at opposite ends of a continuum of explanations and analytical engagements of the phenomenon of ethnicity. What we might refer to here as some middle-ground perspectives help to account for the many questions that fertilize the analytical common ground between these two dominant perspectives. The merger of the two dominant perspectives appear in conceptualizations that focus more on the dimensions and manifestations of change in the strength of ethnic identity. These merger perspectives, referred to as ethnogenesis perspectives, hold that ethnicity is analogous to "a gyroscope which changes form, content, and boundaries over time, and which crystallizes in response to a range of political, social, economic, and cultural forces" (Keyes, 1982).

For the ethnogenesis perspectives, ethnicity in its many variants manifests a momentum which at times "veers toward assimilation and at other times leans toward more highly conscious differentiation," or stated another way, "swings from permeability and fluidity to intense ethnonationalism" (Smith, A., 1981; Stack, 1986). While these perspectives recognize the role and significance of external stimuli in generating and fueling ethnic identity and thus parallel structuralist perspectives, ethnogenesis perspectives also effectively assert the permanency of ethnicity as a more or less residual social formation that may be called forth to assume a forceful and salient position in individual identity and collective group behavior. Ethnogenesis perspectives parallel primordialist perspectives in arguing that it appears difficult, if not indeed wishful, to firmly assert that ethnicity as a significant factor in individual and group identity ever disappears in the sense that it becomes so irrelevant as to be essentially or effectively forgotten, or rendered largely impervious to effective appeals.

Part of the complexity of understanding ethnicity, particularly in some parts of the world, is its very close companionship with other forms of individual and group identity. For example, ethnicity in many settings is reinforced by other major formations of individual and or group identity, such as religion and nationalist identity. In some cases, ethnicity effectively exists coterminously with religion and/or nationalism such that the two are intertwined and effectively inseparable (Gellner, 1994; Smith, A., 1991; Ryan, 1990). While it is relatively easy to comprehend that religious identity is a social adaptation, it is much less readily comprehended that ethnic identity is similarly an adaptation, a mere social construction. Yet many analysts insist that ethnic identity like religious identity are both social constructs.

There are other conceptualizations of ethnicity that similarly constitute middle-range theories. For example, Ted Gurr somewhat sidesteps the primordialist versus structuralist dichotomy and debate by classifying all ethnic groups as communal groups. According to Gurr, communal groups are highly persistent, having antedated the emergence of the modern state system, and are destined to persist and re-emerge independent of the drawing and redrawing of nation-state boundaries. For Gurr, "communal groups are psychological communities: groups whose core members share a distinctive and enduring collective identity based on cultural traits and lifeways that matter to them and to others with whom they interact." Gurr identifies multiple bases for communal identity including shared historical experiences or myths, religious beliefs, language, ethnicity, region of residence, and sometimes customary occupations. We see significant elements of both the primordialist and structuralist perspectives within Gurr's conceptualization. Indeed, in his noted study of comparative communal groups, Gurr "assumes that all collective identities, whether centered on a communal group or a national state, are to a degree situational and transitory."Yet he does not totally embrace the extreme of this position, which regards all communal groups as merely one variation of transitory association created to pursue the material and political interests of the group members. However, Gurr does assert that the emergence of unity among ethnoclasses, such as Asian Americans, is the cumulative consequence of their treatment by dominant groups (Gurr, 1993).

Gurr is one of a few analysts who have included African Americans in globally comparative classification schemes of ethnic or communal groups. Gurr asserts a basic dichotomy between communal groups: national peoples and minority peoples. National peoples are defined as regionally concentrated groups that have lost their cultural and linguistic distinctiveness and want to protect or re-establish some degree of politically separate existence. In contrast, minority peoples are defined as having a defined socioeconomic or political status within a larger society—based on some combination of their ethnicity, immigrant origin, economic roles, and religion—and are concerned about protecting or improving that status. National peoples seek separation or autonomy from the states that rule them; minority peoples seek greater access or control (Gurr, 1993: 15). African Americans are further classified by Gurr as an example of an ethnoclass, distinct in their economic status within the broader society and persistent in their demands for more equitable treatment. The solidarity of ethnoclasses is presumed to be largely a function of their treatment by dominant groups. For Gurr, ethnoclasses differ sharply from other communal groups such as ethnonationalists who might be engaged in fighting a civil war or defending indigenous rights (Gurr, 1993).

Obviously the situation of African Americans somewhat straddles that of ethnonationalists in that they were once the subjects of a civil war, and for various brief moments in their political development, the urge for sectional, cultural, and political separation has been manifest at various levels of saliency. The key determinant of the current status and subsequent classification of African Americans among communal groups is the fact of major changes in the group's status which have been wrought via protest, public policy, and subsequent broad-based social change such that the level of oppression experienced by the group is frequently highly amorphous and generally less than egregious when compared with earlier experiences and conditions. Thus, within the context of theories of comparative communal groups, the status of African Americans as an ethnoclass in American society means that the strength of the ethnic bond between African Americans, while enduring, is not expected to have as firm a basis for persistent social and political mobilization as that of some other communal or ethnic groups.

In sum, how is it that we understand ethnicity? Ethnicity is a highly complex phenomenon and is manifest in myriad variations and complexities in different settings around the globe. Analysts seem to have arrived at general consensus on some major elements and characteristics of ethnicity:

1. Ethnicity emanates from within and among specific groups and has at its base an intentional inclusivity and deeply held sense of identity which has psychological, socio-cultural, and political dimensions.
2. Ethnicity is a form of basic human identity and is more enduring and more amenable to social and political manipulation than other social formations, such as social class.
3. Ethnicity at times appears to be primordial, or socially analogous to a genetically determined condition, however, it derives from a cultural interpretation of descent.
4. Ethnicity is a social construct that varies in its profundity under different circumstances. Ethnicity varies in intensity over time and thus is not fixed.
5. There is little support, theoretical or empirical, for the notion that ethnicity is a "pre-enlightenment" phenomenon that automatically disappears in the face of modernization.
6. Explanatory theories of how the demise of ethnic consciousness occurs are incomplete though various processes have been observed, and analysts agree that history is replete with evidence of the rise and fall of ethnic groups, and the complete demise of some ethnic groups.
7. Explanations of the demise of ethnic groups, through loss of ethnic consciousness or absence of identifiable physical presence include: (a) conquest and coerced assimilation; (b) immigration and eventual voluntary assimilation; (c) conquest and extinction; and (d) successful assimilation and extinction.

The American Ethnic Experience

If, comparatively speaking, African Americans comprise an ethnoclass as Gurr contends, then we might ask what has been the experience of other ethnoclass groups in the U.S. context and how might these patterns inform an assessment of the African American ethnoclass experience? There are, of course, some major differences between African Americans and other minority or ethnoclass groups in the United States. First, the intensity and level of oppression experienced by African Americans has no parallels among the experiences of other groups in the United States. Second, the enduring marker of skin color has not been a part of the ethnic experience of other groups. Both of these factors have at times been immutable obstacles that have at later times appeared to be at least marginally transcendent. The elusiveness of the menace of race needs no explanation here.

Despite the social and political preponderance of a racial divide in America, the nation has had an interestingly rich ethnic experience in which the place and status of multiple ethnic groups or ethnoclasses have evolved over time, and in which ethnic identity among different groups has waxed, waned, and seemingly dissipated as a salient factor in political behavior. In fact, in terms of political empowerment, one can readily identify an extended pattern of ethnoclass succession, of which blacks have been a part.

The main ethnic experience in America that has reached maturity has been that of the groups that are referred to collectively as white ethnics. Other groups have manifest a different and still evolving ethnic experience. For example, Asians have been present in the United States for an extended period of time and the diversity among this group has increased over time. However, their presence has only recently been translated into nascent political capital and we have not seen the use of the kind of ethno-racially based mobilization that has characterized black and Hispanic politics. In characterizing the Asian-American ethnic experience in the United States, one can reasonably argue that it is still evolving. One can make a similar argument about the still evolving Hispanic experience in the United States. Although Hispanics have increasingly utilized ethnic appeals in political mobilization (Kitano and Daniels, 1988).

The core of the American ethnic experience tracks back to: (1) the great wave of immigration that characterized the late 1800s and early 1900s; (2) the unfavorable treatment of these immigrants by the first settler group of white Anglo-Saxon Protestants; and (3) the emergence of majoritarian democracy in America. This specific time period was one of major social and political change. Structural changes expanded the franchise to all white males by elimination of the requirement of ownership of property as a requirement for voting. The adoption of the secret ballot led to the subsequent displacement of one social class group by other groups in the ranks of political leadership. The latter developments were facilitated by the emergence of ethnic voting in which individuals utilized ethnic group identity as the basis for political appeals and group mobilization. Ethnic voting quickly became a reliable mechanism for empowerment of immigrant groups, first by the Irish who also utilized a common religion as a reinforcing factor. The Irish Catholics were followed by Italians, Poles, Jews, and other groups. Robert Dahl characterized the phenomenon of ethnic-based appeals as such: "Any political leader who could help members of an ethnic group to overcome the handicaps and humiliations associated with their identity, who could increase the power, prestige, and income of an ethnic or religious out-group, automatically had an effective strategy for earning support and loyalty" (Dahl, 1961: 33).

In the American ethnic experience, the expression of ethnicity in political form reflected the use of ethnicity as a practical mechanism for securing enhanced rewards from the political system. In terms of broad based socio-political change, a system of cumulative inequalities in which social status, education, wealth, and political influence were united in the same hands gave way to a system of dispersed inequalities in which different groups had access to different kinds of resources (Dahl, 1961). This confluence of structural changes, which made for a more egalitarian political environment, and social change, which made for a political climate that was generally more receptive to participation by out-groups, has been repeated over time in the United States. The result has been a succession of ethnic and racial groups including most recently African Americans and Hispanics who have taken their turn on the political stage. In the latter case, socio-political change and group succession have come as the result of social movement activity and protracted political struggle, which resulted in structural changes that facilitated political mobilization. However, the mobilizing political appeals have been racial and ethnic appeals, made easy by drawing on the stark contrasts in the social, economic, and political status between blacks and whites, with Hispanics having benefited from the policy advances extended to them in the aftermath of the civil rights movement.

Ethnic voting in America saw its apotheosis in the political machine that dominated big-city politics and heavily influenced national politics for decades. The political machine was undermined by the structural changes that were wrought by the Progressive Reform Movement of the early 1920s and that largely reflected a class-based backlash of middle-class WASPs (white Anglo-Saxon Protestants). However, also contributing to the demise of the political machine and the phenomenon of ethnic voting was the social and economic upward mobility of the white ethnic groups that formed the primary support base of these phenomena. In short, successful assimilation led to a diminished need for ethnic-based political support structures and a decline in ethnic political appeals and ethnic responses. While a total loss of ethnic identity in social and cultural dimensions has most likely not occurred, there does seem to have been a real demise in politically significant ethnic solidarity, which is operational on a sustained basis among white ethnic groups in America, with the possible exception of Jews. Jews in the United States form a primary support base for the struggle of Jews in Israel and, according to Gurr's definition, constitute a national people. Many American Jews are very closely identified with the Israeli struggle for a secure Jewish homeland and this is one factor that helps to reinforce their group identity. For other white ethnic groups who were merely "minority peoples" seeking to improve their social and economic status within the mainstream host society, the success of that struggle has resulted in a significant demise in ethnic identity and solidarity as a salient factor in political behavior.

Major analysts of the American ethnic experience in have always assumed that the significance of ethnic identity would wane over time, change forms, and largely persist as a residual effect on voting behavior. It was assumed that ethnic voting would evolve from its manifestation as a reflector of socioeconomic homogeneity within a given ethnic group to a later function as a means of achieving symbolic political representation in electing members of the group to political office by appealing to group members across all socioeconomic strata and to a final stage when the ethnic group became socio-economically heterogeneous such that ethnic appeals alone would be insufficient to win votes (Dahl, 1961; Persons, 1991). One analyst states it in this way: "It seems likely that this will be the legacy of ethnic politics: when national origins are forgotten, the political allegiances formed in the days of ethnic salience will be reflected in the partisan choices of many totally assimilated descendants of the old immigrants" (Wolfinger, 1965).

What might we conclude about the American ethnic experience? We might easily make a compelling argument that "the ethnic moment" for white ethnic groups in the United States, with the possible exception of Jews, has flourished and passed largely because the external stimuli that buttressed such ethnic identity and solidarity have significantly waned. The U.S. ethnic experience has been one in which the place and status of multiple ethnic groups have evolved over time, in which ethnic identification among different groups has been strengthened as a response to hostile treatment by dominant groups, in which ethnic identity has been utilized as a political resource in exacting particularistic political and economic gains from the society, and in which, for many groups, ethnic identity has waxed, waned, and significantly dissipated if not disappeared.

In the main, the legacy of the ethnic experience in America has been a significant flavoring of the national culture and a significant though mainly temporary impact on the nation's politics. Ethnicity has not remained a persistent determinant of the nation's politics nor of the status of different groups. One might argue that the phenomenon of race has had a homogenizing effect on white ethnic identity in the United States, thereby weakening retention of politically connected ethnic identity. Or one might argue the structuralist perspective, that the need for ethnic-based mobilization among white ethnics no longer exists and therefore the level of ethnic identity has waned accordingly.

Incomplete Empowerment and the Issue of Effective Strategies

Clearly, the central question to which this essay points is whether the African-American ethnic moment has passed, or will pass in a manner similar to that of white ethnics in America and that of other ethnic groups around the world. Direct assessment of that question is beyond the objectives and scope of this essay. However, the question is powerfully suggestive of the need for exploring alternative explanatory paths in assessing the situation of post-civil rights black politics, and for contemplating the future state of black America. Much of the lament of post-civil rights black politics and thus the implicit and sometimes explicit explanation of the situation focuses on the issue of strategic failures in the sense of what are perceived as actually defective strategies or a failure to effectively achieve necessary strategy shifts. Indeed, it is worth noting that the focus on strategy has been central to both the scholarly analysis and actual practice of black politics. There has been a consistent focus on the benefits and limitations of identifiable and reasonably well developed strategies for political empowerment, and much of our understanding of black politics is built around an understanding of the significance and consequences of a given strategy in relation to others. Moreover, the significance of strategies, both for analysis and practice, is that they: demonstrate the operationalization of an ideological, philosophical, or strategic/tactical formation over time and its consequences; illumine the evolution and unfolding of specific forms of resource formation and mobilization and permit evaluation of the same; and permit assessment of the efficacy and limitations of specific strategies and attendant tactics.

Although analysts might disagree somewhat on the specifics and the order of the delineation below, there is general agreement that black politics after slavery has evolved along the following sequence of strategies:

1. Efforts on the part of "the race men" to effectively articulate the interests of the black race and thereby secure appreciation and respect for a viable course of sustainable economic and social pursuits for blacks as a separate race.
2. Efforts to establish and/or agree on an overarching political ideology that would anchor and direct the political, social, and economic development of the black race.
3. The convening of national conventions of black leaders over many decades in efforts to develop, agree on, and execute national strategies for the political uplift of the race.
4. Litigation-based efforts to secure basic citizenship and civil rights through the courts.
5. The civil rights movement and mass-based mobilization in protest actions to secure rights and public policy responses.
6. The new black electoral politics and the use of black voter mobilization to support black office holding and a desired institutionalization of black interests within the political system.
7. The leveraging and targeted delivery of black votes in presidential contests tied to demands for specific policy and programmatic benefits.
8. The pursuit of policy gains through a significant presence in policy-making institutions of national government.
9. A partial adoption of deracialization to expand black office holding beyond a constrained tether to black bloc voting in order to secure statewide office, and to increase the number of black elected officials.
10. An absence of strategy and an absence of effective organizational resources within the black community to deal with the black predicament.

The delineation of strategies is useful in that on reflection one observes that this series of strategies, though each might have been somewhat faulty in conceptualization and execution, promised and delivered some progress for the race, or at least a sense of forward movement in the struggle. Comprised of a seemingly reasonably ordered outlook and approach toward securing a better future for the race, this past stands in stark contrast to the major defining characteristics of the current period: a situation in which the notion of racial justice has lost its hold on the nation's consciousness; the absence of a compelling narrative of our future as a race, even at the rhyming, rhetorical level; and a sense that a long-standing embrace of the liberal-integrationist ideology now, in the face of persistent segregation in schools and residential patterns, looms large as a ghastly social chimera.

Given this situation, is it reasonable to assume that "relief is just a strategy away"? If so, then what should be the next strategy; around what assumptions and goals should it be anchored?

In one of the most thorough and compelling analyses of black politics in the post-civil rights era, Robert C. Smith implicitly proffers that the civil rights movement was the quintessential effective strategy for black liberation. It is against this standard that Smith implicitly evaluates several lesser strategies—the leveraging of black votes in presidential elections and the pursuit of administrative appointments in the federal policy-making apparatus—which have been pursued in the wake of the civil rights movement. Smith reaches some strong conclusions in his analyses and I paraphrase them here: (1) black political organizations were not well suited to the demands of post-civil rights politics in America, not for pressing systemic responses and change, nor for sustaining an effective mobilization of the black community; (2) in regard to efforts to institutionalize an effective black presence and effective coalitional support for black interests in the institutions of government, such efforts in the post civil rights era have been woefully inadequate; (3) black political efforts have increasingly been caught up in a game between the Democratic and Republican parties, each of whom have sought to reap the benefits of black voter support without incurring the costs of courting that support; (4) that political, social, and economic gains in the post-civil rights era have been far less than satisfactory because the logic of civil rights legislation—upon which many such gains may have been supported—may well have run its course. Perhaps predictably, Smith calls for a return to effective strategy, for development of a mass mobilization for social change.

Perhaps because the past frequently looks more perfect than the present, in reflecting on past strategies one might conclude that the black political leadership has been reasonably astute in gauging the unfolding of change and circumstances such that they adapted reasonably well in engineering the shift from one strategy to another, that is, except for the current period. There is a general consensus among analysts and activists that black politics lost its anchor at the end of the civil rights movement, and there is a correspondingly implicit explanation that the cause was a defective strategy or defective strategy shift (Walters, 1980). Yet, there is no apparent recognition of how best to institute corrective action, nor any apparent sense of just what should be the thrust of the next strategy.

The contributions of the Robert Smith book are many, but its major contribution is the accomplishment of its stated purpose: providing an explication of how the American political system has processed black political demands in the post civil rights era. Smith refers to this as an assessment of the institutionalization of the civil rights movement. In engaging in this explication, Smith raises a critical question, indirectly and perhaps unwittingly, which continues to haunt this reader: whether by bringing the formal rules and procedures of political and social life into theoretical compliance with the dictates of racial justice, the American political system has reached the limits of its capacity for processing of the race problem beyond symbolic responses. If one gives serious consideration to this question, then the issue of effective strategies takes on a very different meaning.

The Long Pause: An Alternative Explanation

There are other scholarly conceptualizations that inform this discussion and one is particularly worth noting, work by Hanes Walton on what he terms the political context variable. Walton defines the political context in both macro-level and micro-level connotations. In its macro-level connotation, the political context encompasses the total political environment to include a particular time period and a particular place, and the convergence of political leadership dynamics, public sentiments on key issues, the nature of public discourse, and the kind of issues that dominate the public agenda. In its micro-level connotation, the political context may refer to a single key variable, such as race, which produces a contextual effect. Walton argues that the dynamic of race is co-directional in its contextual effect in that white behavior around race can influence black political behavior, and black presence in the physical environment as well as strong advocacy of black issue positions can have a strong effect on white voting behavior and political attitudes. In regard to the current period, Walton defines the changed political context as characterized by the revitalization of race as a wedge issue during the Reagan and Bush administrations and the resulting unfavorable change in the support, interpretation, and enforcement of public policies that had favored black equality and that were the legacies of the civil rights and Great Society eras of black political mobilization and Democratic party dominance (Walton, 1997).

The greater contribution of Walton's thinking to this discussion is his notion of serial contextual revolutions and corresponding counter-contextual revolutions. Walton sees contextual revolutions as total transformations of the socio-political environment in which politics occurs. He identifies two recent partisan driven contextual revolutions as having occurred during the Kennedy-Johnson years of 1960–1968, and that of the Reagan-Bush era that continues to define the current period. He identifies two counter-contextual revolutions that were launched by blacks as having occurred during the period 1800–1865 ensuing from actions at the state level to eliminate slavery and racial oppression, and during the 1950s and 1960s when the black struggle to end racial segregation ushered in social and legal support for desegregation. Walton concludes that blacks must continually seek to wage counter-contextual revolutions just to ensure and reestablish their constitutional and legal rights, and that blacks will continue to find novel responses to contextual transformation (Walton and Generett, 1997).

We can easily interpret Walton's argument to suggest that the current period is just another in a series of long pauses in which blacks must work towards a convergence of factors that will make for a political context, inevitable in its coming, which will be more favorable to black interests. The implications of this theory point to an implicit but strongly held assumption that underlies scholarship on black politics: that there will be continual progressive development in black political life leading to an ultimate goal of liberation. It should be pointed out that Walton's thoughts as presented and interpreted here are not part of an extended presentation of a theory of contextual revolutions and the scholarly community must await his full development of such a theory.

Politics and Social Change: After the Long Pause

Hanes Walton's analysis of contextual revolutions resonates with a consistent theme in American political history of a kind of periodicity or cyclical pattern in the formation of a temporally bound, but determinative socio-cultural ethos that forms the crucible out of which politics emerge and that shapes the bounds of that which is acceptable and possible within the political realm at any given time (Burnham, 1970; Huntington, 1981; Schlesinger, 1986). This phenomenon may also be subsumed under the conceptual rubric of social change. By social change I refer to broad-based change or evolution in public values, attitudes, and sentiments, which in turn have varying ramifications in all aspects of human existence, including changes in gender roles, family life, politics and culture, religion, civic life, scientific thinking, and more. Among the forces that spur broad-based social change are major technological developments; major economic change, especially changes in the nature of work; large-scale movements of human populations; natural and man-made disasters such as famine and war; and collective action such as social movements. Social change redefines expectations, values, and preferences, both individually and collectively, thereby transforming society. In reflecting on the evolution of the various strategies delineated earlier in this essay, one can discern some of the broad contours of social change that have undulated across time and altered the proximate contexts within which various strategies have been deployed. What may have appeared to be defective strategies may, on closer examination, yield insights into how strategies were overtaken or undermined by the forces of social change.

Analysts are much accustomed to focusing on how some dimensions of social change affect and alter the context of black life although one can easily argue that much more research in this vein is urgently needed. However, we have not focused much on how black life, in terms of behavioral manifestations, is shaped and altered by broad-based social change. Contemplation on a few questions will illumine this point. For example, it is easy to think of African-American identity as significantly primordially determined. However, to a non-negligible extent the identity of African Americans has been defined by the black-white racial bifurcation that has characterized American society. What will be the impact on black identity as that bifurcation breaks down? To state the question differently, how will a growing multicultural society affect African-American identity? We have recently seen that a gradual assimilation via interracial marriages has led to demands for non-racial or multi-racial identities on the U.S. Census by individuals who would have earlier accepted the heretofore inevitability of being labeled African-American (Cose, 1997).

What will be the long-term impact of a growing public discourse and much informal public policy that suggests an interchangeability of minority groups? Increasingly African Americans are being morphed into a generic category of minorities or people of color, suggestive of a kind of multicultural pacifism in which the disadvantaged status of blacks ceases to warrant a claim on national politics and public policy. We might contemplate the fact that African-American descendants of Generation X will have no links to the civil rights movement, neither in direct memory nor via direct connections of their parents to this defining moment in African-American life and identity.

The notion of the African-American ethno-racial moment in demise suggests that, due to major social change, the experience of blacks in America has reached a critical point of transition in which both the behavior of the larger political system towards blacks and the behavior of blacks as a group will manifest profound changes. There is inherent in the structuralist view of ethnic identity a co-directionality of behavior between the host political system and the ethnic group that is mutually re-enforcing. System behavior induces group behavior and group behavior induces system behavior, at least up to a certain point. The "certain point" is largely an unknown as analysts have little understanding of the life cycle of ethnic conflicts nor any meaningful cross-national understanding of the peaceful resolution of ethnic conflict. Peaceful resolution seems to occur within the context of ineluctable change with critical turning points and key variables being largely unidentifiable except as historical conjecture. Clearly one cannot argue with great confidence that we are indeed witnessing the demise of the African-American ethnic moment. We can only raise questions of whether there is something peculiarly different and extraordinarily meaningful about the nature of these times in regard to the future status of blacks in America, for African-American group identity, and for the theory and practice of black politics.

References

Burnham, Walter Dean. 1970. *Critical Elections and the Mainsprings of American Politics.* New York: Norton.

Cose, Ellis. 1997. "Census and the Complex Issue of Race." *Social Science and Modern Society,* 34, 6 (September/October): 9–13.

Dahl, Robert. 1961. *Who Governs? Democracy and Power in an American City.* New Haven: Yale University Press.

Geertz, Clifford, 1973. *The Interpretation of Cultures: Selected Essays.* New York: Basic Books.

Gellner, Ernest. 1994. *Encounters with Nationalism.* Cambridge, MA: Blackwell Publishers.

Gurr, Ted. 1993. *Minorities at Risk: A Global View of Ethnopolitical Conflicts*. Washington, DC: United States Institute of Peace.

Huntington, Samuel P. 1981. *American Politics: The Politics of Disharmony*. Cambridge, MA: Harvard University Press.

Isaacs, Harold. 1975. *Idols of the Tribe: Group Identity and Political Change*. New York: Harper and Row.

Keyes, Charles F. 1982. "The Dialectics of Ethnic Change." In *Ethnic Change*, ed. Charles F. Keyes. Seattle: University of Washington Press.

Kitano, Harry, and Roger Daniels. 1988. *Asian Americans: Emerging Minorities*. Englewood Cliffs, NJ: Prentice Hall.

Nagel, Joane, and Susan Olzak. 1982. "Ethnic Mobilization in New and Old States: An Extension of the Competition Model." *Social Problems*, 30, 2 (December): 122–37.

Persons, Georgia. 1991. "Politics and Changing Political Processes in Urban America." In *Contemporary Urban America*, ed. Marvel Lang. Lanham, MD: University Press of America.

Rothchild, Joseph. 1981. *Ethnopolitics: A Conceptual Framework*. New York: Columbia University Press.

Ryan, Stephen. 1990. *Ethnic Conflict and International Relations*. Brookfield, VT: Dartmouth Publishing Company.

Schlesinger, Arthur, Jr. 1986. *The Cycles of American History*. Boston: Houghton Mifflin.

Smith, Anthony. 1981. *The Ethnic Revival in the Modern World*. Cambridge: Cambridge University Press.

———. 1991. *National Identity*. Reno: University of Nevada Press.

Smith, Robert. 1996. *We Have No Leaders: African Americans in the Post-Civil Rights Era*. Albany: State University of New York Press.

Stack, John F., Jr. "Ethnic Mobilization in World Politics: The Primordial Challenge." In The Primordial Challenge: Ethnicity in the Contemporary World, ed. John F. Stack, Jr. Westport, CT: Greenwood, 1986.

Walters, Ronald. 1980. "The Challenge of Black Leadership: An Analysis of the Problem of Strategy Shift." *The Urban League Review*, 5 (Summer 1980): 77–88.

Walton, Hanes, Jr. "The Political Context Variable: The Transformation Politics of the Reagan, Bush, and Clinton Presidencies." In *African American Power and Politics*, ed. Hanes Walton, Jr., 9–32. New York: Columbia University Press, 1997.

Walton, Hanes, Jr., and William O. Generett, Jr. 1997. "African Americans, Political Context, and the Clinton Presidency: The Legacy of the Past in the Future." In *African American Power and Politics*, ed. Hanes Walton, Jr., 373–78.

Wolfinger, Raymond. "The Development and Persistence of Ethnic Voting." *American Political Science Review* 59 (1965): 896–908.

Part VII

A New Structure of Ambition in Black Politics

Beyond the Boundaries, Volume 12; pp. 139-162

The Third Wave: Assessing the Post-Civil Rights Cohort of Black Elected Leadership

Andra Gillespie
Emory University

Introduction

By all accounts, African Americans[1] are being introduced to a third generation of black elected leadership. Ironically, this new phase, like the phases that preceded it, is called "new black politics." What distinguishes this new batch of leaders from their predecessors is their generation (i.e., they were born or came of age after the civil rights movement), their education (i.e., they were educated in Ivy League and other white institutions), and their potential (i.e., they have realistic chances to hold higher executive and legislative positions more frequently than any other generation of black leaders) (Reed and Alleyne, 2002).

This latest wave of black politicians is not immune from criticism. Not least among critics' concerns is whether these new black politicians will advance the substantive and strategic policy goals of the African American community. Yes, some of these women and men can realistically become senators and even president, as Barack Obama has so aptly demonstrated, but at what price? Will they have to abandon a civil rights agenda to gain the electoral advantage needed to attain high office (Martin, 2003)?

Implicit in this discussion of new black politicians is their relative chance for success and the means by which these politicians emerge onto the political spectrum. Is the emergence of this cohort of leadership an organic development emanating from black communities, or are these politicians overly ambitious instrumentalists who are exploiting their racial background for political traction? What is more, does this cohort of elected leadership have a chance at developing a loyal base of black voters, or are they being propped up by white elites seeking to divide and conquer black communities?

The answers to these questions are important because the stakes are so high. The new cohort of black elected officials receive such notoriety because their probability of attaining high office is perhaps greater than it has been for any generation of blacks in the United States. If this cohort of elected leadership meets expectations, ascending in critical numbers to governor's mansions, the U.S. Senate and even the White House, what are the implications for black communities? Clearly, these leaders will be in an unprecedented position to shape public policy. Thus, it seems that the big question is not just what pundits think about new black politicians, but what constituents think about these candidates and whether the material conditions of African Americans will improve under their leadership.

In the pages that follow, I trace the emergence of this new cohort of black leadership. I draw on the Black Leadership literature to see how scholars in the past defined and assessed black leadership. Indeed, they created multiple, yet similar typologies to evaluate leadership. I then use the basic demographic record of the current crop of young black elected leadership to introduce a new model of black leadership, which I in turn apply in describing the post-civil rights cohort.

New Black Politics throughout History

There have been three iterations of new black politics in the post-civil rights era: the widespread election of the first black elected officials in the 1970s; the successes of black candidates in major elections in majority-white jurisdictions in the 1980s; finally, the current rise of young, black moderates, many of whom challenge members of the first wave of black elected officials in majority-black cities and congressional districts. Each wave of black politicians is significant for the barriers that its members traversed. They are also important to study because the rise of each class of black elected officials is concurrent with innovations in campaign strategy. However, despite the campaign innovations, scholars studying these waves of black elected officials have been careful to question whether the programmatic agenda of these black elected officials aligns with the interests of black constituents.

New Black Politics: Phase I

Charles Hamilton notes that after the passage of Voting Rights Act, the focus of black politics, in a literal and academic sense, shifted from the judicial to the legislative/electoral arena. Now that blacks largely had the franchise, the goal became to channel that electoral power into legislative policies that would benefit blacks (Hamilton, 1982). Putting black officials in office was a key first step in achieving that agenda. Indeed, from 1965 to

1988, there was a more than thirteen fold increase in the number of black elected officials (Tate, 1994: 1; see also Williams, 1987: 112).

The elected officials of the first wave of new black politics faced tremendous obstacles. As trailblazers coming on the heels of the civil rights movement, they had to run in still racially tense environments. Furthermore, they had to reconcile with the white portions of their constituency that may have been skeptical of them as leaders (Smith, 1990).

Furthermore, these new black elected officials had difficulty implementing their agenda. As Linda Williams notes, "urban blacks today have reached city hall precisely at the moment when the real power to deliver jobs, money, education and basic services is migrating to higher levels of government and the private sector" (Williams, 1987: 129). She observes that first-wave black politicians came to power during a period of national economic decline and decreased federal aid to cities. As a result, first-wave black mayors were hampered in their efforts to provide redistributive relief to their constituents. What little aid they were able to provide tended to focus on ameliorative policies such as affirmative action and set-asides, which disproportionately benefited middle-class black residents. What is more, blacks ascended to the mayoralty in cities, which severely proscribed their power, limiting some from having control over important functions such as taxation (Williams, 1987: 128-129).

William Nelson further notes that the notion of new black politics being the collective agent for improvement of the whole black community is easier said than done. Using Cleveland as an example, he notes that uniting blacks around a permanent agenda is difficult. Carl Stokes was able to unite blacks under one political banner. However, that union dissolved when Stokes stepped down as leader of Cleveland's black political organization. Diversity of opinion and ambition, then, undermined some attempts for political unity (Nelson, 1982). Moreover, Robert Smith observes that the legislative record of these officials, with respect to their progressive, black politics agenda, has been limited. They only have been able to develop downtown space, implement municipal affirmative action programs, and respond to police brutality (Smith, 1990).

New Black Politics: Phase II

One of the distinguishing features of each wave of new black politics has been the new black candidates' campaign style. While candidates in each wave of new black politics have had some measure of crossover appeal, observers have attributed more crossover appeal to each subsequent generation of new black political candidates. For example, Ardrey and Nelson (1990) note that black elected officials elected in new black politics' first wave, who were largely civil rights leaders, transferred the confrontational style from the movement to the electoral and legislative arena.

Many scholars viewed 1989 as a watershed year for black politics. In November 1989, blacks ascended to the mayoralty for the first time in Seattle (Norm Rice), New Haven (John Daniels), Durham (Chester Jenkins), and New York City (David Dinkins). Most notably, Douglas Wilder was elected governor of Virginia, making him the country's first black governor since Reconstruction. This cluster of elections is particularly important given that these men were elected in majority-white jurisdictions with at least 40 percent of the white vote (McCormick and Jones, 1993: 66, 68).

With their elections, Wilder and his peers ushered in the second wave of new black politics. The second wave is characterized by the prevalent use of a deracialized campaign strategy. McCormick and Jones define a deracialized campaign as one being "in a stylistic fashion that diffuses the polarizing effects of race by avoiding explicit reference to race-specific issues, while at the same time emphasizing those issues that are perceived as racially transcendent, thus mobilizing a broad segment of the electorate" (McCormick and Jones, 1993: 76). McCormick and Jones (1993) go further to articulate this strategy by noting that candidates employing such a strategy convey "a nonthreatening image," (76) "avoid employing direct racial appeals in organizing the black community" (76), and "should avoid emphasis of a racially specific issue agenda (77).

Douglas Wilder clearly exemplifies the deracialized strategy. Strickland and Wheeler note that Wilder, "adopted mainstream and even fiscally conservative positions. He was also able to avoid discussing overtly racial issues" (Strickland and Wheeler, 1992: 210). For example, Wilder's campaign theme was "the 'New Virginia Mainstream,'" and he made law and order, drug enforcement, and his support for the death penalty a key part of his platform (Jones and Clemons, 1993: 140).

While this strategy may be electorally effective, some find it morally troubling and wonder what the implications are for the pursuit of a pro-black political agenda. Earl Sheridan (1996), in his article, "The New Accommodationists," implicitly likens such a strategy to Booker T. Washington's Atlanta Compromise when he writes that instead of lauding black elected officials who deemphasize race to get elected, "America needs Black leaders who will continue the legacy of the 1960s, not the 1890s—men and women who will call for meaningful change in our society" (Sheridan, 1996: 169). He fears that in an attempt to gain office by any means necessary, these officials would abandon the issues of concern to the black community to get votes and would shortchange black interests to stay in power (Sheridan, 1996: 165-166).

McCormick and Jones are a little less fearful of the implications of using a deracialized electoral strategy, but they, too, brace for less progressive politics as a result of the strategy. They write that "In the absence of such demands from a politically organized African American community, there is little reason to expect African American elected officials who capture office in predominantly white political jurisdictions to be in the vanguard of articulating racially-specific policy issues"(McCormick and Jones, 1993: 78).That being said, they proffer that even these politicians will occasionally have to make some explicitly racial overtures to their black constituents, lest these officials lose an important base of support in their communities (McCormick and Jones, 1993: 78).

However, much of the handwringing over the implications of deracialization as a strategy of second-wave black politicians was short-lived. Second-wave politicians experienced a number of setbacks that prevented that cohort from making a long-term impact on the communities they represented. Some setbacks were structural. Doug Wilder, for instance, was constitutionally barred from seeking a second consecutive term as governor of Virginia. Others, such as David Dinkins, had very short tenures in office due to poor public perceptions. (See Kim 2000 for an example of Dinkins alienating black constituents.) However, for a number of politicians in the second wave, they suffered electoral defeats that marked the end of their electoral pursuits. For instance, Harvey Gantt twice lost his bid to represent North Carolina in the U.S. Senate to Jesse Helms in what were racially vitriolic campaigns. Andrew Young lost a bid to be Georgia's governor by wasting time campaigning for white votes in southern Georgia at the expense of campaigning in his base in and around Atlanta. Thus, according to the various authors studying the rise of second-wave politicians in the late 1980s and early 1990s, deracialized candidates overestimated racial goodwill outside of the black community and paid a high electoral price for ignoring black voters (Wilson, 1993; Davis and Willingham, 1993).

Moreover, from an academic perspective, many authors challenged the notion that pure deracialization was even going on in the first place. Mary Summers and Phillip Klinkner, for instance, argue that John Daniels did not run a deracialized campaign in his successful bid to become New Haven's first black mayor. They point to his progressive campaign platform, his integral role in introducing community policing to New Haven and his creation of a needle exchange program, in addition to his willingness to discuss his race on the campaign trail, as evidence that Daniels was not a deracialized candidate (Summers and Klinkner, 1996). Additionally, Lenneal Henderson studied Kurt Schmoke's ascendance to the mayoralty of Baltimore and reached similar conclusions. He contends that Schmoke's efforts at economic redevelopment were racially transcendent, but that Schmoke was not trying to distance himself from black communities. Thus, Schmoke was a "transracial[ized]" black politician and not a deracialized black politician (Henderson, 1996: 172-173).

New Black Politics: Phase III

The current wave of new black politics very much resembles the second wave in that this wave is characterized by ambitious politicians with more moderate politics. What distinguishes this group from its predecessors is its youth and connection to civil rights history. The figures associated with the third wave of new black politics were born after 1960, immediately before or after the passage of all the major civil rights legislation (see Traub, 2002). For example, Barack Obama was born in 1961; Cory Booker was born in 1969; Harold Ford, Jr. and Kwame Kilpatrick were born in 1970. As a result, these figures benefited from the fruits of the struggle and were able to grow up in integrated neighborhoods and attend predominantly white schools from kindergarten to graduate school. However, their youth also means that some perceive this generation as being less likely to relate to the civil rights struggle (see Bositis, 2001: 3-11). While second-wave new black politicians were charged with deliberately not having been active in the civil rights movement, they at least had the benefit of having been eyewitness to the monumental changes that took place in the 1950s and 1960 (see Sheridan 1996: 166).[2] In addition, others view this generation as being untested and unable to point to any record upon which to base their claims of being better legislators or government executives or to a clear agenda around which to organize their candidacies (Martin, 2003).

This perceived lack of identification with the struggle is what raises so much skepticism among older black elites when evaluating this emerging generation of leadership. In an interview with *Savoy* magazine, Ronald Walters voiced the suspicion that this new generation was merely a tool of white elites who wanted to replace more acerbic, older black leaders with less threatening, younger black leaders:

> [The white power structure] would rather supplant [the old guard] with a far more accommodating leadership. They are going to pit them against the so-called old leadership because they have been threatened by the interests and power of the black leadership who really have the influence and control of black people (Walters, quoted in Martin, 2003: 56).

In addition to having had their race consciousness questioned, this generation has also been accused of hubris. David Bositis acknowledged in an interview that young black leaders "imagine themselves as governors, United States Senators, and even President" (Bositis, quoted in Martin, 2003: 56). When Harold Ford, Jr. ran to unseat Nancy Pelosi as House minority leader in 2003, his efforts were rebuffed even by members of the Congressional Black Caucus. Walters notes that Ford's attempted power grab failed because he had not spent years currying favor and garnering support from his colleagues in the House Democratic Caucus. "To step out there because you've got a pretty face and no agenda," Walters said, "you're going to lose every time" (Walters, quoted in Martin, 2003: 56).

If there is anything that does distinguish the third wave of new black politics from the first two waves, it may be that it is the synthesis of the first and second waves. Where we witnessed civil rights activists turned legislators challenge the white power structure in the first wave, and where we witnessed second-wave politicians attempt to join the white power structure, we now see third wave politicians who behave like second-wave politicians and challenge first-wave incumbents for power,[3] often in majority-black jurisdictions, and often with extensive mainstream media support. For instance, Alexandra Starr predicts that moderate politics would probably propel more black candidates to national office (2002). James Traub goes so far as to say that the success of people like Cory Booker and Artur Davis against the Sharpe Jameses and Earl Hilliards of the world would be a "balm to white liberals, whose politics have been so heavily determined by an agonized sense of 'what black people want,' as defined by the black leadership class. And it will be a boon to the Democrats, for it will help heal the ideological rifts within the party" (Traub, 2002: 1).

Analytical Concerns with Phases II and III of New Black Politics

The academy has not been immune from being infatuated with second- and third-wave new black politics because of the non-threatening dimension of their electoral strategy. Strickland and Whicker acquiesce to racism in American society and propose a crossover model for black electoral success. This model calls for espousing conservative positions on issues, deemphasizing race, and having worked outside the civil rights movement. While they do all this, these candidates are supposed to excite and maintain a black voting base (Strickland and Whicker, 1992: 208-209).

Strickland and Whicker acknowledge that catering to whites while not alienating blacks is easier said than done. However, their key mistake is assuming that black voters will be loyal to any black candidate. While that is a gross overgeneralization of black voting preferences in and of itself, Strickland and Whicker fail to account for the situation when two blacks would run against each other. Who should black voters choose, then? In their study of congressional elections, Canon, Schousen, and Sellers (1996) studied the electoral success of black candidates pitted against other black candidates in majority-minority districts. They argue that when first-wave new black politicians run against second- or third-wave new black politicians, the second- or third-wave new black politician will win if whites, who should be a sizable minority of the constituency, vote as a bloc. They assume that whites are more likely to support moderate blacks. However, they do concede that if blacks vote as a bloc, the first-wave new black politician has a better chance of winning.

This focus on which black candidates appeal to white voters (as opposed to which black candidates can best represent the interests of black voters) is what is so troubling to students of black politics. Ronald Walter's aforementioned quote captures this concern (Martin, 2003, 56). Indeed, it is this fixation with keeping whites happy that seems to be an anathema to black self-determination, if only because the focus on this type of black politics shifts the focus away from blacks.

Critics must respond to the question, though, of whether these candidates are out of touch, though. Reed and Alleyne note that the hallmark of third-wave new black politics is their "philosophic mix of political pragmatism, pro-business sensibility, and social progressivism"(Reed and Alleyne, 2002: 84). Martin notes that,"today's black elected official may be more concerned with closing the digital divide, increasing economic opportunities for people of color, and school vouchers..."(Martin, 2003: 54). Are these positions really out of touch with the policy preferences of black constituents? David Bositis would have to concede that these candidates may not be out of touch with their constituents. Reporting the results of the Joint Center's 2002 National Opinion Poll, he notes that a majority of blacks were in favor of vouchers, that younger blacks identified less with the Democratic Party, and that blacks are far more concerned about the economy, foreign affairs, and education than they are about racism (Bositis, 2002: 6, 7, 10). What is more, when the Joint Center compared the political attitudes of black elected officials to the black electorate, they found that generational differences in attitudes among blacks generally paralleled generational differences among black elected officials (Bositis, 2001: 21).

Skeptics need also to consider the substantive critiques levied against older generations of black leadership. While Walters chided the younger generation of black elected officials for being overly ambitious but substantively unfocused and proclaimed that the older generation of black leaders "really have the influence and control of black people" (Walters, quoted in Martin, 2003), he has also acknowledged elsewhere that the earlier vanguard of leadership encountered institutional barriers that limited their effectiveness in providing benefits for blacks (Smith and Walters 1999, 135). His colleague, Robert Smith, argued that post-civil rights elected officials assumed power, but were co-opted by the establishment and thus accomplished very little of their intended programmatic agenda to improve the lives of African Americans. The reality that even the first wave of black politicians failed to deliver policy redress to their black constituents led Smith to boldly proclaim in the title of his book that"We Have No Leaders"(Smith, 1996). This reality begs the questions of whether younger, post-racial candidates really can do more harm than good, relative to the previous generation of leadership, for the advancement of basic African American policy interests, such as ending systemic inequality.

Examining the Typologies of Black Leadership

The exercise of classifying a new, post-racial cohort of leadership is deeply rooted in previous studies of black leadership. In those studies, scholars went to great efforts to classify leaders. The classification scheme they chose varied on the margins, but all focus on identifying distinct leadership styles within the black community based on the leaders' style in dealing with the white power structure.

The extant typologies of black leadership go back to the late 1930s. In 1937, Guy Johnson defined black leaders as either "gradualists" or "revolutionaries" (Ladd, 1966: 148). As their names suggest, gradualists acquiesced to the realities of second-class citizenship in the United States, and revolutionaries challenged the racial caste system. In the classic tome *An American Dilemma*, Gunnar Myrdal created the accommodationist/protest paradigm to classify black leaders. Accommodationists are akin to Johnson's gradualists; and protesters are analogous to Johnson's revolutionaries (Ladd, 1966: 148; see Myrdal, 1944: 720).

Walters and Smith (1999) outline other major typologies created in the early 1960s to define black leadership. James Q. Wilson, for instance, defined black leadership styles on two dimensions. In his view, black leaders were either militants or moderates, basing his typology on the methods these leaders used to achieve specific classes of civil rights goals. Militant leaders used direct action or protest techniques to achieve racial integration, which Wilson termed a "status" goal; moderate leaders, in contrast, tended to try to negotiate with whites to achieve concrete, "welfare" goals for black communities (Wilson, 1960: 218, 235). Thus, a militant leader would lead a protest to achieve a measure of social accommodation for blacks equal to whites while moderate leaders might appeal to white power structures behind the scenes to achieve goals such as more goods and services targeted to black communities (Wilson, 1960: chapter 9).

Drawing on Wilson's scholarship, Everett Ladd uses the notion of welfare and status goals, along with rhetorical style and tactics to create his own typology of leadership. Like Wilson, he notes that at the extremes are conservatives and militants. However, he also notes that there is an intermediate class of leaders known as moderates. Militant leaders seek status goals using confrontational tactics and rhetoric. Conservative leaders seek welfare goals using acquiescent, non-confrontational strategies and rhetoric (usually behind the scenes). Moderate leaders are a hybrid: they seek welfare and status goals depending on the situation using non-confrontational rhetoric. However, they often take advantage of the presence of militants to achieve their goals. They are able to position themselves as the reasonable alternative to the militants and attempt to get access to dominant power structures along these lines (Ladd, 1966: chapter 4).

In her study of black politics in Durham, North Carolina, Elaine Burgess also extends the definition of black leadership beyond the protest-accommodation binary to include other, intermediary types of leadership. In her typology, there were four types of black leaders. On one end of the spectrum were conservative leaders, the old, established black leadership which acquiesced to racial domination and with which the white power structure was more comfortable. Moderates tended to be upper-class blacks who did not devote their full-time and energy to addressing racial issues. They tended to emerge to prominence working on non-racial issues, and they were committed to being part of biracial groups working to address city challenges. Liberals were those black leaders, often from professional backgrounds, who were uncompromising in their commitment to achieving civil rights for blacks. However, their tone was non-confrontational, and they were perceived to be non-threatening, especially in relation to radicals. Radicals were the leaders most prone to be outspoken and to engage in direct action to achieve civil rights. In Burgess' view, they were clearly inspired by Martin Luther King (Burgess, 1962: 181-185; Walters and Smith, 1999: 18).

While there are some clear differences in the typologies mentioned above, their similarities are striking. All of them use a linear continuum to judge a leader based on how radical he or she is. They judge the extent to which a person is radical based on the extent to which these leaders wish to work with powerful whites and whether or not a leader tries to achieve his/her goals through protest or negotiation.

All of the aforementioned studies took place in the midst of the civil rights movement and reflect the diversity of opinion about the efficacy of certain tactics. It would seem logical that in the wake of the legislative victories of the civil rights movement that there would perhaps be some changes in how leadership was defined and categorized. For instance, at the time Burgess was writing, she noted that conservative leaders were losing their prominence in the black community and even white leaders realized that this cohort of leadership's influence in the black community was waning. It seemed to be that racial moderates would fill the role of racial conservatives (Burgess, 1962: 181). Moreover, Robert Smith (1980) contends that in the wake of the Black Nationalist movement, many black elites were radicalized. Thus, even some of the more conservative elements of the black community would likely have been socialized into affirming some measure of race pride, whether it be through membership in a racially specific professional association or some other avenue of racial particularism.

Despite these radical social changes, our understanding of the basic types of black leadership has not changed that much, though there has been some innovation. Walters and Smith acquiesce to the protest-accommodation paradigm in their book. They concede that protesters are far less prevalent, and they contend that most leaders are now accommodationists. They do provide some innovation when they identify different ways black leaders gain legitimacy. One can argue that Walters and Smith define leadership legitimacy on a two-dimensional scale, with white and black acceptance being the x and y axes respectively. Leaders accepted by both black and white communities are "consensus" leaders. Those embraced by the white community and not the black community are called "external" leaders. Those embraced by the black community and not the white community are called "community" leaders. Those who lack credibility in both black and white communities are considered "auto-selected" leaders (Walters and Smith, 1999: 217).

While Walters and Smith's two dimensional rendering of racial accept-ability is helpful, in reality, they are only judging legitimacy on racial accep-tance. Still, others have continued to use the simple binary to define black candidates and politicians. David Canon, Matthew Schousen and Patrick Sellers (1996), for instance, used the terms "old style" and "new style" to describe black candidates running against each other in majority-minority congressional districts. Old-style candidates ran in the protest, confron-tational spirit of the civil rights movement and were thus the racialized candidates; new-style candidates ran racially transcendent campaigns that were more palatable to some of the blacks and the remaining whites in these districts.

Lenneal Henderson (1996), in contrast, creates perhaps the most complex version of race leadership to date. While keeping with the one-dimension-al model of racial radicalism (He defines black leaders on a continuum from non-racial to hyper-racial, with deracialized, racialized and tran-sracialized candidates as the intermediate points), he argues that both electoral and policy considerations should factor into how one categorizes black politicians. Black candidates run differently when running against whites and when running against other blacks, and that should be taken into account. Moreover, race politics plays out differently in different parts of the policy process. An elected official could set the agenda for a policy in a racially transcendent tone, for instance, but once the policy was implemented, it could be judged to be highly beneficial for blacks. Likewise, a policy could be introduced as explicitly helping blacks, but by the time it was passed and implemented, might not achieve its in-tended purpose. Thus, Henderson suggests the importance of looking at the ends elected officials achieve in office rather than the means by which they get to office before judging them (Henderson, 1996: 172-171). Unfortunately, Henderson's typology is very preliminary and in the end, still very unidimensional.

A Multi-Dimensional Assessment of Black Elected Leadership

Is there a better, perhaps more complex way to judge and examine black leadership? For this new cohort of elected officials, I would like to proffer a new model of leadership that creates more complex typologies and presents a more nuanced, and hopefully, more accurate picture of what we know about the post-civil rights cohort of black leadership to date. While this model incorporates the traditional militant to moderate axis (under the rubric of crossover appeal), it also adds two more important dimensions: expected career trajectory (ambition) and preexisting connections to the black establishment. These axes are far from simple, and in the next para-graphs, I will explain the criteria that go into determining a politician's position on these axes.

Crossover Appeal

As shown before, the militant-moderate continuum has figured prominently in studies of black leadership for nearly seventy years (Walters and
Smith, 1999; Ladd, 1966; Burgess, 1962; Wilson, 1960; Canon, Schousen and
Sellers, 1996). While it is extremely antiquated to judge black politicians on
whether they believe in acquiescing to second-class citizenship for blacks
anymore (Indeed, it would be hard to find a credible black leader arguing
for a rollback on the gains of the civil rights movement), the dimension still
has analytic merit. Politicians who run deracialized campaigns, for instance,
would naturally be far less militant and more likely to have greater levels
of crossover appeal than those who do run racialized campaigns.

Additionally, perceptions of moderation and militancy also spill over into
policy issues. An elected official's degree of crossover appeal can affect his
policy agendas and/or how she frames issues in the pursuit of achieving
certain racial policy goals. For instance, a militant official, or one with less
crossover appeal, may pursue the ending of police brutality and frame it
as a racial issue. A moderate counterpart may either not address the issue
entirely or frame it as being disadvantageous to the pursuit of law and order
in order to maintain his/her crossover appeal. A more militant leader may
champion affirmative action, while a moderate leader seeking crossover
appeal may focus on more racially neutral issues such as traditional economic development.

Perceived Career Trajectory

If one reads the mainstream press, he or she can often find examples
of black politicians in the new cohort being touted as presidential material (see Dionne, 2004: Benson, 2006). Clearly, there are members of this
cohort besides Barack Obama who clearly aspire to be president one day
and appear to be better positioned to achieve their goals than any other
generation of black politicians. However, there are members of this cohort
who seem content to remain in the positions they currently hold for the
foreseeable future.

The career trajectory dimension seeks to make distinctions between politicians who appear to be upwardly mobile (i.e., they aspire to statewide or
national office) and those who do not. Often, the personal backgrounds of
politicians influence their ambitions. Pauline Stone studied the ambitions
of black elected officials in Michigan in the late 1970s. Using a typology
developed by Joseph Schlesinger (1966: 10), she identified politicians with
"progressive" ambitions (those who wanted to seek higher office), "static"
ambitions (those who wanted to maintain their current positions), and
"discrete" ambitions (those who wanted to step down from their current
offices) (Stone, 1980: 96). She found that politicians with discrete ambitions
were more likely to have been drafted from the grassroots. In contrast,

politicians with progressive ambitions were more likely to be young, well educated, and less committed to pure partisan politics (Stone, 1980). For the purposes of this analysis, politicians with long trajectories will have progressive ambitions, while politicians with short trajectories will have static or discrete ambitions.

There are three factors that influence a politician's being categorized as having a long or short career trajectory. First, a politician has to want (or appear to want) to pursue higher office. This is important for a number of reasons. Because these officials have not served in prominent office for a short period of time, their future ambitions figure prominently into popular evaluations of them because for now, we really cannot judge their record of achievement. Moreover, the perceived ambitions of these officials have been a point of criticism. Recall that Ronald Walters criticized this cohort of politicians for being too ambitious, for seeking higher office before they had paid their dues (Martin, 2003: 56).

Second, the media also plays a role in generating buzz about a black candidate's future prospects. Adolph Reed, Jr. noted in his analysis of Jesse Jackson, Sr.'s 1984 presidential campaign that the mainstream media hyped Jackson's candidacy. Jackson had no chance of winning the Democratic nomination for president, yet because of the inordinate amount of media attention afforded to Jackson, he emerged from that campaign as the per-ceived spokesman for black America, with no consideration of his actual legitimacy as a leader in the black community (Reed, 1986: chapter 8). It may very well be that some of these officials are media constructions; or conversely, the perception that some of these candidates are mere media constructions could have a very negative impact on their legitimacy in black communities (Walters and Smith, 1999: 217).

Finally, there are structural and political considerations that do impact the future career trajectories of some of these officials. Black elected of-ficials representing majority-minority enclaves in overwhelmingly white states may have difficulty winning statewide elections. Similarly, ambitious black elected officials living in the District of Columbia, such as Mayor Adrian Fenty, would have to move to a state to pursue higher political office. Finally, elected officials who fail to achieve policy goals in office or get mired in scandal jeopardize their chances to make credible runs for higher political office.

Connections to the Black Establishment

The final dimension of the model assesses the strength of young black politicians' connections to the black establishment. Part of this analysis looks at political socialization. Some young black politicians have clear connections to traditional centers of black political power. They are either the scions of political or activist families (i.e., Harold Ford, Jr. and Jesse Jackson, Jr.) or have been politically socialized in traditional black institutions, whether it be serving on the staff of an established black politician or working with prominent civil rights organizations such as the NAACP. Others are clearly new players to the body politic and lack the traditional political connections to the black establishment. Having connections to traditional black centers of power can be invaluable. Those with access to the establishment could gain a fundraising or endorsement advantage, while those without those establishment ties have to raise money or win endorsements from scratch.

Being part of the establishment or being a newcomer to the political scene could have significant implications for the types of agendas young black politicians advance and the tone they use to advance those agendas. Someone who is a newcomer to the political scene may be more likely to ruffle feathers or to challenge the elders. Those with establishment connections may be less likely to challenge their elders, who literally could have raised them or their childhood friends. This decreased likelihood to challenge the system could have significant consequences for the advancement of black politics and the improvement of the material lives of black people. Those less likely to challenge the status quo may in fact be less likely to provide the needed innovations to advance African American interests.

Assessing linked fate also figures prominently into evaluations of a young black politician's connections to the black establishment. Michael Dawson (1994) noted that middle-class blacks, who may physically remove themselves from core black communities when they gain affluence and move to the suburbs, often maintain physical and psychic connections to black communities through a number of means. They can return to these communities for things as mundane as church and hair appointments. They may still leave relatives behind in these core communities, which solidifies their connections to these communities. Finally, the fact that middle-class blacks still experience racial discrimination still plays a radicalizing force. These factors combine to give middle-class blacks a sense that their fate is tied to the fate of other blacks, which in turn leads them to support policy positions (such as welfare spending) that non-blacks of the same class status are far less likely to support. Thus, some young black politicians with no roots in traditional black communities at all may be far less likely to advance a political and policy agenda that would advance the civil rights interests of black communities.

Typologies of the Third Wave

Having articulated the factors that contribute to the political identities of young black elected officials and aspirants of the post-civil rights generation, it is important to see how those factors interact and how this affects the classification of young black politicians.

If we look at the three definitional axes (crossover appeal, perceived career trajectory, and connections to the black establishment), and scale them dichotomously (ranking people as low or high relative to each other on the scales), this yields eight possible archetypal permutations, as shown in Table One. For the rest of this section, I will provide a thumbnail sketch of these typologies, devoting most of the attention to the observed archetypes.

New Black Politicians with Strong Credentials

Ivy League Upstarts

The Ivy League Upstarts, which include Senator Barack Obama and Newark, New Jersey Mayor Cory Booker, are among the most visible of the post-civil rights cohort of black elected leadership. This subset is defined by high crossover appeal, high levels of ambition, and weak ties to the black political establishment. This sub-cohort tends to be highly educated, graduating with advanced degrees from prestigious, majority-white institutions. For example, Obama graduated from Columbia University and Harvard Law School; Booker graduated from Stanford, Oxford University (as a Rhodes Scholar), and Yale Law School. They are also receive a lot of buzz in the mainstream media and appear to be anointed as members of the next wave of black leaders because of their credentials. For instance, a month before Barack Obama delivered his now-famous keynote address to the 2004 Democratic National Convention, columnist E.J. Dionne dubbed Obama, "a media darling in this year's election…. Already there's speculation that he may be the first African American president of the United States—and he's only a state senator" (Dionne, 2004: A29). The week after Cory Booker won his election to lead New Jersey's largest city, *New York Times* columnist Josh Benson noted that people were already discussing Booker's next political office (Benson, 2006, 14:1). Indeed, these gentlemen receive a lot of attention for their poise and for projecting a non-threatening image, similar to the deracialized candidates of Phase II.

However, these candidates are also embattled, at least at first, in black communities. Both Booker and Obama suffered defeats early in their careers, when they challenged established black leaders in Newark and Chicago for political power. Those campaigns were marked by noticeably high levels of racial vitriol, where they were condemned for not being black enough and for being interlopers who at best did not know enough about they communities they aspired to represent to lead them and at worst were insincere instrumentalists who planned to exploit and gentrify their communities for political gain (see Curry, 2005; Lawrence, 2000). While Ivy League Upstarts typically rebound from these initial defeats, their emergence onto the political scene raises important normative questions about class, racial authenticity, and linked fate.

In addition to the normative debate surrounding these candidates about linked fate and their ability to hold the best interests of black communities

Table 1
Typologies of Third Phase Black Politicians

Dominant Characteristic	Typology	Crossover Appeal	Ties to the Black Establishment	Perceived Trajectory	Example	Political Opportunity Structure	Challenges Facing This Sub-Cohort
Dominant Characteristic: Strong Credentials	*Ivy League Upstarts*	High	Weak	Long	Obama, Booker	Systemic Failure in Their Jurisdiction	They have to answer the charge that they are racially inauthentic and only seek to exploit black communities for their personal political gain.
	Local Kids Made Good	High	Weak	Short	Fenty, Davis, Ellison, McTeer-Hudson	Systemic Failure in their Jurisdiction	The political environment in which they run makes it more difficult (but not necessarily impossible) for candidates to achieve higher office, either because of structural constraints or unresolved racial tension.
Dominant Characteristic: Strong Connections To Black Establishment	*Rebrands of Their Parents*	High	Strong	Long	Ford	Generational Succession + Long Term Dynastic Planning	Their ties to the black establishment, and their parents' racialized political records could undermine their crossover appeal.
	Deracialized Sequels	High	Strong	Short	Mitchell	Generational Succession + Demographic Shift Privileging Non-Blacks	This group largely limits themselves deliberately from attaining higher office.
	Chips Off the Old Block	Low	Strong	Short	Kilpatrick, Clarke, Meek, Jackson	Their Parents Pave the Way	This group may face the most pressure to maintain the political status quo, even if that hurts black advancement.
	New "Old Standard Bearers"	Low	Strong	Long	Jackson?	Demographic Shift Favoring Blacks	In order to have viable long term career trajectories, they have to cultivate crossover support.
Dominant Characteristic: High Levels of "Street Credibility"	*New Activists*	Low	Weak	Long	Powell	Rising Internal Class Warfare; Increased Lower Class Participation	It is extremely difficult to maintain a long career trajectory without cultivating crossover appeal and establishment ties.
	Rebels Without a Chance	Low	Weak	Short	Hutchins	Most Likely To Emerge as the Result of a One-Time Disturbance	The emergence of viable candidates from this cohort is unlikely without other resources.

Source: Author's compilation. 2008.

at heart is the inherent pressure to perform that is placed on these officials. These candidates often run on good government platforms, in response to what they perceive to be failures of previous administrations to deliver goods and services effectively to their communities. When they get elected to office, they are expected to produce results immediately, and if they do not produce, then their constituents may be less forgiving at the next election.

Local Kids Made Good

The Local Kids Made Good, which include Washington, D.C. Mayor Adrian Fenty, Greenville, Mississippi Mayor Heather McTeer Hudson, Minnesota Congressman Keith Ellison and Alabama Congressman Artur Davis, are very similar to the Ivy League Upstarts, but they receive far less attention. They, like the Ivy League Upstarts, are extremely well educated, have crossover appeal, are committed to good government and are generally political newcomers, but they are perceived to have shorter career trajectories. As a resident of Washington, D.C., Fenty does not have the option of running for governor or being able to run to be a voting member of Congress. Thus, barring Washington, D.C. obtaining statehood, the D.C. delegate earning full voting privileges in Congress, or Fenty moving to an actual state, his elected political career is probably limited. Ellison, the first Muslim elected to Congress, has expressed no interest yet in running for statewide office at either the state or federal level, so we have to code his progressive ambitions as low for now.

Artur Davis and Heather McTeer Hudson, on the other hand, are potentially constrained by the political and racial conditions in their respective states. While Davis has actively contemplated seeking higher office, he has already had to rule out a 2008 U.S. Senate bid. Alabama voters are predicted to support the Republican candidate for president, and Davis figured that voters would be unlikely to split their ballots to vote for him as the U.S. Senate candidate. While Davis is actively considering a gubernatorial bid in 2010, he will have to overcome the hurdle that race may pose in his election. Alabama has never elected a black to any statewide office (Evans, 2007). Thus, while he harbors similar political aspirations to Obama and Booker, it is unclear at this point as to whether race relations in the Deep South will hamper his efforts to achieve his long-term goals.

Hudson is notable because unlike Fenty and Davis, she was the first black person to be elected to her post. In fact, Hudson is the first black mayor in the Mississippi Delta, which is 70 percent black (Byrd, 2004). As such, her obstacles relate to larger issues of political incorporation. With blacks in her region being largely unable to translate their numerical dominance into political power, it is difficult to project that Hudson would be able to easily win higher political office.

New Black Politicians with Strong Ties to the Black Establishment

Chips off the Old Block

The Chips off the Old Block are the children of prominent black politicians or civil rights leaders who used their lineage as a steppingstone to a political career. This sub-cohort includes people such as Florida Congressman Kendrick Meek, New York Congresswoman Yvette Clarke and Detroit Mayor Kwame Kilpatrick, all children of prominent politicians (former Congresswoman Carrie Meek, former New York City Councilwoman Una Clarke, and Congresswoman Carolyn Cheeks-Kilpatrick respectively). This sub-cohort is probably most diverse in terms of its orientation. While most of them espouse more moderate politics than their parents, they are perceived to have less crossover appeal than their counterparts who are largely defined by their credentials and who lack political lineages. These politicians clearly have connections to the black establishment and are thus less likely to have their commitment to black communities called into question. However, they are less likely to be perceived as having a long career trajectory. For those serving in the House of Representatives, if they continue their congressional careers, they are likely to gain seniority and committee chairmanships, but as of yet, they do not appear likely to take the risk of running for statewide or national office. As illustrated by the case of Mayor Kilpatrick, they may become implicated in political scandals that circumscribe future political opportunities (see Star News Services, 2005).

Rebrands of Their Parents

Rebrands of Their Parents are a different breed of black dynastic heirs. They have high crossover appeal, strong ties to the black establishment and long perceived career trajectories. Rebrands are very similar to Ivy League Upstarts, but they differ on the establishment dimension. Because these politicians have ties to the black establishment—indeed, they are often children of Phase I and II politicians—they tend to be less susceptible to charges of racial inauthenticity levied at Ivy League Upstarts.

Former Tennessee Congressman Harold Ford, Jr. typifies this category. Ford assumed the Memphis congressional seat held by his father in 1996, but he clearly had higher political ambitions and cultivated a national political presence. Al Gore chose him to deliver one of the keynote addresses at the 2000 Democratic National Convention because "He's a rising star. He has a bright future. And he's from Tennessee" (Gore, quoted in Brosnan, 2000). After the 2002 midterm elections, Ford made an unsuccessful bid to be minority leader of the House of Representatives. In 2006, Ford came within three percentage points of becoming Tennessee's first black United States senator. Therefore, unlike the Chips off the Old Block, who currently do not publicly evince an interest in seeking office beyond the posts they currently hold, Rebrands of Their Parents use their parents' old seats as springboards to seek high offices that their parents could only dream of attaining.[4]

However, because Rebrands got their political starts at their parents' knees, they could be constrained by their families no matter how hard they try to escape the proverbial apple tree. If a family's reputation is mixed, it can cause problems for the Rebrand candidate. When Ford ran for the Senate in 2006, his family's ethical issues became a campaign obstacle. For instance, his opponent, Bob Corker, ran an ad ("Family Ties") noting that Harold Ford, Jr. was a puppet for his father, (Strategic Perception, 2006). This ad clearly was meant to prime antipathy for members of the Ford family, who has had more than its share of ethics charges levied against them (see Davis and Sher, 2006).

New "Old Standard Bearers"

There is the potential for an ambitious black politician to emerge with strong black establishment ties and low crossover appeal. The New "Old Standard Bearer" embodies these characteristics. They would likely be the scion of an established black activist or political family whose political base is rooted in the black community. If the conditions were ripe, A New "Old Standard Bearer"would then try to use his/her family's good name to reap win elective office. Certain conditions must be in place first, though, in order to make this a viable possibility. For instance, these candidates would have to generate just enough crossover appeal to effectively split the white vote, thus making black voters the crucial swing vote in their particular contest. In any case, the demographics of a particular jurisdiction would have to change such that blacks made up a decisive portion of the electorate. Currently, no one really fits the description of a New "Old Standard Bearer." However, there is a chance that Jesse Jackson, Jr. (who otherwise is a Chip off the Old Block) could fit this category. In fall 2006, Jackson began to publicly explore the possibility of challenging Richard Daley for the Chicago mayoralty. While he ruled out a run in November 2006, the possibility remains for him to consider a mayoral, gubernatorial or senatorial bid in the future—though one cannot speculate about his chances at this time (see Mihalopoulos, 2006; Mihalopoulos and Washburn, 2006; "Rep. Jesse Jackson, Jr. Won't Run...", 2006). That Jackson even publicly considered running for another office suggests that he might have higher political ambitions.

The Other Types—Deracialized Sequels; New Activists; and Rebels without a Chance

The final three typologies represent different permutations of the three relevant dimensions by which to judge the black politicians of this generation. However, as of yet, no one has been elected at the national or large city executive level who embodies these combinations of characteristics. The paragraphs that follow describe the characteristics of lesser known politicians who could emerge and fit this type and will explain why it may be difficult (though not impossible) for some types of black politicians to emerge.

It is most likely that a Phase III new black politician will emerge onto the national stage who fits the characteristics of a *Deracialized Sequel*. Like Rebrands of Their Parents, these politicians have high crossover appeal and strong ties to the black establishment. However, unlike Rebrands of Their Parents, they choose to have short career trajectories. A Deracialized Sequel politician is most likely to emerge in an area accustomed to black leadership, but has a large enough non-black population that requires that black candidates reach out to non-black constituents in order to be politically viable.

While one cannot point to a prominent mayor or member of Congress who fits this type, former Baltimore City Councilman and mayoral candidate Keiffer Mitchell does provide an example of this type of politician. Mitchell, the grand-nephew of the late Maryland Congressman Parren Mitchell and scion of a legendary black activist family in Maryland, served on Baltimore's City Council for 11 years before running for the Democratic nomination for mayor of Baltimore in 2007. Mitchell represented a diverse city council ward and was comfortable reaching across racial and class lines. Mitchell clearly attempted to capitalize on his family's reputation to be elected mayor of Baltimore. However, at an August 14, 2007 debate (which the author attended), Mitchell announced that he had no intention of running for higher office after serving as mayor.

Despite Mitchell's pledge to devote his career to Baltimore politics, his campaign efforts were hampered in part because of family drama. Mitchell's father, who initially served as treasurer of his campaign, was forced to resign after it was alleged that he had used campaign funds for non-campaign expenses. Mitchell's father then evicted his son's campaign out of office space he rented to them. By the time that this scandal emerged, Mitchell already trailed the eventual nominee and winner, Sheila Dixon, in polling by double-digit margins. The scandal, though, presented a new distraction at best and further hampered his efforts. In a *Baltimore Sun* poll taken weeks before the September 11 primary, 16 percent of voters said that the scandal did make it less likely for them to vote for Keiffer Mitchell (Brewington, 2007).

New Activists are characterized by low crossover appeal, weak ties to the black establishment and long perceived trajectories. Because of the low crossover appeal and weak ties to the black establishment, it is hard to conceive that any successful, young, black politician would emerge who fits this type. However, there are certain conditions which make the emergence of a New Activist more plausible. If class divisions between upper- and lower-class blacks exacerbate and the black lower class organizes politically around a new and different set of leaders than middle- and upper-class blacks (see Dawson, 1994: 208-209), those leaders would likely fit the description of New Activists. The New Activists would be able to maintain their political power so long as lower-class blacks remain a politically cohesive voting bloc; and they might even be able to expand their political base beyond a city or even a congressional district if they were able to effectively use a populist appeal to reach out to poor non-blacks. However, given the fact that all of these conditions have to emerge simultaneously in order for this to be a viable type, it is less likely that New Activists will make up a sizable subset of Phase III black politicians.

That being said, potential candidates are emerging who fit the mold of New Activists. Kevin Powell, a reality TV star turned author/activist, challenged Brooklyn Congressman Edolphus Towns for the Democratic nomination in New York's 10th Congressional District in 2008. Towns, a thirteen-term congressman, won his 2006 primary against New York City Councilman Charles Barron with only a plurality of the vote in a three-person field. This showing, on the heels of narrow primary wins in 1998 and 2000, suggested that he was politically vulnerable. Towns also made a big strategic misstep when he endorsed Hillary Clinton in the 2008 Democratic presidential primary. Fifty-eight percent of Towns' district voted for Barack Obama. Powell hoped to use all of these vulnerabilities, plus his own assertion that Towns was unresponsive to the needs of his constituents, to gain a foothold in the congressional primary. Despite his notoriety as an original cast member of MTV's *The Real World* and his potential appeal to young people, though, Powell was not successful. Towns eventually beat Powell by a two-to-one margin in 2008 (Hicks, 2008a; Hicks, 2008b; Gross, 2008).

Rebels without a Chance are characterized by low crossover appeal, weak ties to the black establishment and a short career trajectory. Because Rebels without a Chance lack conventional resources that are needed to win elections (i.e., support from black elites and non-black voters), they only succeed in cases where they have massive grassroots support among largely disaffected black voters, who would certainly have to comprise a majority of the electorate. Given the structural obstacles impeding Rebels without a Chance (i.e., they may not have majority support in their constituency depending on the demographic makeup of their jurisdiction; they may not have access to the resources needed to run campaigns such as money or professional staff; and they have to mobilize potentially discouraged and inefficacious voters), it is difficult for a successful Phase III black politician to emerge in this mode.

Despite the long odds of success, though, Rebel without a Chance candidates have emerged recently. Markel Hutchins, an Atlanta minister, rose to prominence as the spokesperson for the family of Kathryn Johnston, a 92-year-old Atlanta woman who was shot to death by police during a bungled no-knock warrant arrest in 2006. In February 2008, Hutchins challenged Congressman John Lewis for the Democratic nomination for Georgia's 5th Congressional District. Clearly, Hutchins was attempting to translate his stature as a young activist into political power. He also hoped to tap into voter disappointment with Lewis' original endorsement of Hillary Clinton over Barack Obama in the 2008 presidential primaries. However, he was unable to unseat Lewis, who won nearly 70 percent of the vote in a three-person field. Hutchins only garnered 16 percent of the vote (see Galloway, 2008; Smith, 2008).

It is still too early to predict the political futures of both Kevin Powell and Markel Hutchins. They will first have to win elective office before we can predict their career trajectories and properly categorize them. However, it is clear that they tried to capitalize on their opponents' strategic errors (i.e., supporting a losing presidential candidate) and public dissatisfaction with that political error to win political office. They are clearly presenting themselves as "men of the people" and not overly qualified technocrats or scions of political families in their political campaigns.

It is important to note the differences between candidates like Powell and Hutchins. Powell has fashioned himself as a telegenic political organizer (Hicks, 2008a), while Hutchins, in his causes and cadence, assumes the role of a classic civil rights leader. This framing may put Hutchins at a disadvantage (even in Atlanta) if voters prefer more moderate black candidates (see Canon et al., 1996). Powell still lacks complete crossover appeal, as he is perceived to be an "activist of the hip hop generation" (Hicks, 2008b). However, given Powell's small celebrity, he may be able to cultivate a political base of voters under 45, which could serve him well in future elections (He has already vowed to run again in 2010) (Hicks, 2008c). For this reason, I tentatively classify Powell as a New Activist, and Hutchins as a Rebel without a Chance.

Analysis and Further Questions

The typologies listed above serve a two-fold purpose. First, they are designed to show the diversity among this class of individuals—a diversity that is often obscured in the popular press with their preoccupation with a few of these elected leaders. Moreover, the typologies help to organize our assessment of these leaders and give us some uniform metrics by which to judge them.

They typologies are not meant to be a monolith, though. There are other important considerations that the typologies do not take into consideration. I would like to briefly touch on these points.

Where Are the Women?

One of the interesting and troubling aspects of this research into the third wave of black elected officials is the relative absence of women on the national scene. Not until Yvette Clarke's election in November 2006 had any black woman born after 1960 achieved any measure of prominence in a federal office (She has since been joined by Congresswoman Laura Richardson, who replaced the late Juanita Millender-McDonald). While

Heather McTeer Hudson is an example of a young, black, female mayor, she leads a city with a population of less than 50,000 residents (United States Census Bureau, 2007).

There could be a reason to explain this apparent dearth of young, female black politicians. Jennifer Lawless and Richard Fox (2005) have found that women who are well situated professionally to run for political office (i.e., they come from the pipeline professions of law, education, politics, or business) are less likely to consider running for office and less likely to actually run for office once they have considered the possibility. Moreover, when they do consider running for office, women are more likely to consider running for a lower-level office (i.e., local government as opposed to state government) than men. On a small scale, Lawless and Fox's findings mirror what we observe in the cohort of young black politicians. The women who are running for office are concentrating their efforts at the state and local level. Yvette Clarke started out as a city councilwoman; Heather McTeer Hudson is mayor of a small city. Similarly, Alicia Thomas Morgan of Georgia, Jennifer McClellan of Virginia, Jill Carter of Maryland, and Grace Spencer of New Jersey are examples of Phase III female elected officials who serve as state legislators. These women stand in contrast to Harold Ford, Jr. and Jesse Jackson, Jr., whose first elections were for their congressional seats. However, only time will tell if these observations are temporary and these women use these first seats as steppingstones to higher political office.

Phase 2.5

In addition, there are also some elected officials who by virtue of their age, were not considered in this analysis, but who deserve mention because their politics closely resemble the politics of the younger cohort. Massachusetts Governor Deval Patrick is especially notable. (Congresswoman Donna Edwards also fits into this category.) Born in 1956, Patrick is too old to be considered part of the post-civil rights cohort, but he has the profile and politics of an Ivy League Upstart—he is Harvard-educated and worked in the Clinton administration. In many ways, Patrick's personal narrative draws on the themes of being on the racial vanguard characteristic of previous phases of black leadership and melds it with the post-racial pragmatism of some of the Phase III leadership. He is from the South Side of Chicago and was one of the first blacks to be afforded a prep school education through a program targeted to poor students of color. As a young lawyer, he worked in Darfur and for the NAACP Legal Defense Fund. He followed that with a stint in the Clinton Justice Department (Civil Rights Division) and work in the private sector (Anderson, 2006). Thus, because of his age and the breadth of his experience, Patrick and those like him are able to appeal to both blacks and whites apparently without the same need to prove their racial authenticity that the ways that their Ivy League Upstart counterparts have had to prove.

Conclusion

To be sure, the younger generation of leadership has not amassed enough power or seniority as a whole to affect widespread change in the black community. Thus, it remains to be seen whether their strategies and agenda produce favorable or unfavorable outcomes for blacks. However, we can apply what we now know about this emerging generation of black leadership to developing important questions to guide future research. I conclude with three of these questions, which will hopefully lead to more questions and further lines of inquiry on this topic.

First, we know that the new crop of young, black elected officials is more diverse than it would appear to be in the mainstream media, who focuses mostly on those with Ivy League credentials and crossover appeal. Indeed, most young black politicians inherited their seats from their parents. Will the exodus of Phase I and II black politicians from the scene free this sub-cohort to innovate black politics? Or will this group of dynastic heirs assume the oppositional mantle of their parents and vie for influence with their popular peers who have fewer ties to the black establishment?

Second, the age, class status and upbringing of these politicians raises larger questions for the study of black public opinion. Does this new generation of leadership reflect the larger generation that they came from, or are their preferences artifacts of calculated political ambition? If the values, perspectives and policy preferences of these politicians reflect the values of their cohort of blacks generally (as Bositis [2002] suggests), then this means that we have to reevaluate conventional wisdoms about how blacks develop linked fate and about how they choose parties, candidates and policy preferences. Further study of this cohort may provide further credence to Adolph Reed's argument that class differences within the black community betray multiple black agendas (see Reed, 2000: chapter 1).

Finally, we will eventually have to ask whether the campaign, legislative, and governing approach of this new generation of politicians will actually be more successful in delivering goods and services to African American communities. This question becomes especially important as more minority groups make legitimate claims for recognition, representation, and scarce resources. Moreover, the question reflects the nearly 20-year skepticism over deracialization generally. Robert Smith gloomily predicted that deracialization "is not likely to be able to arrest and reverse the decline of the black community, and ... it suggests that even black leadership itself may be turning away from the problem"(Smith, 1993: 220). If the new generation of black leaders turns away from problems that face the black community or is unable to deliver on their promises, then this could have a negative impact on already deep divisions within black communities. Moreover, it could lead to a deeper secondary marginalization of blacks deemed less socially desirable even within the black community (see Cohen, 1999). By reflecting on these issues sooner rather than later, hopefully this line of research can use lessons from the past 40 years of black elected leadership to chart a course for greater policy advancement in the future.

Notes

1. The terms"black"and"African American"will be used interchangeably in this chapter to describe people of African descent living in the United States.
2. Sheridan uses Douglas Wilder as a example of a second-wave politician who refused to identify with the civil rights struggle, saying that he opted to make money than advocate for change in the 1960s. Whatever one can say about Wilder's personal politics, given his age, no one can argue that he missed being personally affected by Jim Crow growing up in Richmond, Virginia (Sheridan, 1996: 166).
3. To be sure, there are earlier examples of young, moderate blacks challenging leaders from the older, civil rights generation as early as the 1980s. Ardrey and Nelson note that Michael White challenged the combative, divisive tactics of George Forbes and beat him for the mayoralty of Cleveland. There are other examples of black politics going against other black politicians in the 1980s and early 1990s. The notable victors include Dennis Archer (Ardrey and Nelson, 1990; Nordlinger, 2002).
4. Please refer to footnote 3 for a definition of high office. If I define a Rebrand broadly as someone who wins his/her parent's seat and then seeks higher office, then Congresswoman Yvette Clarke qualifies as a Rebrand. She took over her mother's New York City Council seat. Winning a congressional seat could qualify as a step up. However, because this analysis defines high offices as offices higher than congressional seats, Congresswoman Clarke is classified as a Chip off the Old Block until she pursues a U.S. Senate seat, the New York governorship, or the presidency of the United States.

Bibliography

Anderson, Lisa. 2006."Chicago-born, Leading in Mass: Deval Patrick Rose from Poverty, Bids to Be State's 1st Black Governor." The Chicago Tribune. 29 October 2006.

Ardrey, Saundra C. and William E. Nelson."The Maturation of Black Political Power: The Case of Cleveland." PS: Political Science and Politics. 23(2): 148-151.

Benson, Josh. 2006. "Next for Booker? (Get Used to the Question)." The New York Times. 14 May 2006, 14:1.

Bositis, David A. 2002."2002 National Opinion Poll: Politics. Washington: Joint Center for Political and Economic Studies. Retrieved from www.jointcenter.org.

Bositis, David A. 2001. Changing the Guard: Generational Difference among Black Elected Officials. Washington, DC: Joint Center for Political and Economic Studies.

Brewington, Kelly. 2007. "Mitchell, Father Renew Their Feud." Baltimore Sun. Retrieved from baltimoresun.com. 24 September 2007.

Brosnan, James W. 2000."Youngest Congressman to Speak To Democrats."Cleveland Plain Dealer. 6 August 2000.

Burgess, M. Elaine. 1962. Negro Leadership in a Southern City. Chapel Hill: University of North Carolina Press.

Byrd, Veronica. 2004. "'My Generation Can't Just Complain. We Have To Get Involved." Essence. October 2004. Retrieved from findarticles.com, 14 June 2007.

Canon, David T., Matthew Schousen, and Patrick Sellers. 1996."The Supply Side of Congressional Redistricting: Race and Strategic Politicians, 1972-1992. The Journal of Politics. 58(3): 846-862.

Cohen, Cathy. 1999. The Boundaries of Blackness: AIDS and the Breakdown of Black Politics. Chicago: University of Chicago Press.

Curry, Marshall (Director). 2005. Street Fight [DVD]. United States: Marshall Curry Productions.

Davis, Marilyn and Alex Willingham. 1993."Andrew Young and the Georgia State Elections of 1990."In *Dilemmas of Black Politics*. Georgia Persons (ed.). New York: Harper Collins. 147-175.

Davis, Michael and Andy Sher. 2006."State GOP Mailing Focuses on Ford Family." *Chattanooga Times Free Press*. 2 November 2006. B2.

Dawson, Michael C. 1994. *Behind the Mule*. Princeton: Princeton University Press.

Dionne, E.J. 2004."In Illinois, a Star Prepares."*The Washington Post*. 25 June 2004. A29.

Dovi, Suzanne. 2002."Preferable Descriptive Representatives: Will Just Any Woman, Black or Latino Do?"*American Political Science Review*. 96(4): 745-754.

Evans, Ben. 2007."Davis Won't Challenge Sessions for Senate Seat In 2008."*Associated Press State and Local Wire*. 8 January 2007.

Galloway, Jim. 2008."Hutchins to Seek Lewis' Seat."*Atlanta Journal-Constitution*. 23 February 2008. Retrieved from ajc.com. 20 September 2008.

Gross, Courtney. 2008. "Democratic Primary Results by Congressional District." Posted on *The Wonkster* blog (http://www.gothamgazette.com/blogs/ wonkster/2008/02/06/primary-results-by-congressional-district/). 6 February 2008. Retrieved 20 September 2008.

Hamilton, Charles V. 1982. "Foreword." In *The New Black Politics: The Search for Political Power*. Edited by Michael B. Preston, Lenneal J. Henderson Jr. and Paul Puryear. New York and London: Longman Publishers. xvii-xx.

Henderson, Lenneal J., Jr. 1996. "The Governance of Kurt Schmoke as Mayor of Baltimore." In *Race, Governance, and Politics in the United States*. Huey L. Perry (Ed.). Gainesville: University of Florida Press. 165-178.

Hicks, Jonathan. 2008a. "Brooklyn Congressman and Veteran of Tough Primaries Faces New Fight." *New York Times*. 28 April 2008. Retrieved from nytimes.com. 20 September 2008.

Hicks, Jonathan. 2008b. "Accused of Being Out of Touch, a 25-Year Congressman Campaigns for Dear Life." *New York Times*. 4 September 2008. Retrieved from nytimes.com. 20 September 2008.

Hicks, Jonathan. 2008c. "Towns's Challenger Vows to Run Again." Posted on *City Room Blog* of nytimes.com. *New York Times*. 28 April 2008. Retrieved from http:// cityroom.blogs.nytimes.com/2008/09/16/townss-challenger-vows-to-run- again/#more-3963. 20 September 2008.

Jones, Charles E. and Michael Clemons. 1993."A Model of Racial Crossover Voting: An Assessment of the Wilder Victory." In *Dilemmas of Black Politics*. Georgia Persons (Ed.). New York: Harper Collins. 128-146.

Kim, Claire. 2000. *Bitter Fruit: The Politics of Black-Korean Conflict in New York City*. New Haven: Yale University Press.

Ladd, Everett C. 1966. *Negro Political Leadership in the South*. Ithaca: Cornell University Press.

Lawless, Jennifer and Richard Fox. 2005. *It Takes a Candidate: Why Women Don't Run for Office*. Cambridge and New York: Cambridge University Press.

Lawrence, Cynthia. 2000."Rush Wins in 1st: Did Obama Deliver a Wake-Up Call to Rush?"*Chicago Sun-Times*. 22 March 2000. Retrieved from www.jessejacksonjr. org. 14 June 2007.

Martin, Roland. 2003."Ready or Not…"*Savoy*. March 2003. 52-56.

McCormick, Joseph II and Charles E. Jones. 1993."The Conceptualization of De-racialization: Thinking Through The Dilemma." In *Dilemmas of Black Politics*. Georgia Persons (Ed.). New York: Harper Collins. 66-84.

Mihalopoulos, Dan. 2006."Jesse Jackson Jr. Will Probably Run for Mayor of Chicago."*The Chicago Tribune*. 6 September 2006.

Mihalopoulos, Dan and Gary Washburn. 2006."Jesse Jackson Jr. Said to Decide Against Running for Chicago Mayor."*The Chicago Tribune*. 8 November 2006.

Myrdal, Gunnar. 1944. *An American Dilemma.* New York: Harper and Brothers.

Nelson, William E.. 1982. "Cleveland: The Rise and Fall of the New Black Politics." In *The New Black Politics: The Search for Political Power.* Edited by Michael B. Preston, Lenneal J. Henderson Jr. and Paul Puryear. New York and London: Longman Publishers. 187-208.

Nordlinger, Jay. 2002. "Some 'Dissident.' Doin' the Skin-Color Nasty. A Bit of Righteous Kvetching. Etc." *National Review Online.* 28 May 2002. Retrieved from LexisNexis Academic Universe (web.lexis-nexis.com/universe). 20 January 2003.

Reed, Adolph. 1986. *The Jesse Jackson Phenomenon.* New Haven: Yale University Press.

Reed, Adolph. 2000. *Class Notes: Posing as Politics and Other Thought on the American Scene.* New York: The New Press.

Reed, K. Terrell and Sonia Alleyne. 2002. "What It Takes to Win." *Black Enterprise.* November 2002: 82-95.

_____. "Rep. Jesse Jackson Jr. Won't Run for Chicago Mayor." *Jet.* 27 November 2006.

Russakoff, Dale. 2002. "In Newark Race, Black Political Visions Collide." *The Washington Post.* 14 May 2002. Retrieved from LexisNexis Academic Universe (web.lexis-nexis.com/universe) January 2003.

Schexnider, Alvin J. 1996. "Analyzing the Wilder Administration Through the Construct of Deracialization Politics." In *Race, Governance, and Politics in the United States.* Huey L. Perry (Ed.). Gainesville: University of Florida Press. 15-28.

Schlesinger, Joseph. 1966. *Ambition and Politics: Political Careers in the United States.* Chicago: Rand McNally and Company.

Sheridan, Earl. 1996. "The New Accommodationists." *Journal of Black Studies.* 27(2): 152-171.

Smith, Ben. 2008. "US HOUSE: Incumbents win all primary races. Lewis Avoids Runoff Despite Two Opponents." *Atlanta Journal-Constitution.* 16 July 2008. Retrieved from ajc.com. 20 September 2008.

Smith, Robert C. 1990. "Recent Elections and Black Politics: The Maturation or Death of Black Politics? *PS: Political Science and Politics.* 23(2): 160-162.

Smith, Robert C. 1993. "Ideology as the Enduring Dilemma of Black Politics." In *Dilemmas of Black Politics.* Georgia Persons (Ed.). New York: Harper Collins. 211-225.

Smith, Robert C. 1996. *We Have No Leaders.* Albany: State University of New York Press.

Smith, Robert C. and Ronald Walters. 1999. *African American Leadership.* Albany: State University of New York Press.

Star News Services. 2005. "Kwame's Woes: Conflict Follows Detroit Mayor In His Battle for a Second Term." *Windsor Star* (Ontario, Canada). 16 July 2005.

Starr, Alexandra. 2002. "We Shall Overcome, Too." *Business Week.* 15 July 2002. Retrieved from LexisNexis Academic Universe (web.lexis-nexis.com/universe). 20 January 2003.

Strategic Perceptions (Producer). 2006. "Family Ties" [Political Advertisement]. Hollywood: Strategic Perceptions, LLC. Retrieved from http://nationaljournal.com/members/adspotlight/2006/11/1106tnsen2.htm, 14 June 2007.

Strickland, Ruth Ann and Marcia Lynn Whicker. 1992. "Comparing the Wilder and Gantt Campaigns: A Model for Black Candidate Success in Statewide Elections." *PS: Political Science and Politics.* 25(2): 204-212.

Summers, Mary and Phillip Klinkner. 1996. "The Election and Governance of John Daniels as Mayor of New Haven." In *Race, Governance, and Politics in the United States.* Huey L. Perry (Ed.). Gainesville: University of Florida Press. 127-150.

Tate, Katherine. 1994. *From Protest to Politics: The New Black Voters in American Elections.* New York and Cambridge: Russell Sage Foundation/Harvard University Press.

Traub, James. 2002. "The Way We Live Now: 9-8-02; The Last Color Line." *The New York Times Magazine*. 8 September 2002. Retrieved from LexisNexis Academic Universe (web.lexis-nexis.com/universe) 20 January 2003.

United States Census Bureau. 2007. "American Factfinder: Greenville, Mississippi." Retrieved from http://factfinder.census.gov 14 June 2007.

Williams, Linda. 1987. "Black Political Progress in the 1980's: The Electoral Arena." In *The New Black Politics: The Search for Political Power*. Second Edition. Edited by Michael B. Preston, Lenneal J. Henderson Jr. and Paul Puryear. New York and London: Longman Publishers. 97-136.

Wilson, James Q. 1960. *Negro Politics: The Search for Leadership*. Glencoe, Illinois: The Free Press.

Wilson, Zaphon. 1993. "Gantt Versus Helms: Deracialization Confronts Southern-Traditionalism." In *Dilemmas of Black Politics*. Georgia Persons (Ed.). New York: Harper Collins. 176-193.

Beyond the Boundaries, Volume 12; pp. 7-22

Making History, Again, So Soon?
The Massachusetts Gubernatorial Election

Angela K. Lewis
University of Alabama at Birmingham

Introduction

On November 6, 2006, the voters of Massachusetts made history—for only the second time in the United States, voters elected a black governor. It was seventeen years earlier when Douglas Wilder became the nation's first elected black governor. Deval Patrick, a political novice virtually unknown before the election, states he did not campaign as the black candidate, in fact he comments "If all I was offering was to be the first black governor of Massachusetts, I wouldn't have won" (Pierce, 2006). Running a grass-roots campaign rejecting large monetary donations from supporters, for two years Patrick visited neighborhoods and spoke to voters across their kitchen tables about restoring hope back into politics and how to make Massachusetts better. What he offered was an approach that transcended race.

The purpose of this chapter is to provide an in-depth analysis of the 2006 Massachusetts gubernatorial election where Deval Patrick ran against Kerry Healey. First, this chapter provides a history of Massachusetts politics, followed by information about the candidates and the campaign. The chapter concludes with an analysis of how Patrick, unlike so many past black candidates in other states, successfully navigated the campaign trail to attain a high-level statewide office as a governor or U.S. senator.

Massachusetts Politics

"Massachusetts is the most liberal and Democratic state in national elections" (Sonenshein, 1990). Known as the home of the Kennedys and John Kerry, the Democratic nominee for president in 2004, Massachusetts is also the first state to recognize and make legal same-sex marriages. For some time, Massachusetts was under one-party control. Voters last elected a Democrat to the office of governor in 1986 with the election of

Michael Dukakis. It was 1990 when Republicans took the governor's office, with William Weld beating John Silber. Voters were angry over the state's economy, the budget, and one-party leadership and they wanted change. Although Massachusetts is a blue state, after the 1990 Republican takeover, Republicans held it up as an example, "that they could win even in the bluest state" (Mehren, 2006).

Similar to the 1990 Republican takeover, voters in the 2006 election also wanted change after an increase in the cost of living in the state and the state's steady population decline. Voters were also displeased about how their incumbent governor, Mitt Romney, made fun of the state, for being too liberal and being the first to allow same-sex marriage, while he traveled the country campaigning for president. In addition, state funding for education had decreased tremendously, causing it to fall behind Alabama and Mississippi in higher education funding (Mehren, 2006). In the end, voters were upset and wanted change. "Many are considering a vote for Patrick because they are upset by the Big Dig, the high cost of living, and the negative tone of the Healey campaign" (Mooney and Wangsness, 2006). Whichever way the election would have gone, Massachusetts would make history by electing the state's first black or female governor.

The Candidates

Both candidates were self-made millionaires. Although Patrick's story is more revealing of his character, both candidates have a mix of experiences that would have made them qualified governors.

A single-mother that was briefly on welfare raised Deval Patrick in his grandparent's South Side Chicago apartment. Although Patrick grew up around crime and gangs, he avoided them. At age 14 he received a scholarship from A Better Chance program to attend Milton Academy in Massachusetts, a move that would change his life forever.

The first in his family to attend college, he graduated from Harvard College with honors, and later Harvard Law School. Before attending law school, he traveled overseas to Sudan and South Africa on a youth training project funded by a Rockefeller Foundation grant.

At fifty years old, Patrick had a variety of work experiences, which included work as a law clerk to a federal appellate judge, work at the NAACP Legal Defense and Education Fund, at Day, Berry & Howard, and as a partner at Hill & Barlow, two leading law firms. Patrick also served as a federal prosecutor and as the assistant attorney general for civil rights under President Clinton.

In the private sector, two multi-national companies, Texaco and Coca-Cola, hired Patrick as vice president and general counsel. He also served on numerous corporate and charitable boards. He has been married to Diane Patrick for over twenty years and they have two children in college.

The Republican candidate, Kerry Healey, then current lieutenant governor, grew up in Daytona Beach, Florida. Her mother was a public school teacher and her father served 27 years in the US Army and Army Reserves. Healey graduated Harvard with a degree in government in the early '80s. She later received a Ph.D. from Trinity College in Dublin, Ireland.

Healey had two unsuccessful bids at political office, both for state representative in 1998 and 2000. In 2002, she ran successfully in the primary for lieutenant governor beating Jim Rappaport. She later became lieutenant governor as the running mate of Mitt Romney. She was active in numerous community organizations. Her work experience includes work as a law and public safety consultant at Abt Associates and as an adjunct faculty member at Endicott College and the University of Massachusetts at Lowell where she taught social policy and criminal justice. She has two school-aged children with her husband Sean Healy. They have been married for twenty years.

The Primaries

The Democratic Party's rule in Massachusetts is that in order for a candidate's name to appear on the primary ballot, they must receive at least 15 percent of the delegate's votes at the State Convention. Two other Democratic candidates besides Deval Patrick vied for the governor's office, Attorney General Tom Reilly, and millionaire Chris Gabrieli. Even in early March, Patrick was well ahead of his contenders in gaining the Democratic Party's nomination for governor. In his first run for elective office, Patrick received his party's nomination with 58 percent of the convention delegates' votes, while Reilly received 27 percent and Gabriela received 15 percent. Therefore, all three candidates received positions on the ballot. There was some speculation that Reilly and Gabrieli swapped votes to ensure they both had a spot on the ballot although both denied it (Johnson, 2006).

By August, Patrick continued his lead over Reilly and Gabrieli. Polls showed Patrick at 35 percent, Gabrieli at 30 percent and Reilly at 27 percent (O'Sullivan, 2006). Before the primary election, in preparation for one of the debates, Patrick spoke of the problems with school districts charging fees for extracurricular activities and transportation. He argued that the activities are part of a child's education and the parent's ability to pay should not determine a child's participation. He wanted to create a fund to help schools with these programs so parents will not have to pay fees. Gabrieli focused on transportation, more specifically how to make commuting easier for workers. Reilly focused on how his opponents were millionaires who did not understand the significance of a state income tax rollback because they were rich. As a result, Reilly released both he and his wife's tax returns hoping other candidates would do the same, although they did not. This move earned Reilly the endorsements of 15 mayors across the state.

Both Gabriela and Patrick attacked Reilly about two critical issues during his tenure as attorney general—his lack of supervision of the Big Dig Project and how he handled the gay marriage ballot question. The Big Dig is a massive tunnel and bridge road project in Boston that ended up costing much more than forecasted. Moreover, the finished parts of the project were plagued with defects. The project caused outrage because of over-spending and the failure of the Romney administration to be accountable for its failure. They both stated that Reilly could have done more to hold elected officials and contractors accountable for the Big Dig's massive cost overruns and defects. They also argued that Reilly should have blocked attempts to put the gay marriage question on the ballots because the issue was already decided by the courts.

Although both Reilly and Gabrieli criticized Patrick for his work with Texaco and Coca-Cola, as well as his board membership with Ameriquest, Patrick won the Democratic primary election in September by nearly a 30 percentage-point margin. Patrick's victory in the primary is related to Reilly's poor performance as attorney general and Gabrieli's lack of a broad spectrum of support. Most of Gabrieli's campaign was self-funded. Although, he counted on support from the 50 percent or more of voters who were unregistered as Democrats or Republicans, in the end, independent voters were more likely to support Patrick.

Other candidates in the general election for governor included Christy Mihos and Green Rainbow Party candidate Grace Ross. Mihos, who some hoped would run against Healey in the Republican primary, decided to run as an independent, a move that would challenged Healey because it took away her ability to garner votes from independents.

The Campaign

Patrick's candidacy gave voters a comfortable candidate that offered an opportunity for change. A *Boston Globe*/CBS 4 Poll found that a large percentage of respondents had unfavorable views of Healey. In fact, 42 percent of respondents had unfavorable views of Healy, compared to Patrick's 16 percent although voters agreed with Healey on many issues. What damaged Healey during the campaign was her past association with Governor Romney, who was very unpopular at the time (Moynihan, 2006). Voters were unhappy with the previous four years of the Romney-Healey administration and they wanted change. The fact that Patrick had no prior experience as an officeholder did not matter much to voters because he emphasized that his corporate experience was just the experience needed to run a state government and to make it more fiscally responsible.

Healey's unfavorable ratings were likely associated with her negative campaign ads. She consistently attacked Patrick for his work as an attorney involved with rape and death penalty cases. She even went as far as to state that Patrick's experience as a lawyer should disqualify him for running for governor. For example, in one televised debate, Healey suggested that Patrick was soft on crime because of his support of Benjamin LaGuer, a man convicted of raping a 59-year-old woman who was his neighbor.[1] Patrick responded by pointing out that Healey did not care about crime because during her tenure as lieutenant governor the Romney/Healey administration cut police resources to local communities.

Voters believed Patrick was a promising leader often rising above the negative attack ads ran by Healey. He refused to respond with his own negative ads. Former Governor Michael Dukakis honed in on the negative campaigning and remarked, "This has been the dirtiest campaign in the history of the commonwealth" (Mehren, 2006). The ads ran by Healey reminded some of the Willie Horton ads George W. Bush ran against Michael Dukakis in his bid for the presidency. There were two particularly negative ads by Healy. One was of an elderly white woman in a garage at night. It shows Patrick complimenting the man convicted of the crime while in the background stating that Patrick should not be governor because he spoke of a convicted rapist highly and he contributed money to the man's cause. The second set of ads criticized Patrick as an NAACP defense attorney for successfully minimizing a death sentence for a man convicted of killing a state trooper. Even though initially the ads narrowed the margin between the candidates, they eventually worked against Healey giving Patrick the advantage (Anderson, 2006).

Other attacks by the Healey camp included the leaking of information about Patrick's brother-in-law, referring to him as a convicted rapist. Patrick responded by clarifying the situation between his sister and husband and stated that their marriage had problems in the past, but they recently celebrated their twenty-fifth wedding anniversary through a rededication ceremony and that their children had no knowledge of their past before the press leaked the story. Although Healey denied leaking the story, Patrick's response was that the negative campaigning had to end. His specific response "We are going to ask the people to choose whether the politics of fear, division, and personal destruction is what they want, or whether we're better than that, and are ready to finally throw out those who dump this trash in the public square" (Monahan, 2006).

Despite Healey's attacks, Patrick, continued to work on his grass-roots campaign by holding town hall meetings. Polls immediately following the leak showed Patrick 25 points ahead of Healey (Anderson, 2006). Instead of launching his own negative ads, Patrick's response was to focus exclusively on Healey's record during the Romney administration. Patrick argued that Healey utilized negative ads to keep voters off track and off her record. Patrick went on to state that her campaign was nasty and she had set a negative tone for Massachusetts that politics in the state was toxic. Healey's negative campaign did more to hurt her credibility than to move voters over to her side. In fact, polls indicated that 45 percent of voters stated that her negative ads made them less likely to vote for her for (Anderson, 2006).

Both candidates raised a large amount of money for the campaign. Healey received nearly $12 million in donations compared to Patrick's nearly $7.5 million. However, Healey outspent Patrick by a 2:1 margin in advertising (Mooney, 2006).

The Issues

Several issues featured as part of newspaper reports and in the debates were important to voters in the election. Among them were the candidate's positions on fiscal issues such as taxes, the state's economy and the cost of living, healthcare, education, crime, and immigration, and social issues such as abortion and gay marriage. Most important to a large percentage of voters was the cost of living. According to voters, one solution was to lower the state income tax, passed in 2000. Healey supported rolling back the state income tax from 5.3 percent to 5 percent while at the same time increasing aid to local communities. Patrick opposed rolling back the state income tax, arguing that it would be fiscally irresponsible and it would shift the burden to local communities, which would result in higher property taxes. He instead wanted to reduce property taxes and provide more funding to local communities by proposing a local-options or meal tax to help ease their tax burden.

In one televised debate, the moderator questioned the candidates about the cost of living and the problem of residents relocating out of state, Patrick's responses were to propose increasing the minimum wage, building more affordable housing, and making transportation easier for citizens who work in Boston but cannot afford to live there. Healey focused on reducing the cost of unemployment insurance for employers and creating a tax-free savings account for workers saving to purchase their first home.

Related to the cost of living is the cost of health insurance. Massachusetts is ahead of the nation, recently passing legislation requiring all residents to have health insurance. The new administration will shoulder most of responsibility for executing the law, specifically how much businesses and lower income residents will have to pay. The new law expands the state's Medicaid program by covering uninsured adults and children. Adults with incomes 300 percent below the federal poverty level will be subsidized and those greater than the 300 percent threshold are required to purchase an affordable health plan developed by insurance companies. The major difference between the candidates was the fee per worker charged to employers who cannot afford to offer health care benefits to employees. Healey opposed the fee and Patrick supported it.

Patrick and Healey both have criminal justice backgrounds; Patrick as an assistant attorney general for civil rights under Clinton and Healey as a professor of criminal justice. Two major issues in the area of public safety separated the candidates; the death penalty and how the state issues gun licenses. Healey was supportive of the death penalty and Patrick opposed it. Late in the campaign, Healey changed positions on how the state issues gun-licenses. The current policy allows local police chiefs to issue licenses. Worcester Police Chief Gary J. Gemme came out against Healey after she spoke before the Massachusetts Major City Chiefs Association. Healey's proposal for a uniform policy in issuing gun permits, took power away from local police. The proposal included a statewide panel of police chiefs who would decide if an individual receives a permit to carry a gun. Gemme had recently started a new gun issuing policy in Worcester that was more restrictive than the state's. His policy denied permits to anyone who was arrested for drugs, driving-under-the-influence, affiliated with gangs, or any misdemeanor that was punishable by more than two years in jail. Gemme argued that neither the state nor other police chiefs knew what was happening in a community enough to be able to determine whether a person should receive a permit. Moreover, the move for one overarching statewide policy seems antithetical to the Republican view of decentralization of power (Croteau, 2006). On the other side of the issue was the Gun Owners Action League, which believed police chiefs had too much authority in deciding who should receive gun licenses. The League believed local police chiefs would eventually abuse this power. Patrick supported the decentralized policy and adding more police officers to local communities.

Although both candidates' children went to private schools and both wanted to improve public education, they had different approaches. Healey desired to change the age that a student can drop out from 16 to 18. Patrick did not have a position on this proposal. While both candidates supported charter schools, Patrick wanted a cap on how much local governments spend on charter schools. He was also supportive of a bond measure to help fund higher education. The major disagreement in education between the candidates was whether illegal aliens should receive in-state tuition rates. Patrick supports this proposal and like many voters, Healey opposes it.

On the issue of gay marriage, Patrick was supportive of and believed the courts had resolved the issue. Patrick argued that people should stand before the law equally although black ministers criticized him for his stance. Healey opposed same sex marriage, but supported civil unions. She also supported the proposed constitutional amendment banning same sex marriage.

Other issues important in the campaign supported by Patrick included giving driver's licenses to illegal immigrants and limiting employers' access to criminal records. Healey and most voters disagreed with Patrick's positions on these issues.

The position each candidate took on abortion was also important to voters. Both candidates were pro-choice but there was speculation as to where Healey stood on this issue because of her association with Romney who changed positions on abortion frequently.

Endorsements

Because of this speculation, three notable women's groups, the Massachusetts chapter of the National Organization for Women, the Planned Parenthood Advocacy Fund, and NARAL Pro-Choice Massachusetts endorsed Patrick over Healey who would have been the state's first female governor (Wangsness and Simpson, 2006). Healey refused to respond to a survey about her stance on abortion, prompting these groups to support Patrick.

Patrick also received support from a myriad of black political leaders and raised more money from out-of-state contributors than any other candidate in the early days of the campaign. Among the notables who may have had appeal to whites were former National Urban League president Vernon Jordan, former labor secretary Alexis Herman, and Illinois state senator, Barack Obama. Reports suggest that 24 percent of Patrick's funding were from grass-roots sources, black voters who would like to increase the number of black victories for statewide offices, particularly the office of governor and senator (Williams, 2006). Even former President Bill Clinton stomped for Patrick at a rally. The fundraiser in which Clinton appeared raised $2 million for the campaign. Clinton's major appeal to voters was a message that was very similar to Patrick's theme throughout the entire campaign. Clinton urged supporters to speak with their neighbors about Patrick regardless of their political leanings. He stated that Americans were tired of "politics as usual." Voters want, Clinton said, a civil and calm discussion about the issues. His message was one of taking the moral high ground and of bringing out the best in people to make the world better, the foundation of Patrick's campaign. Others in attendance at this rally included Senators Edward M. Kennedy and John F. Kerry.

As common in most political campaigns, major newspapers in Massachusetts also weighed in by endorsing candidates. Among those supporting Patrick were the *Boston Globe, Worchester Telegram & Gazette, MetroWest Daily News, Providence Journal, Berkshire Eagle, Boston Phoenix, Newton Tab,* and the *West Roxbury & Rosindale Transcript.* Major newspapers supporting Healey included the *Boston Herald, The Eagle-Tribune, Sentinel & Enterprise, Lowell Sun,* and *Cape Cod Times.* The most common themes in the newspaper endorsements were the fact that those who supported Patrick believed in his campaign rhetoric of restoring hope back into politics and a desire to make Massachusetts better. They also complimented Patrick on running a campaign that was free of negative advertisements. In the end, Patrick's campaign was one of consensus building and compromise. Those supporting Healey pointed out that the bulk of voters in Massachusetts had the same issue positions as Healey. They also pointed out that Healey agreed to uphold the tax rebate voters supported in 2000.

Other endorsements for Patrick included the Massachusetts Teachers Association and the Service Employees International Union Local 119. The Teachers Association supported Patrick's education policies, pointing to the failure of the Romney administration, which included Healey. The union supported Patrick's promise to make healthcare more affordable.

The Gun Owners Action League endorsed Healey because of her position on creating a state board to issue gun licenses. However, Chief Gemme of Worcester endorsed Patrick (Croteau, 2006).

Depoliticizing Race

In today's political climate, it is often the norm for black candidates to depoliticize race in order to appeal to white voters. It is very unlikely for white voters to elect a passionate civil rights activist to a statewide office. Depoliticizing race is tempting to black candidates who must garner white votes to win.

Most blacks who have won statewide office take race off the table as a part of the dialogue while others have such impeccable credentials that most reasonable Whites do not consider their race while casting their vote. This approach certainly helped Patrick in this campaign. Part of his appeal is that he has had access to an Ivy League university education, experience in the top levels of corporate America, and had a broader political agenda than previous black candidates. Patrick's resume and campaign style was an integral part of this election.

In a state that is nearly 90 percent white and approximately 7 percent black, it was necessary for Patrick to appeal to whites just as Edward Brooke did in his bid for the United States Senate in 1966. Brooke was the nation's first popularly elected black United States senator. He represented Massachusetts from 1967-1979. Since then, only two other blacks have held this prestigious position—Carol Mosely Braun representing Illinois from 1993 to 1999 and, most recently, Barack Obama also representing Illinois (2005-2008). Brooke, however, did extensive research before launching his candidacy for the Senate. According to Becker and Heaton (1967), Brooke's research was part of one of the largest research programs carried out for a statewide election. This intensive research program proved quite beneficial in helping Brooke win the election.

Almost forty years later, Patrick's campaign for governor has some strong similarities to Brooke's campaign. Both had opponents that the public viewed as unfavorable based on their record of service while in office and their previous unsuccessful campaigns. For example, Brooke's opponent, Endicott Peabody, was a former governor who was defeated in his reelection bid in the Democratic gubernatorial primary by Francis X. Bellotti in 1964. Healey had previously run for state representative twice unsuccessfully and was part of a past administration that was unpopular. Brooke's popularity and favorability ratings never slipped in the polls, neither did Patrick's. However, both of their opponents had unpopular records with voters, Peabody as governor and Healey as lieutenant governor. Peabody had a blemished record because voters did not believe he accomplished much in office as governor. Healey's popularity plummeted because of her negative ads and her affiliation with Romney. Brooke had a record of honesty in pubic office. As attorney general, he was part of the investigation that uncovered corruption that indicted many state officials. Voters knew Patrick as a United States assistant attorney general in the civil rights division of the federal government who worked for underrepresented groups. Voters also appreciated the positive tone of his candidacy despite the negative ads run by his opponent, which served to lower her popularity throughout the course of the campaign.

All of these circumstances as well as others that are discussed below, factor into both Brooke's and Patrick's success in Massachusetts. Research suggests there are a variety of conditions necessary for blacks to win state-wide office. Sonenshein (1990) notes the following factors that influence a candidates chances of winning; the candidate's campaign strategy, the political leaning of voters in the state, and the viability of the party. Jeffries (1998) agrees with this assessment but adds and stresses that the black candidates must have an appropriate apprenticeship. For both authors, an ideal political situation for black candidates is a state with a large enough black population to help the candidate win in the general election so that the party will not publicly oppose their candidacy. The voters in the state should also have liberal attitudes. There is, however, a point of departure between Sonenshein (1990) and Jeffries (1998) pertaining to this condition. The latter argues that blacks should not limit their choices to states with liberal attitudes; doing so would severely limit choices where blacks could run for office. Patrick's candidacy in Massachusetts met one of these conditions, having voters with liberal attitudes.

Secondly, black candidates must work within the party structure and have as much party support as their opponent. Support from the party legitimizes the black candidate's campaign and provides him with a myriad of resources. Black candidates should also have extensive previous political experience. Being a former mayor,[2] representing an area that is majority black, or losing their last election is a liability to the black candidate. Beyond the black candidate's control is the quality of the opponent. When the opponent has major flaws, it strengthens the black candidate. Nevertheless, the black candidate must keep their liabilities to a minimum. Patrick had the support of the Democratic Party, which provided him with the vast resources of the party. Former President Clinton and Senators Ted Kennedy and John Kerry both made public appearances to support Patrick. However, he did not have previous experience in elected office. His work as a United States assistant attorney general and the experiences as vice president and general counsel at two of the country's largest corporations, he argued, gave him just the experience need to run a state government responsibly.

Finally, most appealing to whites is a black candidate that is middle class, highly qualified, and one that has a deracialized political strategy. The candidate should have a conciliatory style that "attempts to defuse the divisive effects of race by avoiding references to ethnic or racially construed issues, while at the same time emphasizing those issues that appeal to a wide community"(Jeffries, 1998: 167). The candidate should transcend race and focus on issues that appeal to all voters regardless of race, issues like education, healthcare, and transportation. However, the black candidate must delicately balance their deracialized approach while at the same time utilizing race as an asset. In short, they must appeal to blacks without alienating whites.

Patrick did not have to appeal to blacks as much as others candidates do because of the small number of blacks in the state. Moreover, according to some reports, the fact that Patrick was black did not register with the electorate. At a meeting with the local Chamber of Commerce, Patrick's race did not come up. In fact, one business owner commented, "I don't even see him as black. It looks like to me that he has a deep tan" (Page, 2006). In addition, at the same meeting, Patrick never mentioned his race or any potentially racially divisive issues. Instead, he talked about public education and the state's economy. Unfortunately, the fact that some voters looked at Patrick as having a "deep tan" may lend some credibility to Strickland and Whicker's (1992) assertion that in order for black candidates to win statewide office, they must look white.

Despite Patrick's success, historically, black candidates do not win state-wide elections because a proportion of whites will not vote for a black candidate (Williams, 1989; Jeffries, 1998; Jeffries and Jones, 2006). In fact, Hutchings states that "There remains a non-trivial faction of white voters who will not vote for a candidate simply because (the candidate is) black. We are kidding ourselves if we argue these people have disappeared from the landscape" (Page, 2006). If the candidate is a strong advocate for civil rights for blacks or if the candidate makes this issue prominent during the campaign, this phenomenon is exaggerated. The candidate will likely alienate whites and prompt them to cast a vote for the other candidate. What helped both Brooke and Patrick is their failure to place civil rights on the agenda of their campaign. Becker and Heaton (1967) stated that even though voters knew Brooke was black, they did not associate him with the civil rights movement. Similar to Brooke's campaign, race was not an integral part of Patrick's dialogue while campaigning.

What helped Patrick win the election was voters' dislike for Healey. When pollsters asked voters why they were supporting Patrick, many suggested because they disliked Healey because of her negative ads. On the other hand, when voters mentioned why they supported Healey, a larger percentage said they disliked Patrick. This dislike for Patrick could be related to his race or to the fact that Healey made light of Patrick's support of LaGuer who turned out to be guilty. This in fact made quite a few voters upset with Patrick. However, Patrick said he sincerely believed the justice system mistreated LaGuer. In the end however, Healey's missteps helped Patrick win the election. The fact that this was an open seat also helped Patrick.

Data Analysis

Although the data in Table 1 cannot yield rigorous statistical analysis, I do observe patterns in how the voters of Massachusetts made their decisions in the gubernatorial election. First, neither candidate made much crossover appeal to independents or to voters identifying with the opposing party. Exactly the same percentage of Republicans voted for Patrick as Democrats voted for Healey. This is one area where a larger percentage of voters voted for Healey over Patrick. Furthermore, only a four-percentage point difference separates the candidates' support from Independents. It appears that Patrick had more crossover appeal to conservatives than Healey had with liberals. Only 9 percent of liberal leaning voters cast their ballots for Healey while Patrick was able to garner a fifth of conservative voters.

The data on community size indicates that Patrick had more support from voters in urban and rural communities than in the suburbs. He also garnered more votes from large cities and the Boston area. In North and South Shore Massachusetts, there is an even split between voters.

Looking at the data on gender and vote choice, no patterns emerge. There was no gender gap in this election. Conversely, upon examining the data dissected by race and gender two facts emerge. First, white women gave more support to Patrick than white men. While only 45 percent of white men voted for Patrick, 57 percent of white women voted for him. What is also clear is that white women preferred Patrick almost by a 2 to 1 margin; only 35 percent voted for Healey while 57 percent voted for Patrick. The strong support white women showed for Patrick could be the result of the endorsements from three major women's groups, the Massachusetts chapter of the National Organization for Women, the Planned Parenthood Advocacy Fund, and NARAL Pro-Choice Massachusetts and that Healey's position on abortion was ambiguous. Although during the campaign Healey stated she was pro-choice, she was part of an administration that was pro-life.[3] Moreover, when directly asked about her position in a survey from women's groups, she refused therefore a majority of white women opted for Patrick in the election.

When examining the data by race, it is clear that a large percentage of African Americans, 89 percent, voted for Patrick and 11 percent voted for Healey. These numbers are congruent with nationwide data, which indicate that blacks overwhelmingly vote for Democrats, but a small percentage, usually between 5-10 percent, votes Republican. Because Patrick was a black candidate, he should have garnered more support from blacks, especially considering the fact that the state has such a small black population and he would be the first black governor elected. Notwithstanding blacks who identify with the Republican Party, Patrick outraged some black ministers and voters because he supported gay marriage. It seems that Patrick made a strong appeal to blacks to overlook his stance on gay marriage because issues that are more serious should be their focus like unemployment and crime. It may be, however, that some blacks withheld their votes from him because of his position on gay marriage.

Table 1
Exit Poll Data

Vote by Gender			
	Healey	Patrick	Mihos
Male (46%)	38%	51%	9%
Female (54%)	32%	61%	5%
Vote by Race			
	Healey	Patrick	Mihos
White (83%)	39%	51%	8%
Black (9%)	11%	89%	*
Latino (6%)	*	*	*
Asian (0%)	*	*	*
Other (2%)	*	*	*
Vote by Race and Gender			
	Healey	Patrick	Mihos
White Men (37%)	42%	45%	11%
White Women (45%)	35%	57%	7%
Non-White Men (95)	13%	78%	1%
Non-White Women (9%)	21%	78%	*
Vote by Party ID			
	Healey	Patrick	Mihos
Democrat (41%)	9%	85%	5%
Republican (19%)	85%	9%	6%
Independent (39%)	41%	45%	10%
Vote by Ideology			
	Healey	Patrick	Mihos
Liberal (26%)	9%	83%	6%
Moderate (51%)	36%	55%	8%
Conservative (23%)	72%	20%	6%
Vote by Age			
	Healey	Patrick	Mihos
18-29 (11%)	22%	66%	10%
30-44 (23%)	35%	57%	7%
45-49 (35%)	34%	55%	8%
60 and older (32%)	41%	53%	5%

Table 1 (cont.)

Vote by Income			
	Healey	Patrick	Mihos
Under $15,000 (3%)	*	*	*
$15-30,000 (9%)	37%	51%	7%
$30-50,000 (20%)	34%	51%	11%
$50-75,000 (20%)	31%	57%	9%
$75-100,000 (20%)	34%	62%	4%
$100-150,000 (19%)	40%	56%	4%
$150-200,000 (5%)	*	*	*
Would Romney Make a Good President?			
	Healey	Patrick	Mihos
Yes (31%)	76%	18%	6%
No (65%)	20%	69%	8%
Would Kerry Make a Good President?			
	Healey	Patrick	Mihos
Yes (25%)	8%	85%	5%
No (71%)	49%	40%	8%
Vote by Size of Community			
	Healey	Patrick	Mihos
Urban (22%)	29%	63%	7%
Suburban (67%)	38%	52%	8%
Rural (11%)	30%	65%	2%
Vote by Region			
	Healey	Patrick	Mihos
Boston Area (25%)	28%	65%	6%
Other Large Cities (12%)	31%	59%	7%
N. Shore/S. Shore (17%)	44%	46%	8%
Eastern Mass (35%)	40%	50%	8%
Western Mass (11%)	30%	65%	2%

Source: http://edition.cnn.com/ELECTION/2006/pages/results/states/MA/G/00/epolls.0.html. n=655

More than half of whites voted for Patrick. While neither candidate made race part of the campaign, it is clear that for some whites, Patrick's race did matter. It is also clear that a generation gap exists. There is a forty-point difference between 18-29 year olds who voted for Patrick over Healey. Becker and Heaton's (1967) study of the Brooke campaign revealed that the most prejudiced group in Massachusetts were older people and this group had the lowest percentage of individuals who favored Brooke in the 1966 election. They concluded that race had an impact on candidate preference in that election, and this appears true today.

Whatever the case, it is clear that the hopeful campaign Patrick ran appealed to younger voters. In an article the Sunday before the election, candidates sent messages directly to voters. Patrick's comments were simple and straightforward in that it asked voters how they are doing. He then goes on to asks voters if they are tired of the way things are, particularly with the cost of living, school fees, and friends and family leaving the state because of the cost of living. Patrick's message was one of hope, one that inspired voters to work with him to bring Massachusetts back to its glory. His message was color-blind and it resonated with most voters. As Mooney and Wangsness (2006) point out, most voters just wanted a change from the Romney administration. They wanted to be able to afford to live in Massachusetts. Walker (2006) makes the point painfully clear by speaking to a couple who are residents at a teaching hospital in Boston. The couple commented, "Even on our salaries, we can't afford it here," and they were pediatric dental surgeons. Thus if a family of surgeons find it difficult to live in Massachusetts, one could only imagine how a blue-collar worker would feel pinched. In the end, Patrick's candidacy appealed to all types of people in Massachusetts regardless of race and income.

Healey's message in the same article did not have the same positive appeal as Patrick's. Her words were reminiscent of the same vibe that she put off in her campaign. Instead of primarily focusing on her plans if she became governor, within the first sentence of her statement, she refers to Patrick's promises and feel good message. One voter, registered as an independent stated that she considered voting for Healey, but instead would vote for Patrick. She commented: "Enough is enough. More than voting for Deval Patrick, I'd be voting against Kerry Healey."'I don't believe her and don't like the way she is running her campaign. She should be answering the question: What are you going to do for us?" (Mooney and Wangsness, 2006). Other voters in the same article made comments about Healey's negative ads. One made this comment about the campaign, "It's very, very negative, particularly Kerry Healey." "Her ads are totally negative…. If she had things to stand on, she wouldn't have to do these ads" (Mooney and Wangsness, 2006).

Conclusion

Although Patrick's candidacy proved to be successful, there remains a cloud of doubt about whether whites are ready for a black candidate who does not depoliticize race. Patrick always overlooked race. After winning the election he said, "never raised (the race) question. People voted for him because they have confidence in his ability" (Atkins and Sweet, 2006). The odds were with Patrick in that Healey's association with Romney and the failure of his administration in addition to her negative campaigning turned most voters off. Healey's campaign provided Patrick the ideal circumstances for a black candidate to win statewide election. If the conditions were different, would Patrick be the first black governor of Massachusetts? Only time will tell if he decides to run for reelection, different circumstances and a different candidate. In the meantime, the fact that one of the states with the smallest black population was able to elect a black governor should show promise for the future of the black candidate for statewide office in states with larger black populations.

Acknowledgments

This chapter is dedicated to my son Aiden Lewis Wilson. You are my inspiration. I also thank his cousins Jazmin Nikole Welch and Jessica Victoria Welch who provided him with love and care while I worked on this chapter. I also send a special thanks to my sister, Regina Warren, and my parents Joseph and Cynthia Lewis. And a final thanks to my graduate assistant, Yvonne Simms.

Notes

1. Deval Patrick was supportive of a Latino man convicted of rape. Various other individuals supported the man while in prison because they believed he was mistreated by the criminal justice system and was a victim of juror misconduct. Evidence of several letters written by Patrick to LaGuer surfaced. DNA evidence later proved LaGuer was guilty of the crime.
2. Judson and Jones (2006) find that several unsuccessful statewide black candidates were former mayors (Thomas Bradley, Ron Kirk, Harvey Gantt, and Andrew Young). They go on to state that historically the office of mayor has not been a stepping-stone to a higher elected office.
3. It is clear those voters who support a Romney candidacy for president supported Healey more by nearly 60 percentage points. Although her affiliation with Romney as lieutenant governor may have cost the election, she does have a base of support, albeit small. The total percentage of those supporting a Romney candidacy for president was only 31 percent. An equally important fact to note is that an even smaller percentage supports a Kerry candidacy for president. They split their support between Healey and Patrick evenly.

References

Anderson, Lisa. Massachusetts gubernatorial candidates wage brutal campaigns. (October 27, 2006). Chicago Tribune. Retrieved from http://web.lexis-nexis.com.fetch.mhsl.uab.edu: Lexis Nexis.

Atkins, Kimberly. Battle for Governor; Deval turns up heat on Healey. (October 20, 2006). The Boston Herald, 005. Retrieved April 19, 2007, from http://web.lexis-nexis.com.fetch.mhsl.uab.edu: Lexis Nexis.

Atkins, Kimberly and Sweet, Laurel J. The vote is in 2006; Leaders say 1st black gov a 'bookend' for Mass. Race woes. November 9, 2006). The Boston Herald, 006. Retrieved April 19, 2007, from http://web.lexis-nexis.com.fetch.mhsl.uab.edu: Lexis Nexis.

Becker, John F. and Heaton Jr., Eugene E. 1967. The Election of Senator Edward W. Brooke. *The Public Opinion Quarterly*, 31, 346-358.

Canellos, Peter S. Voters' anger erupts; and the message is a towering no; Primary '90. (September 19, 1990). The Boston Globe, 34p. Retrieved May 25, 2007, from http://web. lexis-nexis.com.fetch.mhsl.uab.edu: Lexis Nexis.

——————. Weld staffers celebrate, but then comes the shock: Silber's the foe. The Boston Globe, 38p. Retrieved May 25, 2007, from http://web.lexis-nexis.com.fetch.mhsl.uab. edu: Lexis Nexis.

CNN Exit Poll Data. http://edition.cnn.com/ELECTION/2006/pages/results/states/ MA/G/00/epolls.0.html. Retrieved April 1, 2007.

Croteau, Scott J. Police chiefs blast Healey on gun permits; Gun group endorses proposal. (October 19, 2006). Telegram & Gazette, A1. Retrieved May 25, 2007, from http://web. lexis-nexis.com.mhsl.uab.edu: Lexis Nexis.

Helman, Scott. Patrick at pulpit, lists his priorities. (February 27, 2006). The Boston Globe, B1. Retrieved May 25, 2007 from http://web.lexis-nexis.com.mhsl.uab.edu: Lexis Nexis.

Jeffries, Judson. 1998. Blacks and High Profile Statewide Office: 1966-1996. The *Western Journal of Black Studies*, 22, 164-173.

Jeffries, Judson L. and Jones, Charles E. 2006. Blacks who run for governor and the U.S. Senate: An examination of their candidacies. *The Negro Educational Review*, 57, 243-261.

Jones, Charles and Clemons, Michael. 1993. A model of racial crossover voting: An assessment of the Wilder victory. In Georgia Persons (Ed), Dilemmas of Black Politics (pp. 128-147). New York: Harper Collins.

Johnson, Glen. Patrick garners most votes; Reilly touts success at convention. (June 3, 2006). Associated Press State and Local Wire. Retrieved May 25, 2007, from http://web. lexis-nexis.com.fetch.mhsl.uab.edu: Lexis Nexis.

Kalke, Rushmie. Patrick, Mihos trade praise, push local aid; Candidates for governor campaign in Central Mass. (September 29, 2006). Telegram & Gazette , A6. Retrieved May 25, 2007, from http://web.lexis-nexis.com.mhsl.uab.edu: Lexis Nexis.

Kiely, Kathy. These are America's governors. No blacks. No Hispanics. (January 21, 2002). USA Today, 1A. Retrieved May 25, 2007, from http://web.lexis-nexis.com.mhsl.uab.edu: Lexis Nexis.

Kush, Bronislaus. Muslims drawn to Patrick; Local community also working against Question 1.. (October 25, 2006). Telegram & Gazette, B5. Retrieved May 25, 2007, from http:// web.lexis-nexis.com.fetch.mhsl.uab.edu: Lexis Nexis.

Lehigh, Scot and Phillips, Frank. Poll finds Weld leading Silber; CLT petition support seen as soft; Politics and Government. The Boston Globe, 24. Retrieved May 25, 2007, from http://web.lexis-nexis.com.fetch.mhsl.uab.edu: Lexis Nexis.

Loth, Renee. Liberal voters struggle with field of irreconcilables; For some, neither candidate is comfortable ideological fit; Campaign '90. The Boston Globe, 1p. Retrieved May 25, 2007, from http://web.lexis-nexis.com.fetch.mhsl.uab.edu: Lexis Nexis.

McNamara, Eileen. Women's Questions. (September 27, 2006). The Boston Globe, B1. Retrieved June 18, 2007, from http://web.lexis-nexis.com.fetch.mhsl.uab.edu: Lexis Nexis.

Mehren, Elizabeth. The Nation; Blue for Beacon Hill?; The man who might be Massachusets' first Democratic governor in 20 years is far from a standard-issue liberal. (October 31, 2006). Los Angeles Times. Retrieved April 19, 2007, from http://web.lexis-nexis.com.fetch. mhsl.uab.edu: Lexis Nexis.

Monahan, John J. Attack ads skew gubernatorial campaign. (October 15, 2006). Telegram & Gazette, A1. Retrieved May 25, 2007, from http://web.lexis-nexis.com.fetch.mhsl.uab. edu: Lexis Nexis.

——————. Gubernatorial candidates do battle in third debate; Patrick, Gabrieli spar with Reilly on gay marriage. (May 25, 2006). Telegram & Gazette, A9. Retrieved May 25, 2007, from http://web.lexis-nexis.com.mhsl.uab.edu: Lexis Nexis.

——————. Democratic gubernatorial debate is tonight. (September 7, 2006). Telegram & Gazette, B1. Retrieved May 25, 2007, from http://web.lexis-nexis.com.mhsl.uab.edu: Lexis Nexis.

Mohl, Bruce and Howe, Peter J. Election becomes battleground in car insurance war. (October 25, 2006). The Boston Globe, C1. Retrieved May 25, 2007, from http://web.lexis-nexis. com.fetch.mhsl.uab.edu: Lexis Nexis.

Mooney, Brian C. Patrick gets help in ad battle with Healey. (October 18, 2006). The Boston Globe, A1. Retrieved May 25, 2007, from http://web.lexis-nexis.com.fetch.mhsl.uab.edu: Lexis Nexis.

——————. Gabrieli readies run for governor; Hires operatives, cites positive polling. (March 22, 2006). The Boston Globe, B1. Retrieved May 25, 2007, from http://web.lexis-nexis.com. fetch.mhsl.uab.edu: Lexis Nexis.

——————. Patrick's path from courtroom to boardroom. (August 13, 2006). The Boston Globe, A1. Retrieved May 25, 2007, from http://web.lexis-nexis.com.fetch.mhsl.uab.edu: Lexis Nexis.

Moynihan, Kenneth. Kerry Healey has work cut out to catch up with Deval Patrick. (October 4, 2006). Telegram & Gazette, A11. Retrieved May 25, 2007, from http://web.lexis-nexis. com.fetch.mhsl.uab.edu: Lexis Nexis.

Nealon, Patricia. Turnout for gubernatorial races set record; crisis in middle east. (November 7, 1990). The Boston Globe, 36p. Retrieved May 25, 2007, from http://web.lexis-nexis.com. fetch.mhsl.uab.edu: Lexis Nexis.

O'Sullivan, Jim. Patrick critic heading for Mass., intending to dog candidate. (August 8, 2006). State House News Service.

Page, Susan. Election test how much race matters; African-American candidates for major state offices try to break some 'old barriers'. (2006). USA Today, 1A. Retrieved November 1, 2006, from http://web.lexis-nexis.com.fetch.mhsl.uab.edu: Lexis Nexis.

Phillips, Frank. Patrick outpaces two rivals in new poll; Democrat surges to a 21-point lead as vote nears. (September 17, 2006). The Boston Globe, A1. Retrieved May 25, 2007, from http://web.lexis-nexis.com.fetch.mhsl.uab.edu: Lexis Nexis.

Phillips, Frank and Samuels, Adrienne. Healey calls for stripping police chiefs of gun-licensing role. (October 18, 2006). The Boston Globe, B4. Retrieved May 25, 2007, from http:// web.lexis-nexis.com.fetch.mhsl.uab.edu: Lexis Nexis.

Pierce, Charles. The Optimist 'I wasn't campaigning as the black candidate.' And because he didn't, because he ran a hopeful, grass-roots campaign that ended with his election as governor, Deval Patrick is our 2006 Bostonian of the Year. (December 31, 2006). The Boston Globe, 28. Retrieved April 15, 2007, from http://web.lexis-nexis.com.fetch.mhsl. uab.edu: Lexis Nexis.

Sonenshein, Raphael J. (1995). Can Black Candidates Win Statewide Elections? *Public Opinion Quarterly*, 105, 219-241.

Strickland, R. and Whicker, M. 1992. Comparing the Wilder and Gantt campaigns: A model for Black statewide success in state wide elections. *Political Science & Politics*, 25, 204-212.

Vennochi, Joan. For Reilly, things go better with Coke. (August 11, 2006). The Boston Globe, A17. Retrieved May 25, 2007, from http://web.lexis-nexis.com.fetch.mhsl.uab.edu: Lexis Nexis.

Wangsness, Lisa. A hushed Clinton speaks proudly of Patrick: Says the electorate wants to be lifted up. (October 17, 2006). The Boston Globe, B1. Retrieved April 19, 2007, from http://web.lexis-nexis.com.fetch.mhsl.uab.edu: Lexis Nexis.

——————. At rally, Patrick tries to turn Healey's ads back at her. (October 16, 2006). The Boston Globe, B4. Retrieved April 19, 2007, from http://web.lexis-nexis.com.fetch.mhsl. uab.edu: Lexis Nexis.

——————. Healey will sign antitax pledge; 3 in4candidates support rollback. (September 4, 2006). The Boston Globe, B1. Retrieved May 25, 2007, from http://web.lexis-nexis.com. mhsl.uab.edu: Lexis Nexis.

Wangsness, Lisa. and Simpson, A. 3 women's group to endorse Patrick. (October 12, 2006). The Boston Globe, B4. Retrieved April 19, 2007, from http://web.lexis-nexis.com.fetch. mhsl.uab.edu: Lexis Nexis.

Williams, Joseph. Black political figures rally around Patrick. (April 18, 2006). The Boston Globe, A1. Retrieved April 19, 2007, from http://web.lexis-nexis.com.fetch.mhsl.uab. edu: Lexis Nexis.

Williams, Linda F. 1989. White/Black perceptions of the electability of Black political candidates. *National Political Science Review*, 1, 45.

Williamson, Dianne. Patrick caught in cross hairs; Support of LaGuer preceded DNA test. (October 5, 2006). Telegram & Gazette, B1. Retrieved May 25, 2007, from http://web.lexis-nexis.com.mhsl.uab.edu: Lexis Nexis.

Beyond the Boundaries, Volume 12; pp. 23-44

Running on Race and Against Convention: Michael Steele, Kweisi Mfume, and Maryland's 2006 Senate Contest

Tyson D. King-Meadows

University of Maryland Baltimore County

Introduction

The 2006 campaign for Maryland's open U.S. Senate seat challenged convention, providing an excellent counterfactual to deracialization theory. On one side was conservative one-term Republican Lieutenant Governor Michael Steele, the state's first black to win statewide elected office in 2002. On the other side, fighting for the Democratic primary win were, among others, ten-year incumbent Democratic U.S. House Representative Ben Cardin in a tight contest against former five-term Democratic U.S. House Representative and former national NAACP president Kweisi Mfume. There were historical, attitudinal, and pragmatic reasons for blacks *not* to have supported Steele. Yet both Mfume and Steele defied expectations by running on race. Steele specifically defied the odds by making the 2006 senate contest competitive in a decidedly blue state and by picking up 25 percent of the black vote despite high national anti-Republican sentiment.[1]

This chapter explains how Steele defied these expectations. It pays particular attention to how Steele spoke about black empowerment, black racial consciousness, and Republican partisanship, and synergies between the three constructs, in ways that were unanticipated by the Democrats. In addition, the chapter addresses how Steele capitalized on black angst over the substantive and descriptive dividends received from Democratic allegiance—including resentment over Cardin's primary defeat of Kweisi Mfume—despite the 2006 Democratic lieutenant governor-nominee being a black State Delegate from Prince George's County. More importantly, this chapter situates the 2006 Senate campaign as a counterfactual to the deracialization construct. While the conventional wisdom of the deracialization construct suggests running away from race, here was a case in which a black Democrat seeking statewide office did emphasize racial issues and in which a black Republican seeking the same office did emphasize race over partisanship. Furthermore, while deracialization largely precludes the possibility that either would occur in the same statewide election cycle, the political context of the 2006 Maryland Senate campaign allowed Mfume and Steele to break convention and to run on race.[2] The conclusion addresses what this campaign may portend about the construct and about the future relationship between blacks and the two parties.

Deracialization Theory

There continues to be a love-hate relationship with the deracialization construct in the literature on black electoral behavior and black political attitudes.[3] The construct refers to a combined rhetorical, electoral, and governance strategy in which black candidates deemphasize "racially-specific issues." In remarking on the distinctions between the agenda setting and the electoral strategy dimensions of the construct, McCormick and Jones define the latter in the following manner:

> Conducting a campaign in a stylistic fashion that defuses the polarizing effects of race by avoiding explicit reference to race-specific issues, while at the same time emphasizing those issues that are perceived as racially transcendent, thus mobilizing a broad segment of the electorate for purposes of capturing and maintaining public office.[4]

Moving further into the analysis, McCormick and Jones assert three components that will enable one to certify the existence of a deracialized campaign. First, the black candidate will employ a political style that seems "non-threatening" to whites. Second, the black candidate will avoid "racial appeals in organizing the black community." Third, the black candidate will avoid a specific racial agenda. At its base, the deracialization construct emerged to explain the value of electoral victories in the 1990s by black candidates in white jurisdictions, the "second wave" of black politics where biracial coalition building replaced direct confrontation as a means of achieving policy goals and elected office.[5]

In offering deracialization as an expression of black politics, McCormick and Jones follow an analytical framework that defines black politics as actions done for the "expressed purpose of improving the material conditions of African Americans" in a way "sensitive to the historical role and continuing impact of white racism in American political life."[6] As such, black candidates who attempt to capture public office for this "express purpose" are working within the analytical parameters of black politics. These authors then conclude with a tacit warning, "If deracialization as a successful electoral strategy lends its practitioners to ignore the policy-oriented concerns of African-Americans, then we should rightly dismiss their political behavior as nonlegitimate expressions of black politics."[7]

The 2006 Maryland Senate Race

In March 2005, Senator Paul S. Sarbanes announced his retirement. This made the 2006 senatorial race the first open seat contest since 1986 when Democratic Representative Barbara Mikulski ran for the seat vacated by Republican Charles McCurdy "Mac" Mathias (1969-1989). Three days later, Kweisi Mfume announced his candidacy. His candidacy seemed inevitable—Mfume was a former Baltimore City council member (1979-1986), former five-term congressman and Congressional Black Caucus (CBC) chair, former national NAACP president (1996-2004), and alumnus of historically black Morgan State University. Yet, his announcement surprised Maryland Democrats, including the state's black federal legislators and CBC members Representatives Elijah Cummings (Seventh District) and Albert Wynn (Fourth District).[8] It also generated both jubilation and consternation. On the one hand, Mfume had expanded the NAACP's membership, had retired organizational debt, and had remained a spokesperson for race-related causes. On the other hand, Mfume's personal and political stories—from gang life, out of wedlock children, and accusations of nepotism and sexual improprieties at the NAACP—produced one tapestry of questions about his judgment.

Even so, black elites saw Mfume's candidacy as an opportunity to break Maryland's glass ceiling of black electoral politics. Mfume characterized it this way: "It's time for the Democratic Party to make a bold statement in a blue state where blacks have always been willing to support white Democrats for office."[9] Without this statement Mfume feared a possible "seismic change in terms of voter loyalty (to the Democratic Party) because the black community will feel betrayed."[10] When other prominent politicians decided against running for the seat, black Democrats hoped the party's leadership would clear the field.

However, the Democratic Party leadership had other plans. Five weeks later Representative Ben Cardin of the Third District announced his candidacy. In fact, one journalist remarked that party leaders "scoured the field for a viable alternative to Mfume" in between the announcement by the former NAACP president and that of the ten-year incumbent from the Third District.[11] Cardin was a relatively unknown commodity outside of his district (representing parts of Anne Arundel, Baltimore, and Howard Counties, and Baltimore City). Cardin, however, secured a host of high-profile endorsements from the "neutral" party leadership (including that of House Minority Whip Steny Hoyer), severely outpaced Mfume's financial backing, made sure that neither Wynn nor Cummings endorsed Mfume until right before the September primary, and paraded out a string of endorsements by black leaders.[12] Despite the genteel nature of the Mfume-Cardin debates, Mfume made it a point to rail publicly against the Democratic leadership who had seemingly "anointed" Cardin as Sarbanes' successor.[13] Mfume surrogates and other blacks echoed these points.

The Cardin team and Democratic operatives took Mfume's candidacy seriously, but not for the reasons one would suspect.[14] Referred to as the "Kweisi Problem,"Democrats feared that an Mfume victory in the September Democratic primary was a lost Democratic Senate seat.[15] To win they had to (a) dismiss the Mfume candidacy; (b) heal wounds from the 2002 gubernatorial race; and (c) attack Steele (who had officially announced in October 2005). All the above was inevitable: This was the first statewide election since the gubernatorial race and wounds from it had festered for four years.

Old Wounds: The 2002 Governor's Race

The 2006 battle for black votes began when Republican Representative Robert Ehrlich chose Steele as a gubernatorial running mate in a campaign against two-term Democratic Lt. Governor Kathleen Kennedy Townsend (daughter of the late Sen. Robert F. Kennedy) serving under two-term Democratic Governor Parris N. Glendening.[16] Ehrlich capitalized on a misstep made by Townsend who, after long speculation, shocked black activists with a late June 2002 choice of retired U.S. Naval Academy superintendent Admiral Charles Larson—a white Republican who had recently switched parties. Townsend's decision negatively resounded on racial and political dimensions: The Democrats held the majority of elected office positions and blacks enjoyed high levels of political incorporation across the state.

A few days later, Ehrlich announced Michael S. Steele as the lieutenant governor-nominee. Steele was two-years into his leadership of the Maryland Republican Party and was a long-term resident of Prince George's County—a predominately black jurisdiction wielding increasing political and economic influence across the state. As the first black elected chair of any state's Republican caucus, the Catholic pro-life, anti-gun control, and pro-school reform candidate had a natural partisan base. He extended it by securing endorsements from disgruntled black Democrats and marketing a black vote for Ehrlich-Steele as payback for the Democrats' disrespect of black interests and as history in the making.[17] Other blacks criticized Republicans for tokenism, playing the race card, and suggesting that Democrats were unwilling to advance black elected office seeking.

The 2002 Ehrlich-Steele victory rippled through national politics. First, Townsend lost by three percentage points. Second, Ehrlich became Maryland's first Republican governor since Spiro T. Agnew (1967-1969). Third, the ticket did well in competitive and minority jurisdictions. Fourth, Steele became Maryland's first black statewide elected officer and the most prominent elected black Republican. Fifth, Ehrlich's victory was attributable to political context: Governor Glendening's approval was low; Townsend's campaign was poorly organized; the election occurred in a midterm year; and black voters were demobilized.

The 2006 Democratic Primary

The 2002 Ehrlich-Steele victory spread speculation about Democratic support of future black statewide office seekers. This speculation turned to consternation when Maryland's Democratic leadership responded unenthusiastically to Mfume's candidacy. However, problems besieged the Mfume campaign from the beginning. It lacked support beyond black circles and experienced fundraising problems. Mfume characterized Cardin as a Democratic insider—beholden to Washington-centered interests rather than state constituents—and as a politician whose votes (e.g., authorizations for military activities in Iraq and the Patriot Act) and campaign contributors (e.g., pharmaceutical companies) placed him out of step with most Marylanders. Mfume's tag lines were that he could not "be bought" and that Maryland could "make history." Cardin countered with his longevity in Maryland politics, widespread backing, and his ability to build coalitions.

Mfume's conundrum was clear: pitch his candidacy beyond black circles without alienating black voters who valued descriptive representation. *The Washington Post's* Marc Fisher put it this way: "But despite his efforts to make white audiences comfortable with him, Mfume has not been shy about mentioning race as one justification for his candidacy...."[18] As detractors of the deracialization construct understood, black candidates had to balance both black voter aspirations and white fear. Fisher then concludes his article with these words, "Race, of course, is the trickiest of weapons in a political campaign. When Mfume uses his prodigious rhetorical skills to neutralize the issue, he is masterful. When he wields race as a threat, he risks losing the advantage he has so carefully gained."[19] Undaunted, Mfume pressed on as Cardin's black gadfly.

Cardin, on the other hand, continued to assail Steele. For example, playing up President Bush's support for Steele; highlighting the endorsement of the MD-Washington Minority Contractors Association for his (Cardin's) candidacy; contrasting his vote to override President Bush's veto on stem cell research with what Senator Steele would do; and criticizing the Bush prescription drug plan. Prior to the September primary, Cardin's press releases mentioned Steele twelve times in the title compared to mentioning Mfume only once. These late 2006 words by Mfume best encapsulate his feelings about Cardin's dismissal: "As I've run this campaign for almost a year and a half, we've always been considered the underdog. We didn't have the same amount of money or the blessing of the party. We're still trying to reach the ears of the voters."[20] By early 2006 Cardin had become a financial juggernaut. His response to Mfume and black discord—"I have not been anointed.... I have a record"—seemed dismissive.

It was politically expedient for Cardin to marginalize the campaign of Mfume and to attack Steele. Polls consistently revealed that an Mfume primary victory could create a competitive general election. For example, an April 2006 survey, suggested that the outcome of the Senate race could turn on who won the Democratic nomination.[21] This poll showed an eight-point Cardin lead over Mfume offset by a large percentage (22 percent) of likely primary voters remaining undecided. According to the poll, if Cardin faced Steele, he would lead by double digits but with an equal number of undecided voters. If Steele faced Mfume, the latter's lead would only be five percentage points with a huge number of undecided voters (17 percent). In either scenario, Steele would pick up between 16 and 21 percent of the African American vote. An August 2006 poll showed Steele picking up 23 percent of this electorate against Cardin but only 8 percent of this electorate against Mfume. The August poll also showed Cardin with a lead of three percentage points over Steele, with 16 percent of voters undecided. Cardin bounced on this news with the only release mentioning Mfume in the title. In the end, Mfume lost the primary election to Cardin, 40.5 to 43.7 percent.

This jockeying for the black vote affected all involved. Cardin's electability forced Mfume into campaigning to *neutralize* race (so that he would not alienate white Democrats) and campaigning to *exploit* race (so that he could mobilize angry black Democrats). Steele's prominence, Mfume's discontent, and the possibility of black defection forced Cardin into obfuscating on issues of race, presenting his candidacy as non-threatening to black interests, and portraying party as more important than race. Along the way, while both Democrats tried to deescalate talk of race and to run a genteel campaign, Steele did neither. Steele, like Mfume, portrayed race as more important than party allegiance: The "Kweisi Problem" had become the "Steele Problem."[22]

The 2006 Steele Campaign

Steele did not run a deracialized campaign. He consistently expressed issues related to race and racism, and made reference to how Democrats responded to his race and party identification before and after he became the lieutenant governor-nominee. For example, Steele often intonated about the 2001 incident where white Democrat and Maryland Senate President Thomas V. Mike Miller called him an "Uncle Tom" because Steele complained about minority vote dilution in the redistricting process. He also referenced a September 2002 "Oreo Cookie" incident, where allegedly some in the crowd "pelted" him with the snacks at Morgan State University during a gubernatorial campaign debate.[23] Although some challenged the veracity of the "Oreo" incident, Steele and others pressed on with the story. He also reiterated the story during an appearance on *Hannity and Colmes*.[24]

Using these incidents as a thematic backdrop, Steele presented his official entrée into the Senate contest as an evolution of independent black politics. "For too long, one party worried more about prices in the stock market than prices in the corner market…. And too many in the other party preached reconciliation at the same time they practiced division," he remarked. Later he said, "As a young man I realized that the front lines in the New Civil Rights Struggle would be different ... instead of the right to sit at the lunch counter ... the New Civil Rights Struggle would be a struggle for the right to own the diner and to create legacy wealth for our children."[25] During the speech Steele criticized both parties and refrained from mentioning his Republican affiliation, proclaiming that he would be "A bridge that not only brings both parties together, but, more importantly, brings all of us closer to one another."

Furthermore, Steele tried to conjoin black racial consciousness with partisanship, and, like Mfume, to present his candidacy an evolution in black perseverance against racism. He brought up the federal investigation of two Democratic Senatorial Campaign Committee staffers for illegally obtaining Steele's credit report. (One pleaded guilty and avoided jail time, the other resigned.) Steele called this a "low point" in the campaign, remarking that the media did not react to the story as it would have if the Republican Senatorial Campaign Committee employed such a tactic against Illinois Senator Barack Obama.[26] Steele also reminded blacks that New Yorker Steve Gilliard, a liberal black Democratic operative, had depicted him as a minstrel in black face.[27] The picture, titled "I's Simple Sambo and I's Running for the Big House," was decried by Democratic Virginia gubernatorial candidate Timothy M. Kaine and was eventually pulled—to the dismay of liberal bloggers. Reportedly, Gilliard defended the picture by saying "Steele invited the portrayal by failing to criticize Gov. Robert L. Ehrlich Jr.'s (R) decision to hold a fundraiser at an all-white country club."[28] Steele also brought up House Minority Leader Hoyer's remark that the lieutenant governor had "a career of slavishly supporting the Republican Party." For Steele, reaction to Hoyer's remark underscored the problem he faced: Steele calls the term racist; Hoyer apologizes but sticks to the underlying sentiment; Cardin calls Steele's reaction an attempt to "change the subject"; the divided response of black elites make headlines; and black Democrats remain sidelined.

It was easy for Steele to connect these above incidents to a controversial strategy memo prepared for the Democratic National Committee and leaked to *The Washington Post* in April 2006. The 37-page internal document, prepared by DNC pollster Cornel Belcher and reportedly in consultation with the Democratic Senatorial Campaign Committee (DSCC), advised the party to "knock Steele down" by identifying Steele as the "hand-picked candidate" of President Bush. The memo hoped Democrats would capitalize on high anti-Bush sentiment amongst black voters. The memo also specifically urged the party to "turn Steele into a typical Republican in the eyes of voters, as opposed to an African American candidate." Why? Because, according to the *Post*, "a sizable segment of likely black voters—as much as 44 percent—would readily abandon their historic Democratic allegiances 'after hearing Steele's messaging.'"[29] The memo also carried a warning, picked up by another news organization, that Democrats might not press Steele about his relationship with President Bush. According to this news report, Belcher warned,"Democrats must be aggressive, Steele is a unique challenge."Part of that unique challenge, according to the memo, stemmed from "Steele's messaging to the African American community [which] clearly had a positive effect—with many voters reciting his campaign slogans and his advertising."[30]

Steele's response to the memo was immediate and direct, labeling the strategy instructive of how Democrats valued black voters:"They're afraid of what I represent. They're afraid of the fact that African American voters have options, and I'm one of them."[31] Steele surrogates labeled the memo another example of race baiting. Others decried the proposed strategy to discredit and "knock down" Steele's candidacy and objected to depicting Steele as a guaranteed, rather than swing or likely, vote for Bush policies on Medicare reform and Social Security privatization.[32]

While prominent black Democrats remained silent about these practices, they did respond to Steele's use of black colloquialisms. In July 2006, blacks chastised Steele for employing the"homeboy"colloquialism in reference to President Bush during a radio interview. It never became clear as to whether black angst centered on the term, the reference point, or belief that Steele was using the term to ingratiate himself with blacks or with Republicans. Either way when pressed, Steele explained it this way,"I've been quoted before as calling the president my homeboy, you know, and that's how I feel."[33] Steele also invoked another colloquialism when discussing prior critical comments about the Republican Party and President Bush:

> "I'm not trying to dis the president ... I'm not trying to distance myself from the president. I'm trying to show those lines where I have a different perspective and a different point of view. If I'm not free to share that as a candidate for the U.S. Senate, how can people expect me to share that and express that as a United States senator?"[34]

These comments came in response to the revelation that Steele was the anonymous Republican whose critiques of the party went public in a July *Washington Post* article,"For One Senate Candidate, the 'R' is a 'Scarlet Letter'."The then-anonymous candidate challenged the president's war policy, the federal response to Katrina, and stated that he would"probably not"want President Bush to campaign for him in the state.[35] The title of the article was derived from Steele's comment,"For me to pretend I'm not a Republican would be a lie ... [to run as a proud Republican is] going to be tough, it's going to be tough to do.... If this race is about Republicans and Democrats, I lose."[36] For Steele and supporters, the campaign was about black political independence.[37]

Unwilling to confront Steele on race, Cardin hammered him as a Bush Republican. A Cardin television commercial even featured President Bush's comments that "Michael Steele is the right man for the United States Senate."Cardin's move was both easy and difficult. It was easy because Republican star power fueled Steele's candidacy. Bush headlined a November 2005 fundraiser and appeared on the same stage with Steele at

Baltimore's M&T Bank Stadium. White House insider Karl Rove, President Bush, Vice President Cheney, and Arizona Senator John McCain hosted or appeared at fundraisers for Steele in Washington and Maryland. White House Chief of Staff Andrew H. Card Jr. headlined a fundraiser in New York, and Bush "Ranger" Mallory Factor (head of the Free Enterprise Fund in D.C.) spearheaded a private fundraiser.[38]

Steele's commercials and campaign zingers also made Cardin's job easy. For example, in television commercials Steele said the following: "politicians in Washington say one thing but do another"; it was time to "show [politicians] the door"; "real change" meant thinking differently about the vote; and, appearing with trash containers that it was time to take "out the trash." In another commercial, Steele appeared with a puppy, that reportedly was not his own. He intonated that Democrats would call him anything other than a "child of God" and say that he "hated puppies." These commercials were edgy, confrontational, and elusive about his stances on the issues. Cardin surrogates pointed out that President Bush, like Steele, was recalcitrant on Iraq, was confrontational to those with dissimilar views, was allusive about solutions, and employed discourse on the edge of acceptable political debate.

Despite this, Cardin surrogates faced a difficult time in rallying blacks to denounce Steele as a black Republican or as an individual. Some notable non-Marylanders with racial and partisan cache failed to campaign for Cardin inside the state. Only Illinois Senator Barack Obama and former President Clinton ventured into Maryland, with Al Sharpton, Jesse Jackson, and John Conyers appearing outside.[39]

To counter the label as a *Bush* Republican, Steele offered a new twist to the "Reagan Democrat" moniker: "Steele *Democrats*." The former label, firmly ensconced in America's political lexicon, explains both process and outcome. The outcome being a vote cast for Reagan by loyal Democrats (e.g., middle class, low-income, blue-collar, and union workers) who had grown increasingly disconcerted about their party's approach to cultural issues, economic policy, and foreign affairs. Envisioning similar success, Steele believed his personal appeal and public policy vision would win over black Democrats whose racial consciousness, religious convictions, and belief in economic empowerment could trump partisan affinity. Unlike the Reagan campaign however, there was never a clear message as to which political orientations differentiated segments of the party. The "Steele Democrat" slogan left constituents wondering about the similarities between a Reagan Democrat (who valued a strong military defense and conservative values) and a Steele Democrat (who valued racial consciousness and conservative values). The ambiguity was an especially strategic error for a campaign targeting young people born after the presidency of George H.W. Bush (1989-1993).[40]

Nonetheless, many Democrats with racial and partisan cache were nervous about the message and visual presentation of the "Steele Democrat" moniker. Presented in white letters against a light blue background, some believed the "Steele Democrat" moniker to be deceptive (akin to partisan identity theft); a position exaggerated by news of filmmaker Michael Mfume, a child of the primary contender, proudly sporting the moniker. Yet the Republican pressed on with its message and its display. For example, in the first debate between Cardin, Steele, and independent Kevin Zeese, Steele chastised Cardin for not learning to "look around the room and shut up and listen." This was, in part, a response to Cardin's attack on Steele for supporting the Bush administration's policies on health care, Iraq, and Social Security. Steele later remarked, "Stop the noise. Stop the race baiting, stop the fear mongering, and deal with me as a man." Steele's hyperbolic comments were strategic. The debate was at the headquarters of the Greater Baltimore Urban League headquarters, notable for being both a former church and a stop on the Underground Railroad. Steele, in effect, charged Cardin with racism, myopic partisanship, and indifference to black voices; charged he hoped would motivate blacks to think of themselves as Steele Democrats.

Finally dealing with the issue of race, Cardin stated, "Voters in the African-American community want change, and if they vote for me, they will get change." He went on, "I voted against [President] Bush's budget because Bush's budget is leading America in the wrong direction, and the people in the African-American community know that." Steele responded, "I appreciate your message of change, but it is an outdated message.... How can you be a change agent if you vote with your party 95 percent of the time?"[41] For Steele, Cardin's loyalty to party trumped loyalty to Maryland, and a citizen's loyalty to his/her economic, social, geographic, or racial interests should then trump (what Steele believed was) atavistic partisan attachment.

During other debates Steele tried again to depict Democrats, and Cardin, as out of touch with non-elite (or black) concerns. The second debate, held in October, occurred on WJLA's *News Talk Live*. At one point during the debate Steele asked Cardin about the beginning and ending of the proposed Metro Purple Line—a point of contention in Maryland's suburbs of Prince George's and Montgomery Counties. For many residents, the state's failure to ameliorate traffic congestion, and the state's federal elected officials refrain from directing traffic funds to solve the problem, was unacceptable. Flustered by Steele's aggressiveness and the unexpected question, Cardin stumbled to answer the question and then refused to answer it. In response Steele uttered "This gentleman has no clue about Metro traffic, congestion in this region ... I know exactly what the needs are because I live here." Steele's words were a not-so-thinly veiled nod to descriptive politics—both racially and geographically; Maryland had yet to elect a senator from the Washington suburbs (a place of growing minority presence).[42] News accounts of the debate characterized Steele as aggressive and Cardin as a policy-wonk unaware of problems outside the Baltimore City/County corridor.

Steele would make another such nod to descriptive politics during a third debate with Cardin in late October on Tim Russert's *Meet the Press*. Steele characterized himself more as a Reagan Republican or Lincoln Republican than a Bush Republican.[43] He also affirmed that Justice Clarence Thomas was his hero, but couched it this way: "In this sense, that, as an African-American, and the only African-American on the bench. You know, I've disagreed with Clarence Thomas on a number of issues." Steele then went on to explain his support for affirmative action. After this, Cardin began to pick up steam with black voters.[44]

It was easy to see why blacks were skeptical of Steele. He vacillated between running a racialized campaign and running a partisan campaign. For example, in a change of tactics, in mid-2006 Steele missed a fundraiser with Bush held at the Baltimore-Washington International Airport Marriott—choosing instead to appear at a fundraiser in Las Vegas. He cited scheduling conflicts. Ehrlich did not miss the fundraiser.[45] When asked about missing the fundraiser, Steele again employed black colloquialisms: "The reality of it is: Friends agree [and] friends disagree.... Where I agree with him, I say, 'Yo, Mr. President. I've got your back.' Where I disagree with him, I'm like, 'Yo, hold up. Let's talk about this.'"[46] These comments reminded voters of Steele's earlier support for the president's position against embryonic stem cell research; a position poorly articulated by horrific turn-of-the-year remarks linking stem cell research to experimentation done on imprisoned Jews and enslaved blacks. Although Steele's later apologies to the Jewish community were accepted, onlookers continued to question the veracity of Steele's moderate image.[47] His attempts to run against the party line—by distancing himself from the Republican president, from the pro-stem cell research Republican Governor Ehrlich, and by presenting himself as an independent thinker—were unpersuasive.

Running back to race, Steele publicized an endorsement by Russell Simmons—hip-hop cultural icon (e.g., founder of Def Jam Records and Phat Farm Clothing) and founder of the Hip Hop Summit Action Network—who hosted an August 2006 Baltimore fundraiser.[48] The Steele-Simmons relationship was below the radar. They had previously hosted financial empowerment summits in the state, and the Senate candidate had addressed Simmons' Hip Hop Summit in Detroit.[49] With the theme of "Change the Game" to mark his senatorial candidacy, Steele employed hip-hop phraseology to connect with young voters and Simmons' endorsement video went viral. Political analyst Donna Brazile characterized Simmon's entrée into the Steele camp as "a major endorsement for Lieutenant Governor Steele that will help him attract young people, as well as black voters." Brazile also noted, "Once again, this should serve as a wake-up call to Democrats not to take their most loyal constituents and voters for granted."[50] David Bositis, of the Joint Center for Political and Economic Studies, however downplayed the endorsement, claiming that Steele would no longer pursue black voters if Mfume won the primary.[51] Steele also secured the endorsement of

Cathy Hughes, founder and chair of Radio One. The Simmons and Hughes endorsement videos were marketed throughout minority communities. Steele's former brother-in-law and former heavyweight boxing champion Mike Tyson (who was previously married to Steele's sister, physician Monica Turner) also advocated for Steele, as did Don King who had endorsed Bush in 2004.[52] Understandably, Tyson's pro-Steele campaign activities were not endorsed by the Steele campaign. While Mfume stated that the Hughes and Simmons endorsements were "lost on him,"[53] others saw potential precursors to an avalanche of weighty endorsements.

While not an avalanche, a flurry of later endorsements did affect how the two party nominees jockeyed for the black vote. In October 2006, early Mfume supporter, and former Prince George's County executive, Wayne K. Curry endorsed Steele. As the county's first black executive and a vocal Democrat, Curry's endorsement gained enormous publicity, as did the endorsement by Major F. Riddick Jr., former aide to then-Gov. Parris N. Glendening. Steele coupled the Curry endorsement with the endorsement of five Prince George's county council members.[54] Donna Brazile dismissed the Curry endorsement and put more stock in current County Executive Jack Johnson's endorsement of Cardin. Political scientist Ron Walters however called the endorsements "audacious." He proclaimed, "This is going to go through the black community like a rocket.... It's going to be the talk of the county, the state, maybe even the nation."[55] Chair of Maryland's Democratic Party Terry Lierman dismissed black angst and defended the party's relationship with blacks. He stated, "[Those doubting the veracity of the party's commitment] are trying to make an issue out of something that doesn't exist."[56]

Some did not share Lierman's conviction or his optimism about how black party resentment could play out. By October 2006, *The Cook Political Report* labeled Maryland's open seat a "Toss Up," a decisive turn from its prior ranking.[57] For many, the Steele-Cardin campaign represented a problem of navigating legacy and partisan loyalty. Many onlookers made mention of a September 27, 2006 meeting between a frustrated delegation of Maryland's black state senators and party leaders. While Baltimore mayor and 2006 Democratic gubernatorial candidate Martin O'Malley described the meeting between himself, the delegation, Cardin, and Lierman as "cordial," non-elites suspected otherwise.[58] Black elites confirmed these suspicions when Prince George's Senator Nathaniel Exum noted, "They don't take us serious. We're the most loyal constituency, and they don't take us serious. They have never done anything, and they pay us lip service.... We'll have to see how it plays out."[59]

Mfume's numerous gaffes were also changing how the Steele-Cardin contest was playing out, opportunities Steele continued to exploit. These gaffes made it easy for Steele to connect the Democrats' dismissal of the former NAACP president, Steele's changing electoral fortunes, and ambivalent black Democratic allegiance, into a larger story about the Republican

Party being "uniquely positioned" to give voice to and act upon black substantive interests. For example, Steele exploited Mfume's decision to wait three days before conceding his primary loss to Cardin. Mfume justified the wait under guise of speculation that absentee and provisional ballots would make the difference. Yet Cardin campaigned as the presumptive victor and challenged Steele to debate. This prompted a statement from Steele's staff: "As much as Congressman Cardin and Democratic Party bosses would like to push Kweisi Mfume out of the race, the Maryland Board of Election still has yet to certify who won Tuesday's primary." Also, "This attempt by Congressman Cardin to anoint himself the nominee is disrespectful to the lieutenant governor's friend, Kweisi Mfume and, more importantly, disrespectful to Maryland voters."[60]

Mfume's concession remarks tried to take the air out of Steele's sails, but his next gaffe, at a pro-unity rally two weeks after the Democratic primary, opened up more space for Steele's appeal to black racial consciousness. This would be the first time that Cardin and Mfume would appear together after the primary election. During the rally headlining Senator Obama, Mfume endorsed Cardin but then added, "We need women in leadership positions in the state. We've got to find a way that African Americans and other minorities are represented statewide in office."[61] That black State House Majority Whip and two-term Delegate Anthony G. Brown was the 2006 Democratic nominee for lieutenant governor seemed unimportant. Steele pounced on Mfume's gaffe by stating: "The challenge of the opportunity is to build a bridge to communities the Democratic Party has taken for granted and has, by its choice of nominee, [decided to tell to wait].… I'm here to say, 'You don't have to wait any longer.'"[62] A *Washington Post* article added legitimacy to Steele's comments when quoting Mfume, who apparently justified his appearance at the event as part "promise keeping" to Senator Mikulski. Mfume remarked, "I am here to fulfill my commitment and my obligation."[63] It was clear that Mfume's endorsement of Cardin came with a "caveat."[64]

Figure 1, which displays the post-primary volatility of public opinion towards Cardin and Steele, makes clear that the lieutenant governor was gaining momentum in his campaign. Notice that a late October poll, conducted by the *Baltimore Sun*, gave the Democrat a six-point lead, with Steele garnering only 43 percent and 5 percent undecided. The *Sun* poll contradicted an earlier *Washington Post* poll that gave Cardin an 11-point lead (with 54 percent) and only 1 percent of respondents identified as undecided. A Mason-Dixon poll conducted at the turn of November reported a Steele disadvantage of three points, and reported that a full 9 percent of respondents remained undecided.

Hoping to build upon Steele's momentum, the Republicans provided another controversial visual depiction of the "Steele Democrats" moniker. It came in the form of a four-page "Democratic Sample Ballot" flier distributed to Prince George's County precincts. It immediately garnered public outcry. The flier was a direct appeal to racial consciousness on multiple

Figure 1
Post-Primary Volatility in Approval of Steele and Cardin

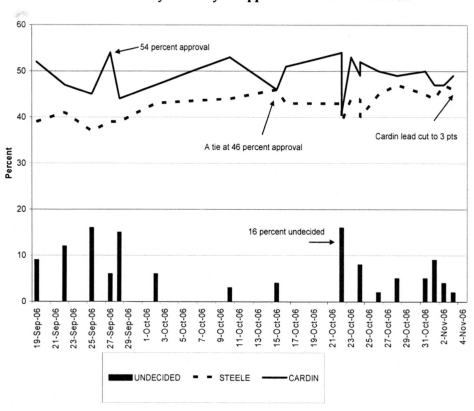

Source: Compiled by author, from data reported at http://www.reealclearpolitics.com and http://www.pollingreport.com, various dates. Data is for both likely and registered voters.

levels. First, the cover displayed pictures of Kweisi Mfume, Executive Jack B. Johnson, and former Executive Wayne K. Curry. Second, the inside contained a checked box for Ehrlich and Steele. Candidates for the other offices listed were Democrats. Third, the text, "These are OUR Choices" and "Official Voter Guide" adorned the cover. Fourth, the flier's colors were red, black, and green. Outraged, the Democrats blasted Republicans for fraudulent electioneering and a veiled attempt at either minority vote dilution or voter deception.[65] The Steele campaign claimed that the fliers were suggestive not deceptive.

Election Results

The Democrats successfully nationalized the 2006 midterm elections. The public had grown increasing discontent with Republican scandals, what they perceived as executive and legislative abuses of power, questionable congressional deference to the executive, the war in Iraq, and with President George W. Bush. Making electoral history, a 2006 vote for Democratic candidates was truly a vote against the president.[66] However, Maryland's election environment was contentious for reasons unrelated to national anti-Republican sentiment.[67] Concerns about electronic voting, voter-verifiable technology, and open-source coding caused citizens to cast 1,608,708 votes at the polls along with nearly 156,000 absentee ballots and over 41,000 provisional ballots.

Turnout and Support Data

Turnout reported at 57.53 percent, higher than in 2002 (30.76) and, understandably, lower than in 2004 (78.03). Steele carried 18 of the state's 24 counties but lost to Cardin by ten percentage points (54.2 to 44.2) and 178,296 votes. Table 1 depicts the breadth and depth of the Steele constituency examined against the constituencies built by other Republican candidates. I measure gains and losses by the proportionate share of votes garnered by Steele in 2006 compared to the votes garnered by Ehrlich as a 2002 gubernatorial candidate, by State Senator E.J. Pipkin (R-36) as a 2004 senatorial candidate against incumbent Senator Mikulski, and by President Bush seeking reelection. Looking across the data for Queen Anne's County, the 0.98 figure indicates that Steele retained 98 percent of the 2004 Pipkin constituency, 81 percent of the Bush reelection constituency, and 95 percent of the 2002 Ehrlich constituency. In Prince George's county, Steele bested Pipkin by 24 percent and Ehrlich by 9 percent.

Table 1 confirms Steele's inability to hold onto and build beyond the constituencies supporting previous Republican candidates. This is especially evident in the 18 Bush counties, varying in size, diversity, and geographical proximity to the state's inner corridor. For example, although both carried eastern Maryland, these counties tend to be predominately white, rural, and to *vote* Republican. Moreover, while Steele carried the 18 Bush counties, he was expected to carry those eight (8) giving Republicans a registration advantage: Calvert, Carroll, Frederick, Washington, Allegany, Garrett, Queen's Anne and Talbot. The greatest loss of the Bush constituency occurred in Washington County, a jurisdiction that gave Bush 64.4 percent of the two-party vote in 2004 but gave Steele only 60.8 percent of the vote (and 12,144 less votes). In Baltimore City, Steele outpaced Bush by garnering a greater share of the vote (23 to 17 percent) even while losing by over 75,000 votes.

As Figure 2 shows, reporting votes for Steele by the percentage of a district's black voting-age population, black constituents rejected the candidate despite endorsements by black elected officials and celebrities.[68] In Montgomery County, Steele garnered 31 percent of the vote and lost by over 108,000 votes. In Prince George's County, the lieutenant governor lost by more than 100,000 votes—a ratio of 3.1:1. Within the county's District 24 (an area with a 90 percent BVAP), Steele received 16 percent of vote. Hence,

Table 1
Steel's Gains and Losses of Republican Constituencies, by County

County	Steele / Pipkin 04	Steele / Bush 04	Steele / Ehrlich 02	Steele Gain / Loss Relative to Bush Vote
Allegany *	1.00	0.68	0.89	+ 4 B
Anne Arundel *	0.99	0.76	0.89	+ 3 B
Baltimore City	1.48	0.97	0.91	+ 6 S
Baltimore	1.06	0.79	0.77	+ 2 B
Calvert *	0.91	0.73	1.03	+ 3 B
Caroline *	1.10	0.81	0.95	+ 1 S
Carroll *	0.95	0.77	0.90	+ 2 B
Cecil *	0.86	0.72	0.96	+ 3 B
Charles	0.92	0.69	1.00	+ 1 B
Dorchester *	1.20	0.81	0.91	+ 1 S
Frederick *	0.90	0.70	0.97	+ 2 B
Garrett *	0.95	0.77	1.06	+ 1 B
Harford *	1.00	0.79	0.89	+ 2 B
Howard	1.01	0.79	0.88	+ 1 B
Kent *	1.10	0.87	0.85	+ 1 S
Montgomery	0.91	0.71	0.85	+ 2 B
Prince George's	1.24	0.89	1.09	+ 5 S
Queen Anne's *	0.98	0.81	0.95	+ 2 B
Saint Mary's *	0.92	0.69	1.02	+ 5 S
Somerset *	1.13	0.81	0.88	+ 6 B
Talbot *	1.14	0.86	0.97	+ 2 S
Washington *	0.85	0.67	0.94	+ 4 B
Wicomico *	1.04	0.78	1.06	+ 2 S
Worcester *	1.13	0.80	1.04	0
Average	1.03	0.78	0.94	-

Rounded figures reported.

* Bush County (N=18); Underlined counties reported a 2006 Republican registration advantage.

Note: + 4 B means in that specific county President Bush (B) did 4 percentage points better in 2004 than did Lt. Governor Steele (S) in 2006. For example, in Allegany County, Bush received 64 percent of the vote whereas Steele received 60 percent. In Baltimore City, the vote percentages were 17% (B) and 23% (S) for a +6 S code.

Source: Author calculations of Maryland State Board of Elections data.

Figure 2
Votes for Steele by Percent Black Voting Age Population, by District

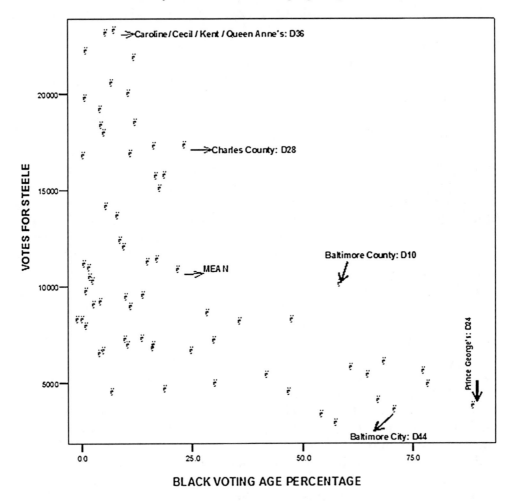

N=65; Votes for Steele = 13650.79 − 129.4 BVAP; p<.000
Source: Author calculations, Maryland State Board of Elections legislative district data.

Steele's greatest support came from non-white jurisdictions within the 18 Bush counties (52 percent of the total Steele electorate); e.g., District 36 (with 8.6 BVAP) gave Steele 60 percent of the vote. OLS regression shows for every percentage increase in BVAP, Steele lost 129 votes (F=26.855; p<.000; adjusted R^2 = .284).[69]

Exit Poll Data

Below I analyze the 2006 National Election Poll General weighted national and state sample—with 13,962 and 1,721 respondents, with 1,334 and 394 blacks, respectively.

Table 2 illustrates that Steele exceeded Democratic expectations by garnering 25 percent of the black vote. Comparatively, Republican House and Senate candidates nationwide received 10 and 12 percent, respectively, of the black vote. The lieutenant governor garnered 35 percent of the 18-24 age cohorts, though this segment was the least mobilized. As expected, Steele did well among married blacks (28 percent) and among the more affluent. Other Republican congressional candidates did comparatively worse among married blacks (average 12.5 percent) and among the affluent (average 22.5 percent) making more than $75,000. Steele also bested his Republican counterparts amongst the most educated blacks. Among black college graduates, Steele received 33 percent of the vote while colleagues received an average of 21 percent. Steele failed to capture the majority of Maryland's most affluent and most educated black voters.

Table 3 confirms similar patterns. Steele earned 17 percent of the black Democratic vote and lost 16 percent of the black Republican vote. He also lost 62 percent of the black conservative vote and 72 percent of the black moderate vote. Among liberal blacks, Steele earned 14 percent of the vote and did better than other Republicans who only earned 5 percent of this segment. Moreover, despite Steele's pro-life stances, he received a small percentage of the Protestant and Catholic vote and of the vote from frequent church attendees. Among those blacks attending church once a week (34 percent of the electorate), Steele received only 25 percent of the vote. This was a 15-point improvement over other 2006 Republican candidates.

The data in Table 4 are most revealing about black perceptions of the Steele campaign. The Democrats effectively portrayed Steele as a *Bush* Republican, and support from Maryland blacks reflected nationwide consternation about the president's agenda. Steele did quite well among blacks who approved of President Bush, voted to express their support for the executive (86 percent), and who believed that Iraq was unimportant to their Senate vote. However, nearly two-thirds of blacks in Maryland and over two-thirds of black nationwide strongly disapproved of Bush's job performance and connected their Senate vote to the Iraq War. Only 5 percent of blacks expressing disapproval of Bush voted for Republican Senate candidates. Steele also fared anemic among blacks who connected the issue of terrorism to their Senate vote (24 percent).

Table 4 shows another dimension of black perception. Thirteen percent of blacks believing that the Democrats only respected their views voted for Steele, and 37 percent of those believing that both parties respected the

Table 2
African American Vote for Steele, by Select Demographic Characteristics

OVERALL (23)	25%
GENDER	
Male (44)	30
Female (56)	20
AGE	
18-24 (6) 35	
25-29 (10)	14
30-39 (17)	25
40-44 (12)	40
45-49 (15)	27
50-59 (24)	22
60-64 (8) 20	
65+ (9) 12	
MARITAL STATUS	
Married (65)	28
Not married (35)	15
INCOME (2005 FAMILY)	
<$15,000 (2)	20
15,000 - 29,999 (7)	12
30,000 – 49,999 (19)	20
50,000 - 74,999 (29)	26
75,000 - 99,999 (19)	31
100,000+ (24)	26
EDUCATION	
Less Than High School (3)	0
High School Graduate (17)	20
Some College (33)	22
College Graduate (31)	33
Post Graduate (17)	24

* Parentheses represent proportion of the Maryland African American exit-poll electorate.

Table 3
African American Vote for Steele, by Party, Ideology, Religion,
Church Attendance, and Perceptions of Maryland Economy

PARTY	
Democrat (77)	17
Republican (8)	84
Independent/Something Else (15)	29
IDEOLOGY	
Liberal (29)	14
Moderate (55)	26
Conservative (16)	38
RELIGION	
Protestant / Other Christian (70)	21
Catholic (14)	37
Something Else (10)	21
None (6)	20
CHURCH ATTENDANCE	
More than Once a Week (20)	28
Once a Week (34)	25
A few times a month (20)	27
A few times a year (20)	20
Never (5)	5
PERCEPTION OF MARYLAND ECONOMY	
Excellent (5)	50
Good (50)	27
Not So Good (41)	17
Poor (4)	21

* Parentheses represent proportion of the Maryland African American exit-poll electorate.

Table 4
The Anti-Bush, Anti-Iraq War, Party Legacy, and
Candidate Approval Impact on the African American Vote for Steele

PRESIDENT G. W. BUSH'S JOB PERFORMANCE	
Strongly Approve (6)	59
Somewhat Approve (7)	62
Somewhat Disapprove (22)	28
Strongly Disapprove (64)	14
IMPORTANCE OF IRAQ WAR IN SENATE VOTE	
Extremely Important (38)	15
Somewhat Important (27)	24
Somewhat Not Important (23)	33
Not Important at all (12)	37
ISSUE OF TERRORISM IN SENATE VOTE	
Extremely Important (31)	24
Somewhat Important (35)	19
Somewhat Not Important (22)	30
Not Important at all (11)	31
SENATE VOTE TO EXPRESS:	
Support for President G. W. Bush (2)	86
Opposition to President G. W. Bush (53)	5
President G. W. Bush not a factor (42)	42
RESPECTS THE VIEWS OF BLACKS	
Only the Democratic Party (43)	13
Only the Republican Party (1)	67
Both do (28)	37
Neither does (25)	25
REASONS FOR STEELE VOTE:	
Strongly favor candidate	51
Like candidate but with reservations	37
Dislike the other candidate	7

* Parentheses represent proportion of the Maryland African American exit-poll electorate.

views of blacks voted for him. Cardin garnered 76 percent of those who believed neither party respected their views. Thirty-seven percent of those blacks who voted for Steele indicated that they had reservations.

Conclusion

The 2006 campaign for Maryland's open U.S. Senate seat reveals the need to modify the deracialization construct for examining the nuances of partisan and racial politics in twenty-first-century America. The deracialization construct is a rational choice explanation of black politics practiced against the backdrop of racial antagonism, socioeconomic stratification, and bloc voting. The construct is therefore akin to the black utility heuristic construct—where individual actions are structured by perceptions of how well blacks are doing and would do under alternative policy regimes.[70] The latter explains black electoral and attitudinal orientations and the former explains black office seeking practices. Both presume future trajectories of black politics will remain amenable to Democratic partisanship. Yet the logic of each construct presents an alternative path, one where black candidates seeking statewide office reject deracialization in order to raise black skepticism about the collective dividend produced by Democratic allegiance.

The campaigns of Kweisi Mfume and Michael Steele were decidedly counter to the proscriptions of the deracialization construct. Each sought, albeit in significantly different ways, to (a) threaten white political power; (b) mobilize black citizens through racial appeals, and (c) to interject issues of race into the contest. Both campaigns reflected consternation over black office seeking under the Democratic banner. Indeed, observers have long pondered about the impact of shifts in black allegiance, with journalists having proclaimed 2006 as the "year of the black Republicans."[71] Of course, the senatorial and gubernatorial defeats of Steele, Lynn Swan (PA), and Kenneth Blackwell (OH) and the black proportion of the Republican vote in 2006 suggest otherwise. On the other hand, harbingers are hard to identify at the time of emergence.

Indeed, voter turnout paved the way for other critiques of rational choice theory. Morris P. Fiorina contended that turnout was "the paradox that ate rational choice theory."[72] The theory was inadequate for explaining the expressive value of participation or for why people voted despite the improbability of their vote being decisive. Similarly, both Mfume and Steele continued to reject deracialization despite the improbability of winning—racial bloc voting within a closed primary system prevented the former from winning and a heavy anti-Republican context prevented the latter. This 2006 Senate contest however could foreshadow bigger problems to come for the Democrats. The Republicans could learn how to organize along *racial* lines as they learned to organize along *organizational* lines to win Congress in 1994; and the Democrats could (as the national party did in 1988 and as Maryland's state party did in 2002) misread black willingness to stay home or to defect. If either occurs, Maryland's 2006 contest could become, in retrospect, the campaign that ate deracialization theory as a prism from which to view trajectories of twenty-first-century black politics. As Prince George's Senator Nathaniel Exum suggested, only time will tell how it "plays out," or, more specifically, how the parties balance black voter aspirations and the need to diversify and solidify their partisan bases.[73]

Notes

1. Jeremy Mayer, *Running on race: Racial politics in presidential campaigns*, 1960-2000 (New York: Random House, 2002); Gary C. Jacobson, "Referendum: The 2006 Midterm Congressional Elections." *Political Science Quarterly* 122 (Spring, 2007), pp. 1-24.
2. Hanes Walton, *African American Power and Politics* (New York: Columbia University Press,1997); Michael C. Dawson, *Behind the mule: Race and class in American politics* (Chicago, IL: University of Chicago Press, 1994); Michael C. Dawson, *Black visions: The roots of* contemporary African-American political ideologies (Chicago, IL: University of Chicago Press, 2001)
3. Joseph McCormick, II and Charles E. Jones, "The Conceptualization of Deracialization: Thinking Through the Dilemma," in *Dilemmas of Black Politics: Issues of Leadership and Strategy,* (ed.) Georgia A. Persons, (New York: HarperCollins College Publishers, 1993), pp. 66-84; Robert B. Albritton, George Amedee, Keenan Grenell and Don-Terry Veal, "Deracialization and the New Black Politics," in *Race, politics, and governance in the United States,* Huey L. Perry (ed.) (Gainesville: University Press of Florida, 1996), pp.96-106; Byron D'Andra Orey and Boris E. Ricks, "A Systematic Analysis of the Deracialization Concept," *National Political Science Review* 11 (2007), pp. 325-334
4. McCormick and Jones (1993:76)
5. Saundra C. Ardrey and William E. Nelson. "The Maturation of Black Political Power: The Case of Cleveland." *PS: Political Science and Politics* 23(June 1990): 148-151.
6. McCormick and Jones (1993:79)
7. Ibid
8. John Wagner and Spencer S. Hsu, "Mfume Jumps In for Sarbanes's Seat," *Washington Post*, March 15, 2005, pg. B05.
9. DeWayne Wickham, "Blacks deserve something in return from Md. Democrats," *USA TODAY,* March 14, 2005, pg. 13A
10. Ibid.
11. Hockstader, "The 'Kweisi Problem'," pg. B07
12. Jon Ward, "Wynn, Cummings back Mfume," *The Washington Times,* August 30, 2006; Matthew Mosk, "Cummings And Wynn To Back Mfume," *The Washington Post,* August 30, 2006; pg. B02
13. Matthew Mosk, "Steele Strives for the Hearts of Black Voters," *The Washington Post,* November 8, 2005, pg. B01
14. Twenty-eight persons filed for the vacant seat, with eighteen in the Democratic primary.
15. Lee Hockstader, "The 'Kweisi Problem'," *The Washington Post,* June 11, 2006; B07
16. Parris N. Glendening served from 1995-2003.
17. The parallel is Douglas Wilder's successful 1986 bid for Lt. Governor of Virginia that laid the foundation for Wilder's successful and historic 1989 campaign. Until the 2006 election of Deval Patrick, Massachusetts, Wilder was the first popularly elected African American governor since Reconstruction.
18. Marc Fisher, "For Mfume, Race Cuts Both Ways," *The Washington Post*, July 2, 2006; pg. C01
19. Ibid.
20. Matthew Mosk and Claudia Deane, "Maryland Senate Race May Hinge On Ethnicity," *The Washington Post,* July 2, 2006, pg. A01
21. Gonzales Research & Marketing Strategies, April 4 – 13, 2006; N=819 registered regular voters.

22. Matthew Mosk, "Steele Strives for the Hearts of Black Voters," *The Washington Post*, November 8, 2005, pg. B01

23. Michael Sokolove, "Why Is Michael Steele A *Republican* Candidate?," *New York Times Magazine,* March 26, 2006; Paul Schwartzman and Matthew Mosk, "'Racist' Label by Ehrlich Riles Democrats," *The Washington Post,* September 1, 2004

24. Andrew Green, "Ehrlich bristles at Oreo skeptics,"The Baltimore Sun, November 13, 2005, pg. 1B

25. Steele Announcement Speech, Prince George's Community College, October 25, 2005

26. Author interview with Lt. Governor Michael Steele, June 22, 2007.

27. A few weeks before Gilliard depicted Ohio Secretary of State Kenneth Blackwell in blackface.

28. S. A. Miller, "Top Democrats duck on Steele hits," *The Washington Times*, November 3, 2005; Matthew Mosk, "Blog Attack on Steele Decried, Doctored Photo Criticized by Republicans and Democrats," *Washington Post,* October 28, 2005, pg. B04; Jeff Jacoby, "Slurs Fly from the Left," *The Boston Globe*, December 28, 2005, pg. A19

29. Survey based on 489 black Maryland voters. See Matthew Mosk,"Poll Finds Steele May Be Magnet for Black Voters," *Washington Post,* April 6, 2006, pg. B05

30. Richard Miniter,"Democrats Plan Race-Based Campaign Against Black Candidate in Maryland," *The New York Sun*, April 13, 2006,

31. Mosk, *Washington Post,* April 6, 2006

32. Jon Ward,"Plans to knock Steele labeled as 'destructive'," *The Washington Times*, April 7, 2006

33. John Wagner, "Steele Addresses Negative Comments on Bush," *Washington Post*, July 27, 2006, B01

34. Ibid.

35. Dana Milbank,"For One Senate Candidate, the 'R' Is a 'Scarlet Letter'," *Washington Post*, July 25, 2006, pg. A02

36. Ibid.

37. Interview with Steele (June 22, 2007) and Steele supporters (November 7, 2006)

38. Rangers were individuals bundling at least $200,000 for the Bush-Cheney 2004 campaign.

39. Interview with Steele (June 22, 2007)

40. Interview with senior campaign advisor (June 28, 2007).

41. S.A. Miller,"Steele, Cardin wrangle over race in debate,"*The Washington Times*, October 4, 2006

42. Interview with senior campaign advisor, June 28, 2007.

43. Transcript for October 29, 2006 edition of Meet The Press, Ben Cardin, Michael Steele. Updated: 10:42 a.m. ET Oct 30, 2006 [Accessed on January 3, 2007; available at ww.msnbc.msn.com/id/15473528/]

44. Robert Barnes and Matthew Mosk,"Poll Puts Maryland Democrats In the Lead,"Washington Post, October 29, 2006, A01

45. Matthew Mosk,"Steele Absent From Bush GOP Fundraiser,"Washington Post, June 1, 2006, pg. B05

46. S.A. Miller,"Missed fundraiser wasn't a slap at Bush, Steele says,"*The Washington Times*, June 4, 2006

47. See Robert Barnes and Matthew Mosk, "Steele Apologies for Holocaust Remarks," *Washington Post*, February 11, 2006, pg. B01

48. Jon Ward,"Steele gaining blacks' support," *The Washington Times*, August 24, 2006

49. Interview with Steele, June 22, 2007.

50. Jon Ward,"Steele gaining blacks' support," *The Washington Times*, August 24, 2006

51. Matthew Mosk, "Angling for Hip-Hop Appeal," *Washington Post*, August 25, 2006, pg. B01

52. Tyson and Turner have two children—a son and a daughter.

53. Matthew Mosk,"Angling for Hip-Hop Appeal," *Washington Post*, August 25, 2006, pg. B01

54. The members were David Harrington (D-Cheverly); Samuel H. Dean (D-Mitchellville); Camille Exum (D-Seat Pleasant); Tony Knotts (D-Temple Hills); and Marilynn Bland (D-Clinton).

55. Ovetta Wiggins, "Black Democrats Cross Party Lines To Back Steele For U.S. Senate," *Washington Post*, October 31, 2006, pg. B01
56. Ibid.
57. *The Cook Political Report*, "2006 Senate Race Ratings," October 20, 2006, pg. 3
58. Doug Donovan, "O'Malley Calls Talk `Cordial'," *The Baltimore Sun*, October 6, 2006, pg. 5.B
59. Jon Ward, "Democrats hit for lack of black candidates," *The Washington Times*, October 6, 2006
60. Jon Ward, "Steele, Cardin: Opening shots," *The Washington Times*, September 14, 2006
61. Ann E. Marimow, "Mfume Endorses Cardin, but Adds Caveat," *Washington Post*, September 28, 2006; pg. A01
62. Ibid.
63. Ibid.
64. Matthew Hay Brow, "Backing Cardin, with a Caveat," *The Baltimore Sun*, September 28, 2006, pg. 1B
65. Ernesto Londono, "Sample Ballots in Pr. George's Misidentify Candidates, "*Washington Post*, November 7, 2006
66. Gary C. Jacobson, "Referendum: The 2006 Midterm Congressional Elections," *Political Science Quarterly* 122(Spring 2007):1-24.
67. A host of problems plagued the September primary—late poll openings, a lawsuit to keep polling precincts open, late or absent election judges, long lines, and concern that electronic voting would disenfranchise the technologically challenged. Governor Ehrlich's comments about ballot security—i.e., that Marylanders vote by absentee ballot, and that those uncertain about their precincts to cast provisional ballots instead of going from site to site—added fuel to the fire.
68. Frequent precinct changes make it impossible to map demographic profile to these small unit lines.
69. A logistic regression running the likelihood of a district giving Steele more than 50 percent of the vote against the percentage of black voting age population produced an Ex(B) for BVAP of .904. This means that a one-unit change in BVAP decreased the odds of a district voting for Steele by 9.6 percent.
70. Michael C. Dawson, *Behind the mule: Race and class in American politics* (Chicago, IL: University of Chicago Press, 1994)
71. Dan Balz and Matthew Mosk, "The Year of the Black Republican?: GOP Targets Democratic Constituency in 3 High-Profile Races," *Washington Post*, May 10, 2006; pg. A01.
72. Morris P. Fiorina, "Information and Rationality in Elections," in *Information and Democratic Processes*, J. A. Ferejohn and J. H. Kuklinski (eds.) (Urbana, IL: University of Illinois Press, 1990), pp.334
73. See the provocative prescription offered to Democrats in Thomas F. Schaller's *Whistling past Dixie: how Democrats can win without the South* (New York: Simon & Schuster, 2006). Black Democrats are, of course, antagonistic towards the sentiment. For an analysis of the dilemma Republicans face in the future, see Michael Fauntroy, *Republicans and the Black Vote* (Boulder, CO: Lynne Rienner, 2007)

Beyond the Boundaries, Volume 12; pp. 45-62

Three Wrongs and Too Far Right:
The Wrong Candidate, the Wrong Year, and the Wrong State: J. Kenneth Blackwell's Run for Ohio Governor

Wendy G. Smooth
The Ohio State University

In January of 2005, Ohio appeared poised to make history by electing an African American as its next governor. At that early moment, both the Democratic and Republican Parties had strong, viable black candidates. From the Democratic Party, Michael B. Coleman, the mayor of Columbus, Ohio (the state's capital city) emerged as the contending frontrunner, while Secretary of State J. Kenneth Blackwell captured the frontrunner position among Republicans. Both candidates had well established bases capable of mobilizing supporters across the state. Coleman, a pro-growth mayor was credited with leading Ohio's largest city and the only in the state to experience growth in the last ten years. As mayor, he was credited with creating new jobs and overseeing a growing economic base. With deep ties to the state's business community, Coleman had learned to strike the always shaky balance between community interests and big business.

Secretary of State Ken Blackwell was even better positioned to run for governor given his record of winning statewide offices, the first black candidate to do so in the state. Blackwell had also developed a national reputation and was deeply favored among Republicans and equally vilified by Democrats. His national reputation developed in the wake of the 2004 presidential election, in which Ohio's balloting proved as controversial as the voting in the 2000 presidential contest in Florida. In his capacity as secretary of state, Blackwell presided over the elections in Ohio and made national news amidst allegations of widespread voter suppression tactics. Blackwell emerged as a national GOP icon and a party hopeful destined to rise in prominence. Political pundits and national political interests watched with bated breath at the prospects of a Coleman/Blackwell match up. This amazing political first would take place in the nation's foremost political battleground state, which would make Ohio central to deciding the 2008 presidential elections.

Despite such great expectations, by November of 2005 Columbus Mayor Michael Coleman announced that he would not seek the Democratic Party's nomination citing the challenges of running Ohio's largest city and the needs of his family as his reasons for pulling out of the race. Coleman's announcement allowed the Democrats to escape a primary contest between Coleman and Congressman Ted Strickland. Strickland went on to win the nomination. Coleman's exit ended the prospects of a nationally watched battle between two formidable black candidates for governor, a campaign that would have been a first for the nation.

Following Coleman's withdrawal from the race, Democrats quickly coalesced around Congressman Ted Strickland of Lisbon, Ohio, a 12-year congressman representing southeast Ohio, covering a portion of the Appalachian region. Strickland, a Methodist minister and psychologist, established himself as a moderate pro-gun Democrat with humble rural beginnings. Known for sharing his story of living in a chicken coop following the burning of his family's homestead, Strickland connected quickly with rural Ohio voters and steelworkers, the occupation of his father. He campaigned on a platform to clean up Republican corruption and create a stronger economic base for the state. In an overwhelming show of unity among Democrats, Strickland captured over 80 percent of the vote against competitor Bryan Flannery. This set the stage for a strong standing among Democrats in the general election that translated into record setting fundraising and aggressive races up and down the Democratic Party ticket.

Unlike the Democrats, the Republicans engaged in a bitter primary fight, the party's first contested gubernatorial primary since 1988. The primary race between candidates Ken Blackwell and state Attorney General Jim Petro left the party severely fragmented. Blackwell cleverly linked Petro as an insider of the embattled administration of Republican Governor Bob Taft, while situating himself as the lone outsider. He also successfully painted Petro as a liberal who only recently discovered moral values. Petro fought back to no avail. Drawing these differences, Blackwell captured the support of social conservatives across the state. After the entrenched mud slinging fest, Blackwell emerged as the winner capturing 56 percent of the vote with Petro garnering 44 percent. Following the primary, the state GOP faced a difficult task to unite their party, which never fully coalesced in support of the Blackwell candidacy.

Ted Strickland and Ken Blackwell ran the most expensive gubernatorial campaigns in Ohio state history. Voters overwhelmingly supported Democrat Ted Strickland, with Strickland carrying 72 of the 88 counties across the state. Blackwell suffered a brutal loss, garnering only 37 percent of the vote to Strickland's 60 percent, the lowest number of votes of any Ohio Republican candidate since the election of 1912. What factors explain Blackwell's poor showing in the general election? Lavished with promise, Blackwell was considered a rising star in the national Republican Party and a major player in increasing Republican support among blacks not only in Ohio, but across the country. Why did such an esteemed candidate suffer such a bitter defeat?

In this chapter, I argue that Blackwell's loss is attributable to an array of factors. Blackwell was the wrong candidate, in the wrong year and in the wrong state. Despite the national GOP's hopes that this was indeed the year to support a black Republican, the political landscape of Ohio made it nearly impossible for any Republican candidate, much less a black Republican candidate to win in 2006. Even more so, the socially and fiscally conservative Blackwell by all accounts was ideologically too far to the right to hold onto party moderates in such a volatile year for Republicans. Likewise, Blackwell, with his extreme conservative rhetoric, was the wrong black Republican to attract sizeable numbers of crossover black Democrats.

Most studies of black candidates running for high-profile statewide offices have focused on moderate Democrats and Republicans or liberal Democrats. The models evolving from this research implicitly assume that future candidates will also hold such ideological positions. The existing literature on blacks and statewide office speaks little to cases like Blackwell, in which a black conservative is a candidate for statewide office. Ken Blackwell's run for Ohio governor sheds light on our understandings of what non-traditional black candidates running for statewide office might encounter in future elections. As the Republican Party continues to seek out black candidates and voters aggressively, we can expect to see more ideological variances among candidates, including more conservative blacks running for statewide office. Such a strategy might prove successful in a state whose values align with the black conservative candidate. The Blackwell candidacy offers an opportunity to build models that account for the unique challenges such candidates face—challenges that differ from those of their more liberal and moderate counterparts.

Data and Methods

This study is based on analyses of election coverage in major national and local newspapers between the winters of 2005 and 2006. I analyzed coverage of the 2006 Ohio gubernatorial race in national papers, including *The Washington Post, The New York Times, USA Today,* and *The Chicago Tribune.* I also analyzed the major local Ohio papers, including the *Akron Beacon Journal, The Columbus Dispatch, The Cleveland Plain Dealer, The Cincinnati Enquirer, Cincinnati Post, Dayton Daily News,* and *Toledo Blade* across the same time period.

In addition to the newspaper coverage, I utilized campaign financing data and the official voter turnout rates from the Ohio Office of the Secretary of State. Finally, I used exit polls conducted by Edison Media Research and Mitofsky International, which consisted of 2, 286 interviews from

Ohio. The exit poll data provided the percentages of votes that each candidate received from voters across racial groups, genders, ideological backgrounds, political parties, and religious affiliations. The exit poll also queried voters on their motivations and priorities that may have influenced their votes in the gubernatorial election. Given the limited number of blacks included in the exit poll, I am able to do limited analyses of black voters, but include data where possible.

The Year of the Black Republican in Politics?

Ken Mehlman, then-chairman of the Republican National Committee (RNC), set the party's agenda with a strong emphasis on aggressively attracting black voters. Mehlman went beyond his RNC predecessors in implementing this agenda and began his campaign for black voters by denouncing the Republican Party's historic use of the "southern strategy." Mehlman acknowledged his party's long-employed strategy of using race-based appeals as a means of garnering the support of some white southerners with racist sensibilities.

Mehlman followed his denouncement of the southern strategy with a series of speeches before predominantly black audiences in which he sought to build connections using moral values arguments and pushing the faith-based initiatives. The black church figures prominently into the RNC plans as President Bush's faith-based initiatives are being used to sway black ministers toward support of their party (Muwakkil, 2005).

The centerpiece of the RNC's strategy to attract black voters hinged on the emergence of a star power team of black Republicans running for high-profile statewide offices in key battleground states. *The Washington Post* touted 2006 as the "Year of the Black Republican" pointing to the candidacies of Maryland senatorial candidate Lt. Governor Michael S. Steele, and Pennsylvania gubernatorial candidate Lynn Swann, the former Pittsburgh Steelers football star. The *Post* included Ken Blackwell's success in winning the Ohio primary as the third pillar of the Republican plan. Together, these three black candidates for high-profile offices represented the RNC's key efforts to reshape relations between blacks and the Republican Party (Balz and Mosk, 1995). If the Republicans sought to truly make inroads with black voters by running black candidates for high-profile offices, the party had simply selected the wrong year for Republicans in the states they selected. The RNC also woefully underestimated the extent to which black voters would look to the issues and their political interests in casting their ballots, rather than relying on a crude, more simplistic type of identity politics. Much like Republicans across the nation, Ohio Republicans used the midterm elections and the governor's race to send a message of dissatisfaction to the national party regarding national party scandals, the policies of the Bush administration, and the war in Iraq.

Wrong Year, Wrong State, Wrong Candidate

By the general election in November of 2006, the political landscape indicated that Ohio voters were primed to "throw the rascals out" after 16 years of Republican Party control. Blackwell could not have selected a less favorable year to run as a Republican. He had the misfortune of running as a Republican in a year in which voters were determined to issue a referendum against the Republican Taft administration. The array of scandals faced by the state's GOP, as well as the dismal condition of the state's economy, heavily weighted the governor's race in favor of the Democratic candidate. The low approval rating of the national GOP and the declining support for the war in Iraq did little to bolster the prospects for Ohio Republicans retaining leadership of the state.

To say Ohio Republicans faced a crisis of public trust is an understatement. The Republican governor, Bob Taft, faced ethics violation charges of which he was later found guilty, becoming the first sitting Ohio governor convicted of a crime. His approval ratings sank deeply providing him the honor of holding the lowest approval ratings in the nation. That same year, investigations began regarding a public finance scandal termed by the local media, "Coingate." Coingate involved Thomas Noe, a major Republican fundraiser, who was awarded a generous contract from the state to manage an investment of over $50 million for the Ohio Workers' Compensation Bureau. Noe invested the state's dollars in a rare coin fund, an unusual investment for a public fund. The questionable investments led to conflict of interest charges for the governor's administration and suspicions that money had been funneled to Republican election campaigns to facilitate the deal. Noe and his associates faced federal criminal and civil charges for the secretive rare coin scheme. Coingate further solidified allegations that Ohio had become strictly a "pay to play" state under the Republican administration. Only Republican supporters with a history of sizeable campaign contributions to party candidates would be awarded state contracts.

Blackwell responded to these political conditions by campaigning aggressively against Governor Taft's administration, criticizing the administration more brutally than if he were a Democrat. Blackwell painted the state's Republican leadership as tax and spend Republicans with utter disregard for fiscal responsibility. Needless to say, this strategy won Blackwell few friends among state GOP leaders. It further stressed an already tumultuous relationship between Blackwell and Governor Taft. As Taft faced ethics violations charges, Blackwell regarded the strained relationship as being of little benefit to his election bid.

These deep party divisions, along with the soiled reputations of the Republican administration, left a void in notable Republicans to campaign on Blackwell's behalf. In lieu of local GOP support, Blackwell capitalized on his national party attachments and brought national Republican star power to the state to fundraise and campaign on his behalf, including visits by President Bush, Senator John McCain, and presidential hopeful Mitt Romney. In the final days of the general election, Rudy Giuliani appeared in television ads endorsing Blackwell's fiscal policies, an ad that came too late to truly benefit Blackwell.

Blackwell was indeed saddled with formidable challenges. Moving into the general election, he needed to first, distance himself from the party in government. He needed to strike the artful balance between appealing to his own base of social and fiscal conservatives while also unifying the party, which meant modifying his campaign rhetoric to appeal to the moderates of his party. Rather than build common ground with moderate Republicans, Blackwell instead moved into the general elections maintaining his extreme fiscal and social conservative agenda. As a fiscal conservative, Blackwell advocated for a state flat tax and an extremely legislatively confining constitutional amendment that placed spending caps on the state's budget. Blackwell heavily advertised his 2004 work on an anti-gay marriage bill in the state and his stance against abortion. With these strongly conservative positions, Blackwell gained the endorsement of the Ohio Restoration Project, a group consisting of 2,000 evangelical, Baptist, Pentecostal, and Roman Catholic leaders in a network of so-called "Patriot Pastors." The group set out to build grassroots coalitions in Ohio's 88 counties in hopes of mobilizing conservative voters across the state for Blackwell (Dao, 2005).

Blackwell, as a key player in the RNC's imperative to increase its support among black voters, also set his sights on attracting that coveted prize for the party. As a conservative black Republican, Blackwell faced an uphill battle to dislodge the state's black voters' commitments to the Democratic Party. However, there were strong possibilities that Blackwell could, in fact, attract sizeable numbers of black voters. He had a solid record of doing so. In past elections, Blackwell successfully swayed black voters, garnering between 30 and 40 percent of the black vote in his previous election bids (Will, 2006). Further, studies show that voters are willing to exercise racial loyalty, if provided the opportunity to select a candidate of their own race (Grose, 2007: 326).

Blackwell never completely ignored race in his campaign. To the contrary, he embraced his own perspective of black politics. Blackwell always regards himself as a civil rights activist with a record of working on urban issues, and he often points out his work at the Department of Housing and Urban Development as proof of such commitments. At the same time, he relishes himself as "Jesse Jackson's worst nightmare" (Jones, 2005). Blackwell's appeals to black voters were on his own socially conservative terms. He counted on the socially conservative beliefs of black voters to trump their more liberal stances on economic and redistributive issues.

Blacks Candidates in High-Profile Statewide Races

Strickland and Whicker (1992) explain that a successful black candidate for statewide office will have crossover appeal with white voters, if the candidate posses certain personal characteristics. A black candidate for statewide office must be a political insider, project a conservative image, and blend with the dominant culture (1992: 208). Based upon this model, Blackwell ran a classic crossover campaign. He was foremost a political insider having served in the state's Republican administration as secretary of state and was also fast becoming recognized as a rising star among party conservatives at the national level. Some even speculated that winning the governor's office in Ohio would place Blackwell in line to secure the 2008 Republican vice presidential nomination (Will, 2006).

Running to the right of the state's GOP, Blackwell positioned himself as a true conservative and keeper of conservative values. Finally he fashioned himself as seamlessly blending with the dominant white culture. Blackwell defied one of Strickland and Whicker most controversial assertions that the ideal black candidate for statewide office must physically "look white" (1992:209). To the contrary, Blackwell physically "looks black" yet maintained an appeal to white voters. Blackwell sought to carefully balance his appeal to white voters with an appeal to black voters. Blackwell understood that securing a sizeable percentage of the black vote was necessary not only to win the race, but also to prove that the Republican Party could appeal to black voters thereby dislodging the Democratic Party's proverbial hold on the black vote. In the midst of his appeals to white social conservatives and white fiscal conservatives, Blackwell used his attachments, albeit limited to the black community, to reach out to blacks, particularly more socially conservative blacks.

Scholars also regard holding prior statewide office, possessing the support of one's party, and having good relationships with the media as fundamental to black candidates winning statewide office (Jeffries, 1995, 1999; McCormick and Jones, 1999; Strickland and Whicker, 1992). Blackwell possessed the appropriate political pedigree to launch a successful bid for the governor's office. He served on the city council of Cincinnati, later served as the city's mayor and by the time of the gubernatorial race had served in two statewide offices as state treasurer and secretary of state. Likewise, Blackwell had carefully steered clear of the pitfalls often afforded to black candidates seeking statewide office. Most importantly, his position as secretary of state meant statewide name recognition beyond his home base of Cincinnati, which would have offered him limited value in a statewide campaign (Sonenshein, 1990; Strickland and Whicker, 1992). In contrast, Blackwell garnered the secretary of state office in a high-profile statewide election immediately before running for governor. He was well supported by the national Republican Party, despite his strained relationships with other state party leaders.

In keeping with the ideal black statewide candidacy, Blackwell staged a largely deracialized campaign with minimal mention of race or race-based issues. Deracialization is a strategy used by candidates to craft a biracial electoral base by de-emphasizing race and avoiding racially divisive issues. The strategy is often used when candidates desire to appeal to voters of other races while maintaining the support of voters of their own race (Wright and Middleton, 2004; McCormick and Jones, 1993). Blackwell strategically used race and pointed out his own blackness in instances when he deemed voters would respond favorably to the idea of making history by electing him the state's first black governor and only the second in the nation's history. This was a successful strategy for Blackwell, one he used in his previous campaigns. He is commonly associated with a series of "first black" honors in Ohio's political history. In lieu of more racialized politics, Blackwell instead focused largely on taxation and moral values as his core campaign issues. Blackwell staged himself as a conservative maverick candidate who stood on his convictions. In contrast to the typical non-threatening image black candidates seeking crossover appeal assume (Wright and Middleton, 2004; McCormick and Jones, 1993), Blackwell presented himself as a passionate conservative unwilling to compromise on his values-driven politics.

Blackwell easily made news and captured the attention of the local and national media. One local journalist captures the sentiment of covering Blackwell writing, "He opens his mouth and news pours out. He has a talent for speaking in quotes and a knack for seeing how they will look in the next day's newspaper, even as he says them." Recognizing Blackwell's charismatic nature, he further writes, "I will miss covering Blackwell. He is fun to be around, blessed with an enveloping personality, and endearing sense of humor and a very big brain" (Hallett, 2006b). Blackwell emerged as a media darling and was often described endearingly as the "six-foot five, broadly built ex-professional football player." Echoing his steadfast, stand on one's convictions persona, Blackwell was drafted by the NFL's Dallas Cowboys after college, but declined his contract during training camp because he refused to play the position he was assigned.

Beyond all of his charismatic personal traits, Blackwell's rags to riches Horatio Alger story enhanced his media appeal. Blackwell's personal story of growing up in the projects of Cincinnati and becoming a millionaire made for the ideal Republican Party narrative. Blackwell earned his millions after selling shares in Blue Chip Broadcasting, a group of 15 urban-formatted Cincinnati radio stations. His rags-to-riches narrative symbolizes what the Republican Party imagines it offers to blacks who are willing to work hard and persevere in the face of hardships. Blackwell's story of racial uplift coincides with black conservative attitudes of self-help through economic empowerment as opposed to blaming whites for the conditions of the black community (Orey, 2004). Together, these factors made Ken Blackwell symbolic of the ideal black Republican and helped to him rise as an iconic figure of the party. He soon became an up and coming, major player for the more conservative factions of the GOP. This positioning on the national forefront made him a media sensation. Quite different from the experiences of many black candidates for high-profile offices (Jeffries, 2002), Blackwell had no problem garnering media attention and coverage.

Blackwell adopted different political strategies from those of most blacks running in statewide races. Opponents wishing to cast black candidates as political outsiders often engage in the "rough politics of values" as a means of defining the black candidate as beyond the mainstream and not in touch with traditional, middle of the road values. This is particularly threatening to black candidates for statewide office who struggle to position themselves as insiders in the eyes of voters (Strickland and Whicker, 1992). Blackwell however used this strategy to his advantage throughout the campaign to attack Strickland as too liberal for Ohio voters. Blackwell portrayed himself as the keeper of morality, often campaigning with a Bible in hand. He took every opportunity to remind voters of his support for the contentious Issue 1, the 2004 ballot issue banning same-sex marriage that rallied Ohio's religious and social conservatives and helped to increase support for President Bush's re-election bid. Blackwell used support of the anti-gay measure as a litmus test of values for Jim Petro during the primary and again with Strickland during the general election.

On two occasions, Blackwell and the state GOP engaged in the lowest form of negative campaigning by using gay-baiting tactics, strategies used to label an opponent as gay or sympathetic to gay issues as a means of distancing the candidate from the mainstream. The first incident involved a state GOP staffer who sent a message to conservative bloggers that Strickland, despite his 18-year marriage to a woman, was in fact gay. The staffer was later fired, but not before the story fully circulated. By mid-October, Blackwell trailed Strickland by 20 percentage point in the polls. At that point, the Blackwell campaign circulated an even more vile story intimating that Strickland was not only himself gay, but also a supporter of child sexual exploitation. Blackwell's campaign built upon a story that one of Strickland's former staffers had been charged with exposing himself to a minor, and suggested that Strickland supported the employee. *The Cincinnati Enquirer* (2006) denounced Blackwell's campaign tactics, labeling them as not befitting of a politician of his stature, yet in the same editorial the paper endorsed his candidacy, the only major Ohio newspaper to do so.

In the end, playing the "rough politics of values" backfired for Blackwell. Since Strickland too had claims to religious convictions and values, Blackwell was ultimately conceived as the extremist. Strickland was able to position himself as a more moderate centrist who also embraced religious values. Strickland, a Methodist minister was often quoted in local papers saying he went into politics "following the example of Jesus Christ." His religious posturing coupled with more moderate politics resonated with Ohio voters as more to the center and Blackwell's values appeared too far out of bounds for Ohio voters.

The Campaign by the Dollars

The 2006 governor's race raised the most money in Ohio's history with the candidates raising a combined $28.3 million. Blackwell raised a total of $12.1 million while Strickland raised $16.2 million. For Blackwell, the primary was an expensive campaign against fellow Republican Jim Petro. The contentious primary race left Blackwell's campaign depleted by more than $5.5 million, over which Blackwell expressed regret (Abraham, 2006). His subsequent fundraising efforts consistently lagged behind those of his Democratic challenger, Ted Strickland. Even after receiving over $1 million dollars from the state Republican Party, Blackwell continued to struggle to match Strickland's fundraising. Strickland raised more money than Blackwell throughout the campaign and ended the campaign with considerable cash on hand. Table 1 shows campaign funds for both candidates across the campaign. Strickland repeatedly attributed his fundraising success to the state's desire for a change in political leadership.

In the last weeks of the campaign, Blackwell's fundraising struggles became more apparent. With limited funds remaining, Blackwell was forced to withdraw his television ads while the Strickland campaign continued a consistent, aggressive television advertising campaign during the final weeks of the campaign (Hallett, 2006).

The General Election: Blackwell and Key Voting Groups

Blackwell successfully motivated his conservative base and they showed up to support him. According to exit poll data, those voters identifying as conservatives supported Blackwell in groves with 71 percent of these voters supporting him (See Table 2). The difficulty for Blackwell was that these voters constituted only 32 percent of the electorate. Moderates constituted a much larger share of the electorate. Nearly half of the voters identified as such and Blackwell garnered only 26 percent of their support.

Similar numbers of voters identified as Democrats and Republicans. However, while Strickland secured 92 percent of his party's support. Republican support for Blackwell was far less strong. Of the 37 percent of voters identifying as Republicans, Blackwell garnered 77 percent of their

Table 1
2006 Ohio Gubernatorial Race by the Dollars

	Strickland	Blackwell
Post-Primary Election Cash on Hand	$5,129,053	$330,000
Post-General Elections Fundraising	$2.8 million	$304,935
Post- General Election Cash on Hand	$258,486	$11,476
Total Campaign Fundraising	$16.2 million	$12.1 million

Source: Ohio Office of the Secretary of State.

votes. Strickland successfully whittled away one in four Republican voters. Roughly a quarter of independents supported Blackwell (see Table 2).

Blackwell banked heavily on the support of religious conservatives and campaigned aggressively with both black and white congregations across the state. However, positioning his religious values as so far to the right served to alienate some religious voters. Those identifying as Protestants or other Christians constituted 59 percent of the electorate and Strickland fared slightly better with this group than did Blackwell (see Table 3). The second largest group, Catholics, comprised a quarter of the electorate and overwhelmingly supported Strickland.

Table 2
Breakdown of 2006 Ohio Gubernatorial Elections by Ideology
and Political Party Affiliation

	Total	Strickland	Blackwell
Ideology			
Liberal	20	92	8
Moderate	48	71	26
Conservative	32	26	71
Political Party			
Democrat	40	92	6
Republican	37	20	77
Independent	23	69	26

Source: Edison/Mitofsky Exit Poll Data based on 2,286 interviews.

Table 3
Breakdown of 2006 Ohio Gubernatorial by Religion and
Religious Service Attendance

	Total	Strickland	Blackwell
Religion			
Protestant/Other Christian	59	57	41
Catholic	25	58	38
Jewish	3	93	7
Other	4	79	18
None	9	80	18
Religious Service Attendance			
Weekly	45	49	48
Occasionally	39	68	30
Never	13	81	17

Source: Edison/Mitofsky Exit Poll Data based on 2,286 interviews.

Beyond religious denominations, the frequency of church attendance is often used to identify religious conservatives across denominational lines. Nearly half of those polled identified themselves as attending church or religious services weekly and these voters were evenly split between the two candidates. Voters attending church or religious services more than once per week comprised 16 percent of those polled and Blackwell fared best among this group garnering 59 percent of these voters' support. Given the small numbers of blacks in the exit poll, I am not able to comment on the number of blacks of various religious denominations supporting Blackwell or those who attend church weekly or more so.

Strickland led Blackwell with every group of traditional swing voters in the state. Women, consisting of 52 percent of the voters polled, supported Strickland in higher numbers with 63 percent of their votes and Blackwell garnering the support of only 34 percent of women voters. Moderate-income families supported Strickland in higher numbers. Three out of five voters with families earning less than $75,000 supported Strickland (see Table 4).

The condition of the state's economy figured heavily in voters' decisions. In general, voters viewed the state's economy in hardship. Sixty three percent of voters interviewed thought the condition of the state's economy was "not so good or poor" and 77 percent of those voters cast ballots for Strickland. In addition, 47 percent of voters considered the job situation in their area as worse off than it was just two years ago while 34 percent viewed the job situation as about the same. Only 17 percent of Ohioans polled viewed the job situation in their area as better than it was two years

Table 4
Breakdown of 2006 Ohio Gubernatorial Elections by Income

	Total	Strickland	Blackwell
2005 Total Family Income			
Under $15,000	7	72	27
$15,000-$29,000	15	66	32
$30,000-$49,999	23	60	36
$50,000-$74,999	24	63	36
$75,000-$99,000	14	55	41
$100,000-$149,000	9	59	36
$150,000-$199,000	3	56	40
$200,000 or more	5	52	46

Source: Edison/Mitofsky Exit Poll Data based on 2,286 interviews.

ago. The pessimistic view of the economy and jobs played to Strickland's strengths and voters supported his position on jobs and the economy. Ohio voters also supported in large numbers an amendment to increase the state minimum wage. Of the 56 percent of voters supporting Issue 2, fully three quarters (75 percent) favored Strickland.

Ohioans views on the war in Iraq bolster the argument that this was indeed a bad year for Republican candidates, as unfavorable feelings about the war informed voters' responses in the gubernatorial election. More than half of those polled (56 percent) disapproved of the war in Iraq and 83 percent of those voters cast their ballots for Strickland. Likewise the declining support for President Bush and his policies were reflected in the gubernatorial race. More than half of Ohioans polled (58 percent) disapproved of the job President Bush was doing and 86 percent of those voters supported Strickland.

Blackwell and The Black Vote

While Blackwell enjoyed name recognition among black Ohioans, he faced the formidable task of persuading blacks to switchover to support a Republican candidate. An equally formidable challenge for Blackwell winning over black voters was overcoming his reputation for engaging in voter suppression tactics during the 2004 elections. Many blacks across the state associated Blackwell with using his power as secretary of state to disenfranchise black voters during the 2004 presidential elections. In going after black voters, Blackwell made several political miscalculations including an over-reliance on black churchgoers, running political ads that were perceived as stereotypical portrayals of blacks, and overstating the connections between black conservatism on social issues and black voting interests.

Concerned that black voters would interpret supporting Blackwell as offering support for Republican candidates more generally, Blackwell launched aggressive black voter education campaigns. The campaigns aimed at convincing blacks to crossover focused on the opportunity to "make black history" by electing Blackwell. Those educating the black community on supporting Blackwell explicitly argued that they were generating support for Blackwell exclusively, and were not asking for general support of the Republican ticket. As one of his black supporters stated, "We don't care what you do further down the ticket, but you need to help this black man get elected" (Hallett, 2006).

As early as the primaries, Blackwell ran ads on urban-format radio stations advising black voters that how they voted in previous election would not prohibit them for casting a ballot for him in the primary. Voters were instructed to request "The Blackwell Ballot" at the polls. In the short span of a radio commercial, these ads cleverly offered voters an education on the open primary system. The ads addressed concerns that blacks who traditionally voted as Democrats would not be able to cast a vote in the Republican primary. The ad offered a short explanation of Ohio's primary system that would allow those traditionally voting as Democrats to vote in the Republican primary. Most importantly, the ads stressed the opportunity to "make black history" by putting the first black candidate in the governor's office in Ohio.

Blackwell relied heavily on black ministers to carry his message and campaigned heavily with black churches seeking to find black voters supportive of the moral values cornerstone of his campaign. Blackwell met with black ministers across the state, including two major black church groups in the Cleveland area—the Black Ministers Conference representing 70 black congregations and the United Pastors in Mission. In addition, Blackwell met with the International Ministerial Alliance in the Dayton area consisting of 35 black congregations.

Beyond the setting of the black church where Blackwell could appeal to blacks on the basis of shared religious values, Blackwell struggled to build connections with other segments of the black community. Blackwell used a series of campaign ads depicting exaggerated caricatures of urban blacks, which many described as offensive. Blackwell's appeals to black voters in urban areas drew criticism across urban newspapers and became a lightening rod among web bloggers. One ad in particular drew widespread attention depicting a black man dressed in an oversized white t-shirt and baggy jeans with bulging eyes suggesting he was frightened beyond extreme. The bulging eyes coupled with the size of his head and hands, which were disproportionately larger than the small body harkened to images of a black Sambo. The ad's commentary encouraged voters to fear Strickland's positions on education, religious freedom, crime, marriage, and economics. Some argued that these ads were reminiscent of previous Blackwell campaigns in which he drew widespread criticism for his portrayal of black men in a barbershop using exaggerated dialect and language that served to mock black cultural spaces (Morris, 2006b). In all, Blackwell's attempts at reaching out to segments of the black community beyond the religious community were strained at best.

Despite these difficulties, at various points in the campaign Blackwell's projection to secure 40-50 percent of the black vote seemed plausible, particularly in light of Strickland's virtual unknown status among black voters across the state. Strickland's congressional district could offer little black support as blacks make up only 2.5 percent of the district. Aware of the critiques that the Democratic Party would simply take the black vote for granted, Strickland aggressively vowed not to do so. Making good on this promise initially proved difficult for Strickland. It appeared that Blackwell would have an opportunity to capitalize on black voters when Strickland struggled to acquire endorsements from key black leaders in the state. A political fault line had developed among Democrats in the state over the selection of the state party chairman and Strickland had supported the candidate that several key black leaders opposed. This cost Strickland initially in the governor's race as several black leaders withheld their endorsements, which were critical to Strickland gaining legitimacy among black voters. After much effort, Strickland narrowly secured endorsements from Congresswoman Stephanie Tubbs-Jones, Columbus mayor and former opponent Michael B. Coleman, and Dayton Mayor Rhine McLin, and only after explicitly addressing concerns for urban areas across the state (Morris, 2006a). Upon gaining these endorsements, Strickland too pursued the black community through visits to black churches across the state, often accompanied by key black community leaders. Further, he ran a series of commercials on gospel and urban formatted radio stations in markets with sizeable black populations.

Blackwell overestimated his appeal to black voters. His staunch social conservative values were not enough to attract the 40-50 percent of the black vote that he projected. Perhaps the largest miscalculation on Blackwell's part was the actual base of black support for a social conservative agenda. Blackwell largely banked on his support for the 2004 amendment banning gay marriage to further solidify his support among black Ohioans. It is commonly understood that the amendment to ban gay marriage in 2004 is responsible for an increase in black voter support for Bush in Ohio and the other 12 states with such amendments on the ballot. However as Smith and Seltzer (2007) illustrate, blacks, while opposing gay marriage, rank this issue as far less important when compared to jobs and the economy or the war in Iraq. Blackwell's experiences with black voters confirm that while blacks in Ohio may hold socially conservative views on issues like same-sex marriage, their voting interests are focused on more traditionally liberal issues such as the availability of jobs, the condition of the economy, and the war.

Black voters are estimated to comprise 8 percent of the overall vote in statewide elections (Hallet, 2006a); however, exit poll data suggest the numbers were higher in this gubernatorial election. Figure 1 illustrates the distribution of the black population across the state and shows the distribution of Blackwell and Strickland's support by county. Ohio's black voting population is clustered in Cuyahoga, Franklin, and Hamilton counties, the three counties make up the urban centers of the state—Cleveland, Columbus, and Cincinnati.

Table 5 indicates that in the precincts accounting for 90 percent or more of the state's black residents—Cuyahoga (Cleveland), Franklin (Columbus), and Hamilton (Cincinnati) counties, it is clear that Blackwell did not capture the 40 to 50 percent of the vote he expected. Instead, his best showing occurred in his home county of Hamilton. Surprisingly, Blackwell did not win Hamilton County, but evenly split the votes with Strickland. Blackwell was able to carry the neighboring counties of Butler and Clermont. Outside of his home county and neighboring counties, as Figure 1 shows, Blackwell's stronghold was located along the western edge of the state. He carried several counties along the western border of the state with largely white populations.

Figure 1

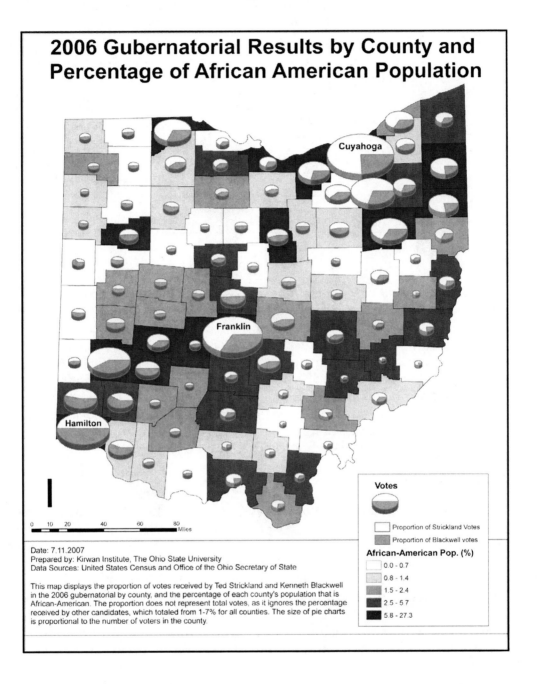

2006 Gubernatorial Results by County and Percentage of African American Population

Cuyahoga

Franklin

Hamilton

0   10   20   40   60   80
                                  Miles

Votes

Proportion of Strickland Votes
Proportion of Blackwell votes

African-American Pop. (%)
0.0 - 0.7
0.8 - 1.4
1.5 - 2.4
2.5 - 5.7
5.8 - 27.3

Date: 7.11.2007
Prepared by: Kirwan Institute, The Ohio State University
Data Sources: United States Census and Office of the Ohio Secretary of State

This map displays the proportion of votes received by Ted Strickland and Kenneth Blackwell in the 2006 gubernatorial by county, and the percentage of each county's population that is African-American. The proportion does not represent total votes, as it ignores the percentage received by other candidates, which totaled from 1-7% for all counties. The size of pie charts is proportional to the number of voters in the county.

Table 5
Registered Voters and Voter Turnout in Ohio Counties with
Large African American Populations

Ohio Counties	Total # of Registered Voters	Total # of Votes Cast	% of Total Votes Cast	Votes for Strickland	Votes for Blackwell
Cuyahoga	1,054,670	468,056	44.38	335,306 (72%)	107,234 (23%)
Hamilton	566,930	296,420	52.29	139,451 (47%)	141,374 (48%)
Franklin	766,652	385,863	50.33	241,536 (62%)	122,601 (32%)

Source: Office of the Ohio Secretary of State.

According to exit poll data in Table 6, blacks constituted 12 percent of exit poll participants. Overall, Strickland garnered 77 percent of the black vote in comparison to 20 percent for Blackwell. A slight gender gap emerges among black men and women, with black men (26 percent) supporting Blackwell more than black women (19 percent). This data is in keeping with studies showing that women, regardless of race are more likely to support more liberal democratic candidates than are their male counterparts (Smooth, 2006). For Blackwell, miscalculations regarding the appeal of socially conservative values to black voters and a series of advertising missteps proved how out of step he was with black voters and their voting interests.

Conclusion

Blackwell's emphasis on moral values, a rarity among Republican candidates in 2006 races made him too far to the right for the majority of Ohio voters, including the state's Republicans who tend to run more moderate campaigns. Blackwell never took into account the need to pull support from moderate Republicans particularly moving into the general elections. Some imagined that he would successfully meld together the most unlikely of coalitions between blacks who tend to be socially conservative and white social and fiscal conservatives. However, Blackwell could not attract a sizeable number of black supporters. These political miscalculations cost him heavily.

While Blackwell's role as secretary of state during the 2004 presidential election earned him star power among the conservative arm of the national Republican Party, we must surmise that his reputation for voter suppression in the minds of black voters made him unacceptable to become the state's first black governor. Black voters in Ohio, as in other states sent the

Table 6
Breakdown of 2006 Ohio Gubernatorial Elections by Race, Gender, and Ideology

	Total	Strickland	Blackwell
Race			
Whites	84	58	40
Blacks	12	77	20
Hispanic/Latino	2	-	-
Gender			
Men	48	58	40
Women	52	63	34
Race/Gender			
White Men	41	55	42
White Women	43	60	37
Non-White Men	7	70	26
Non-White Women	9	78	19

Source: Edison/Mitofsky Exit Poll Data based on 2,286 interviews.

message that in order to appeal to them as voters candidates will have to speak to issues of concern to the black community. Black politics is far more sophisticated than simple appeals based on identity politics, as the Republicans nationally misunderstood. Black voters again showed that they are issue-based voters and will support candidates that appeal to them as such.

Blackwell's gubernatorial bid offers lessons to future black republicans seeking high profile statewide offices and the Republican National Committee which will likely take the lessons learned to heart as they continue to strategize for increasing black support for their party. The question raised by this race is that if Kenneth Blackwell was the wrong candidate, what type of candidate will persuade black voters to crossover? This is likely a question that RNC strategists are pursuing. For students of black politics, we must begin to develop models that account for these possibilities as well.

References

Abraham, Lisa. 2006. "Key Race Days Ahead-Blackwell Not Giving Up. Strickland Not Taking Win for Granted." *Akron Beacon Journal* (October 22).

Austin, Sharon D. Wright and Richard T. Middleton, IV. 2004. "The Limitations of the Deracialization Concept in the 2001 Los Angeles Mayoral Election. *Political Research Quarterly*, 57 (June): 283-93.

Balz, Dan and Matthew Mosk. 2006. "The Year of the Black Republican? GOP Targets Democratic Constituency in 3 High Profile Races." *The Washington Post* (May 10).

The Cincinnati Enquirer. 2006."Blackwell for Governor." *The Cincinnati Enquirer* (October 22).

Dao, James. 2005."Movement in the Pews Tries to Jolt Ohio" *The New York Times* (March 27).

Grose, Christian R., 2007."Cues, Endorsements, and Heresthetic in a High-profile Election: Racial Polarization in Durham, North Carolina? *PS: Political Science* (April): 325-332.

Hallett, Joe. 2006a. "Role of Skin Color is Uncertain in Ohio's Gubernatorial Race." *The Columbus Dispatch* (August 13).

————————. 2006b." Blackwell Never Put His Best Foot Forward, and Paid the Price." *The Columbus Dispatch* (November 19).

Jeffries, Judson L. 2002. "Press Coverage of Black Statewide Candidates: The Case of L. Douglas Wilder of Virginia." *Journal of Black Studies* 32 (July): 673-97.

————————. 1999." U.S. Senator Edward W. Brooke and Governor L. Douglas Wilder Tell Political Scientists How Blacks Can Win High-Profile Statewide Office." *Political Science Quarterly* 32 (September): 583-87.

————————. 1995."Douglas Wilder and the Continuing Significance of Race" An Analysis of the 1989 Gubernatorial Election." *Journal of Political Science* 23: 87-111.

Jones, Tim. 2005."The anti-Obama-Ohio's Bible-quoting Secretary of State Tests the GOP with His Ultraconservative, Unpredictable Style." *The Chicago Tribune* (February 11).

McCormick, Joseph and Charles E. Jones. 1993."The Conceptualization of Deracialization: Thinking Through the Dilemma."in *Dilemmas of Black Politics*, ed. Georgia Persons. New York: Harper-Collins.

Morris, Phillip. 2006a. "Blackwell Taking Aim at Ohio's Black Voters." *Plain Dealer* (Cleveland) (May 2).

————————. 2006b."Blackwell's Stereotypical Appeal to Blacks Isn't Very Appealing." *Plain Dealer* (Cleveland) (July 25).

Muwakkil, Salim. 2005."GOP's Faith-Based Quest for a Touch of Color." *The Chicago Tribune* (April 10).

Orey, Byron D. 2004."Explaining Black Conservatives: Racial Uplift or Racial Resentment?" *Black Scholar* 34 (Spring): 18-22.

Smith, Robert C. and Richard Seltzer. 2007."The Deck and the Sea: The African American Vote in the Presidential Elections of 2000 and 2004"in *The National Political Science Review* 11: 253-270.

Smooth, Wendy G. 2006. "Journeying from the Shadows to the Spotlight: African American Women and Electoral Politics From Shirley Chisholm to Carol Moseley Braun"in *Gender and Elections in America: Change and Continuity through 2004*. eds Susan J. Carroll and Richard L. Fox. New York: Cambridge University Press.

Sonenshein, Raphael J. 1990. "Can Black Candidates Win Statewide Elections?" *Political Science Quarterly* 105 (Summer): 219-41.

Strickland, Ruth Ann. and Marcia Lynn Whicker. 1992."Comparing the Wilder and Gantt Campaigns: A Model for Black Candidate Success in Statewide Elections." *PS: Political Science and Politics* 25(June): 204-12.

Will, George F. 2006. "Governor's race in Ohio could be pivotal." *Desert News* (Salt Lake City) (Feb 19).

Williams, Sherri, Joe Hallett and Mark Niquette. 2006."Lack of Support; Blackwell Won Few of the White Conservative or Black Votes He Thought He Could Expect." *The Columbus Dispatch* (November 19).

Beyond the Boundaries, Volume 12; pp. 63-82

Southern Racial Etiquette and the 2006 Tennessee Senate Race: The Racialization of Harold Ford's Deracialized Campaign

Richard T. Middleton, IV
University of Missouri-St. Louis

Sekou M. Franklin
Middle Tennessee State University

In November 2006, Harold Ford, Jr., an African American congressman from Memphis, Tennessee, ran as the Democratic Party's senatorial nominee against Chattanooga mayor and multi-millionaire, Bob Corker, the Republican Party nominee. The Senate race was among the most closely watched contests of the 2006 mid-term elections, because a Ford victory would increase the Democratic Party's chances of regaining control of the Senate for the first time in a decade. Ford would have also become the South's first black senator who was elected by a *popular* vote and the region's first black senator since Blanche K. Bruce's selection by the Mississippi legislature (1875-1881).

Ford's Senate campaign marked a significant departure from black electoral politics in Tennessee. Although blacks have won many political victories in Tennessee, rarely has an African American candidate campaigned and won in a statewide election. In the nineteenth century, Y.F. Yardley, a Knoxville city councilman, ran for governor in 1872, and Samuel McElwee campaigned for the speaker of the House a decade later. Yet both lost these bids, and between 1887 and 1964, blacks were not even elected to the state legislature.[1] Two blacks ran for governor in the years following the civil rights movement. William Butler of east Tennessee ran for governor in 1974 and Rev. Ed Sanders of Nashville ran as an independent 2002, however, both were soundly defeated.

Similar to most states, especially in the South, Tennessee's racially conservative culture marginalized black electoral politics. Its patrimonial political

culture, which privileges politically powerful families and wealthy candidates, and archaic legislative districts,[2] which for decades, disenfranchised
black and urban voters, also made it difficult for blacks to win statewide political campaigns.[3] Moreover, Tennessee's black population is relative small
compared to other southern states—blacks comprise only 17 percent of the
population—and most blacks reside in the western region of the state in and
adjacent to Memphis-Shelby County. The state's geographic complexity has
allowed blacks to garner victories in the western black belt, and to a lesser
extent, in the mid-state's Nashville-Davidson County, but little success in the
mostly white, homogenous and conservative counties of eastern Tennessee.

Nevertheless, Ford's campaign was enhanced by relatively favorable coverage by the national and state media, not only during the 2006 Senate race,
but throughout his ten years in the House of Representatives.[4] Many political
commentators were impressed by Ford's willingness to work with Republicans
and his active membership in the Blue Dog Coalition and the Democratic Leadership Council, two moderate/conservative Democratic Party organizations.[5]
In fact, they viewed Ford as a race-neutral/non-racial, young black leader and
his centrist brand of leadership as a viable alternative to civil rights leaders
and black progressives inside of the Democratic Party.[6]

Despite Ford's race-neutral centrism, racial politics still had an important impact on the Senate race. On October 20, as Ford and Corker were in
a virtual tie, the Republican National Committee (RNC) aired a political
advertisement, which purported that Ford had associational ties with a
blonde-haired, Caucasian-looking woman who said she met him at a
Playboy party during the 2005 Super Bowl weekend celebrations. The commercial, generally referred to as the "Bimbo" ad,[7] was clearly designed to
prime embedded racial stereotypes, and convince white voters that a Ford
victory would violate the South's traditional customs regulating relations
between black men and white women.

This chapter analyzes the 2006 Senate race in Tennessee and gives close
attention to Ford's electoral strategy and crossover appeal to moderate and
conservative voters. The first part of this chapter explains how racial cues or
symbolic appeals that prime racial stereotypes can limit the potential effectiveness of crossover or deracialized campaigns. This is followed by a discussion
of recent trends in the deracialization literature.[8] We then turn our attention
to Ford's efforts to exert a *normalizing effect* over critical policy issues.[9] The normalizing effect describes what happens when black candidates in statewide
elections or biracial jurisdictions attempt to neutralize racially or ideologically
divisive issues. They will often embrace an electoral strategy that normalizes
their image, or situate their politics as mainstream or centrist, in order to
attract moderates, centrists, and even conservative whites.[10]

We further discuss how the Republican National Committee (along
with Corker's implicit consent) racialized what had essentially been a
deracialized campaign by Ford. The ad was intended to convince a critical
segment of the (white) electorate that Ford did not abide by the traditional

norms and etiquette regulating black-white relations. The advertisement implied that black men (i.e., Ford) must exercise restraint and not encroach upon the sanctity of white women. In addition to the ad, some political observers believed that a Republican Party-sponsored circular in eastern Tennessee counties, which urged residents to vote in order "preserve your way of life," was also racially coded.[11] Other forms of racial priming included a radio commercial criticizing Ford with African drums beating in the background, a campaign flyer that darkened Ford's skin color, and another radio commercial sponsored by a political organization, Tennesseans for Truth, criticizing Ford's connection to the Congressional Black Caucus.[12]

This set of tactics was similar to one that was promoted by white candidate, James Hahn, against Antonio Villaraigosa, a Mexican American, in the 2001 Los Angeles mayoral election primary run-off. Hahn ran an advertisement that depicted images of a crackpipe and graffiti-covered buildings along with Villaraigosa's image. Hahn also promoted print as well as television advertisements that implied Villaraigosa lacked the moral fortitude to thwart gang violence, pedophilia, and drug trafficking.[13] As evidenced by both the 2001 Los Angeles mayoral race, as well as the 2006 Tennessee Senate race, candidates of color have increasingly become the targets of racially coded messages that in effect racialized what otherwise have been deracialized campaigns.

As part of this discussion, we present data from Mason-Dixon Polling Research firm, as well as pre-election data from a November 1-4, 2006 *USA Today/ Gallup* poll and a National Election Poll exit poll. These data allow us to gauge the impact of the "Bimbo" ad and assess whether Ford's normalizing tactics (his infusion of religion (Christianity) in the campaign, and harsh criticisms of gay marriage and illegal immigration) effectively mobilized white and moderate/conservative voters. Additional discussion, using ecological regression, is offered to examine Ford's crossover appeal in select counties.

The Southern Custom of Racial Etiquette as a Framing Device

Research on U.S. southern culture has found that an elaborate etiquette of race evolved during the Civil War era to govern race relations in the South.[14] This etiquette, "created a system of behavior that served to reinforce the supremacy of the white race and the inferiority of the black."[15] One particularly rigid aspect of this etiquette was the belief that "white women were too 'pure' for liaisons with black men."[16] The evolution of this dogma in the U.S. South dates back to the American colonial period when race mixing between blacks and whites was admonished by white governing elites.[17] During this period in American history, the law generally provided for more harsh treatment for interracial relations between *white females* and *black males*. One such example was a 1664 Maryland statute that decreed children born to such relationships carried the status of the father and were to be enslaved for a period of 30 years while the mother was to be banished from the colony.[18]

Anti-miscegenation laws were enacted, beginning as early as 1662 in Maryland, in an effort to stem the mixing of blacks with whites. According to legal historian Christine Hickman, the presence of a relatively large mixed black-white population (mulatto) in the colonies was one of the catalysts for the passage of this race-based type of legislation.[19] White colonial leaders saw the mulatto as evidence that the purity of the white woman and white race was being encroached upon.[20] The rule of hypodescent was legislatively and/or judicially adopted in many states in order to socially stigmatize the participating parties who engaged in interracial fornication as well as their progeny. Pursuant to the rule of hypodescent, any individual of some varying degree of mixed black-white blood was assigned the status of their socially (and, according to some, biologically) inferior bloodline—the Negro. The state of Tennessee espoused a particularly strict form of the rule of hypodescent—the infamous "one-drop" rule, which provided that "anyone having any African blood in their veins was a person of color."[21]

During the post-Civil War period and into the Jim Crow era, punishment for breaching southern racial etiquette came in the form of extralegal repercussions, such as lynchings.[22] As F. James Davis notes, "the racial etiquette was complex, and the penalties for not learning and following it well could be severe. There were countless lessons to be learned...."[23] The murder of Emmett Till, a young black boy, in Money, Mississippi, for having allegedly whistled at a white woman serves as one of the most grim, yet classic examples of the severity of an allegation that a black male breached the most stringent of the rules of southern racial etiquette.

Given the deeply embedded nature of a racial etiquette in the South, one can understand how even in modern-day Tennessee, the Republican National Committee's allegation of Harold Ford having connections to a sexually energized and provocatively dressed, blonde-haired, white woman could foment racial sentiments among conservative and rural white voters and cause Ford's race to become a critical framing device for mobilization against him.

Recent Trends in the Deracialization Literature

At the time of this writing, thirty years has passed since Charles V. Hamilton first posited the idea of African American candidates strategically reaching out to white voters by emphasizing policy issues that would tend to appeal to a broader spectrum of constituents versus focusing on issues salient primarily to black voters.[24] Twenty years after the publication of Hamilton's seminal work, Huey Perry edited a volume in which a number of scholars examined the campaign strategies utilized by various African American candidates in light of Hamilton's thesis.[25] Perry's aim was to test Hamilton's deracialization theory to discern if African American candidates who had ascended to high profile elected offices had actually utilized a deracialized strategy, and if so, what implications did such an approach have on the socio-economic prospects for African Americans.

Recent trends in the deracialization literature present a number of findings that are positioned to shape how political scientists think about electoral politics into the next decade and beyond. Much of this recent literature looks at how candidates of color are portrayed, the amount of exposure they receive by media outlets, and how this affects their ability to attract important crossover votes from whites and moderate conservatives. For example, in a study of the 2001 Los Angeles mayoral election, Timothy Krebs and David Holian analyze how a candidate's race affects the occurrence of negative campaigning.[26] Krebs and Holian argue that one of the major challenges of minority candidates (that is, candidates of color) in a white dominated electoral climate is "how to craft a political style to appeal to, or at least not energize, voters least likely to support a minority candidate, voters for whom a candidate's race matters."[27] Their findings suggest that candidates of color who choose to run deracialized campaigns face an interesting dilemma. On the one hand, such candidates must attack their opponents significantly less than white candidates, in an overall effort to deracialize their appeal. On the other hand, according to Krebs and Holian, when candidates of color are not front-runners, but rather, strong contenders, they have more of a strategic need to attack or at least respond to attacks. In doing so, however, such candidates are more likely to lose the support of voters who are already least likely to support a candidate of color. For example, Krebs and Holian find that Villaraigosa likely did not aggressively attack James Hahn or vociferously respond to Hahn's attack ads because doing so would have reinforced stereotypes of Villaraigosa as an "angry kid from the streets [of a Latino neighborhood]."[28] They go on to note that Villaraigosa could not afford to attack because his low favorability among swing voters was a function, in part, of his race.

Other recent studies have also probed into the role media exposure and portrayals of candidates of color in deracialized electoral contexts. For example, Baodong Liu investigates the interaction between media exposure as an agent of deracialization and its associated effect on white voting behavior.[29] In particular, Liu finds that positive media exposure by white-controlled media outlets can serve as a legitimizing source for an African Americans who desire to present themselves in a racially non-threatening manner. In an analysis of electoral politics in New Orleans, Louisiana, Liu finds that endorsements that emanated from a white-controlled newspaper (*Times-Picayune*) provided legitimacy to African American candidates who ran deracialized campaigns which, in turn, increased their level of white crossover support.[30] Implicitly, then, such media endorsements serve as a racial cue—one that signifies that a candidate of color is a friend of the white community. On the other hand, negative media exposure has been found to limit the effectiveness of deracialized campaigns run by candidates of color.

As mentioned previously, Austin and Middleton investigate negative campaigns advertisements that were employed by James Hahn in the 2001 Los Angeles mayoral election to attack his competitor, Villaraigosa's, character and play upon negative stereotypes of Mexicans as drug dealers and criminals. In particular, Austin and Middleton find that Villaraigosa's, "attempts to widen his appeal beyond white liberals and Latinos failed primarily because the Hahn campaign's print and televisions ads made it impossible for him to maintain a non-threatening image on the issue of crime."[31] In the case of the 2001 Los Angeles mayoral election, Hahn's favorability rating increased dynamically after the negative advertisements made the airwaves and landed on the streets.

The Normalizing Effect

The preceding discussion sets the tone for our following analysis of Harold Ford's deracialized campaign strategy. In our discussion, we focus on how Ford attempted to exert a *normalizing effect* over critical policy issues to enhance his ability to attract crossover votes from whites and moderate conservatives. The normalizing effect describes what happens when a candidate attempts to remove race from a campaign, as well as convince whites that she or he has more in common with them on a host of non-black issues (i.e., gay rights, immigration rights, etc.), which presumably, have been receptive to civil rights and liberal groups. The expectation is that the normalizing effect can neutralize the race variable and liberal issues, and convince white moderates and conservatives that a black candidate subscribes to their preferred belief systems.

Ford tried to normalize his image in the white community by embracing positions that are opposed by many of his liberal supporters. For example, he voted for the congressional bill to ban gay marriage,[32] and he supported Tennessee's constitutional amendment to ban gay marriage that was on the November ballot. His stance on immigration was also in concert with many conservatives in the state and he attacked his opponent, Corker, for being soft on illegal immigrants. In addition, he repeatedly invoked religious symbolism during the campaign, which appealed to state's Bible belt culture and white evangelical voters.[33] This was a surprise since there was no prior evidence that Ford held orthodox Christian beliefs. In addition, Ford was at best moderate on economic issues, and at worse, rejected progressive economic policies.[34]

The RNC-sponsored attack ads raised additional concerns about the effectiveness of deracialization and the normalizing strategies, and whether they can prevail over sophisticated efforts to racially prime, race-neutral campaigns. Despite the contention by some researchers that negative attacks backfire and demobilize voter turnout,[35] some political observers give credence to their effectiveness.[36] When campaign ads are delivered late in an electoral contest, such as the "Bimbo" commercial, they may be more effective in shaping voter attitudes, because it allows voters to use the most recent information they have about a candidate to evaluate their performance.[37] Furthermore, the effectiveness of racial priming tactics is enhanced if the targeted candidates fail to condemn or offer authoritative responses to the attack ads.[38]

Interestingly, a version of the "Bimbo" ad was aired by the National Republican Senatorial Committee during the first week of October. Yet, the national media expressed little outrage about the ad, in part, because unlike the RNC-sponsored ad several weeks later, it didn't make a direct connection between Ford and a Caucasian woman. The ad, designed as a counterattack to Ford's appeal among social conservatives, stated that Ford partied with "Playboy playmates in lingerie."[39] Ford denounced the ad by insisting that Republicans were the ones lacking in moral character, as exemplified in their efforts to hide the scandal involving Congressman Mark Foley, the Florida Republican who made sexual advances to underage, male congressional pages.

Ford also said that Republicans injected his racial background into the campaign after Tennesseans for Truth sponsored a radio ad that said: "[Ford's] daddy handed him his seat in Congress and his seat in the Congressional Black Caucus, an all-black group of congressmen who represent the interest of black people above all others."[40] Yet despite these earlier political advertisements, and despite his strong response to them, he failed to authoritatively condemn Republicans of racial priming after the "Bimbo" ad was first aired on October 20. When asked to respond to the ad, he called it "smutty," and days later explained his reason for attending the Playboy party as, "I like football, and I like girls."[41] Furthermore, he refused to call the ad racist and said about Republicans, "You have to ask them about race. I don't focus on those things."[42] Ford's response underscores the challenge with deracialization. If, as Mendelberg suggests, candidates are better suited to diminish racially charged attack ads by publicly condemning them,[43] this becomes difficult if a candidate is stubbornly committed to race-neutralism. After all, if Ford had publicly condemned the "Bimbo" ad as racist, it would have racialized the campaign, and given legitimacy to the fact that black and white Tennesseans were racially polarized. Ford's response and his bachelor status may have further harmed his image among family values moderates and conservatives.

In the remainder of the chapter, we offer a detailed analysis of Ford's normalizing strategy, while controlling for a host of socio-demographic and political variables. Yet before engaging this discussion, we discuss the data and methodology, and then examine the impact of the RNC-sponsored playboy bunny advertisement on the campaign. Afterward, we discuss Ford's overall support in the week before the election and on the day of the election.

Data and Methods

This chapter draws upon data from a *USA Today*/Gallup poll conducted from November 1-4, 2006 and a National Election Pool (ABC News/Associated Press/CBS News/CNN/Fox News/NBC News) exit poll administered on November 7. The pre-election poll allows us to measure for two outcomes. We look at approval ratings of the "Bimbo" advertisement (1=approve, 0=disapproval), while controlling for socio-demographic variables (race, gender, age, social class (low-income and college-educated respondents), and jurisdiction/locality (rural and east Tennessee voters). Since we are interested in the influence of swing voters, measured as self-identified moderates and independents, we included these variables in the analysis. Finally, we looked at whether general opinions about political advertisements influenced approval/disapproval ratings of the advertisement. Another logistic regression model was constructed with the same variables in order to measure Ford's support among prospective voters a week before the election. Approval of the playboy ad, election interest, and whether the respondents voted in the 2002 election were also added as independent variables.

We conducted a third logistic regression for the exit poll with Senate vote (1=Ford, 0=Corker) serving as the dependent variable. We controlled for socio-demographic variables: race, gender, age (30-59=reference category), jurisdiction (rural/town=reference category), region (East Tennessee voters=reference category),[44] and social class (measured by education). Due to Ford's bachelor status, we included three measures (married voters, single women, parents) to determine his appeal to voters from varying family types. An additional variable was included to determine if concerns about the economy impacted the Senate race.

The exit poll did not ask specific questions about the "Bimbo" ad, but it did ask if "either of the candidates for U.S. senator attacked the other unfairly." We included this as an independent variable, as well as three proxy measures of partisanship (independent voters, approval of George Bush, and approval of Tennessee's incumbent Democratic governor, Phil Bredesen). We expect Bredesen supporters to vote for Ford and Bush supporters to reject him. Three measures are included to test the *normalizing effect*: support for the state's anti-gay marriage amendment; if the respondents believed immigration was an important issue; and support from white evangelicals/born-again voters.[45]

In addition, we performed a secondary analysis of black voter turnout and black-white racial polarization on the day of the election. Ecological inference, refined by political scientist Gary King,[46] is a useful tool for assessing racial polarity between blacks and whites.[47] This approach is commonly used by scholars to study voter intensity and transitions, as well as racially polarized voting.

Findings and Discussion

The RNC-sponsored, "Bimbo" advertisement was designed to convince a critical segment of the electorate that Ford had violated the southern traditionalism and etiquette which forbid black men from associating with white women. Similar to many racially charged campaign tactics, the ad operated as a framing device that appealed to the state's conservative population.[48] As Table 1 points out, voter attitudes shifted after the first airing of the "Bimbo" advertisement. Six weeks before the election, Ford had a six-point lead over Corker, although a sizeable number of voters had neither favorable nor unfavorable views of the two candidates. By mid-October, the race was a virtual dead heat, yet after the ad was aired, Corker's favorability rating over Ford increased by eight percentage points.

It is debatable whether these shifting attitudes were attributed to the advertisement or other factors. The "Bimbo" ad was one of many negative ads levied by both campaigns. Further, Bob Corker reorganized his campaign staff in late September. Though some political observers viewed this as a setback for Corker, it may have worked to his advantage because he brought in Tom Ingram to run his campaign. Ingram, the chief of staff for Senator Lamar Alexander, the Republican senator from Tennessee, refocused Corker's message, and used his in-state networks to boost Corker's image. In addition, Corker survived a brutal primary season, in which his opponents, former congressmen Ed Bryant and Van Hilleary, harshly crit-

Table 1
Favorability/Approval Ratings of Harold Ford, Jr. and Bob Corker
Before and After the "Playboy Bunny" Political Advertisement

Conducted Before Ad First Aired - September 25 – September 27, 2006

	FAVORABLE	UNFAVORABLE	NEUTRAL
Harold Ford, Jr.	44%	30%	22%
Bob Corker	38%	35%	24%

Conducted Between October 18 – October 20, 2006

	FAVORABLE	UNFAVORABLE	NEUTRAL
Harold Ford, Jr.	45%	36%	18%
Bob Corker	46%	27%	26%

Conducted After Ad First Aired - November 1 – November 3, 2006

	FAVORABLE	UNFAVORABLE	NEUTRAL
Harold Ford, Jr.	39%	44%	15%
Bob Corker	47%	33%	17%

Source: The Mason-Dixon Tennessee Polling & Research, Inc. administered the surveys for the Memphis Commercial Appeal and Chattanooga Times Free Press. A total of 625 registered Tennessee voters were interviewed statewide by telephone.

icized him for running negative attacks. Some conservatives also believed Corker was too moderate to adequately represent the Republican Party. This created tension and acrimony among the three camps (Corker, Bryant, Hilleary). In fact, Bryant and Hilleary did not actively campaign for Corker until late in the campaign season. These factors may have harmed Corker's support, and boosted Ford's standing, in September.

To gain more insight into the effectiveness of the Playboy bunny ad, we conducted logistic regression of a pre-election poll conducted a week before the election. Table 2 displays the regression estimates. As expected, disapproval of the ad was found among moderates and respondents who had negative views about the election-oriented, television commercials. However, independent voters and social class did not significantly distinguish sentiments about the ad.

Racial background, as expected, significantly influenced how voters interpreted the ad. Whites were much more likely to approve of the ad and did not find it offensive. Approval of the ad was also found among men. Given Ford's youth, we incorrectly expected young adults/youth to be more critical of the ad. This was surprising since Democratic Party insiders insisted that the party made significant inroads in capturing the youth vote during the mid-term elections.[49] Young people—both Democrats and Republicans—found few problems with the advertisement, perhaps because they have less knowledge about the sophisticated use of racial cues.[50] Young people also have less memory of southern traditionalism. In contrast to their parents and grandparents, the state's young voters are more cosmopolitan

Table 2
Logistic Regression Measuring Approval of the "Bimbo" Advertisement

(Pre-Election Poll, November 1-4, 2006)

Independent Variables	B	
Independents	-.05	(.51)
Negative Political Ads	-1.1*	(.31)
East TN	-.41**	(.24)
College Ed.	-.33	(.26)
Whites	1.81*	(.75)
Rural TN	.23	(.25)
Men	.64*	(.23)
Moderates	-.73*	(.73)
Young Adults	.94*	(.37)
Low-Income	-.42	(.31)
Constant	-2.24*	(.80)

-2 Log Likelihood	499.745	*$p<.05$, **$p<.10$
Chi-Square	53.195*	

Source: The survey is a USA Today/Gallup Poll, November 1-4, 2006. The survey was obtained from the Roper Center. The N=1,001, but because of missing data, only 616 respondents were included in the logistic regression.

(urban and suburban) and may not have entrenched predispositions against interracial relationships. If racial priming activates pre-existing racial schemas,[51] then this may have less of an effect on young voters than older ones. Further, Ford's refusal to admonish the ad as racist—he condemned the ad, but for other reasons—may have misled younger voters about the intention of the "Bimbo" advertisement, especially since young adults (18-29) have historical distance from southern etiquette and Jim Crow politics.

We further expected rural voters and eastern Tennesseans to approve of the ad, because it may have allied hidden stereotypes they had about Ford. Yet there was no statistical significance between rural and urban/suburban voters, and surprisingly, voters from eastern Tennessee, the state's conservative stronghold, disapproved of the ad compared to those from other parts of the state. Sentiments among rural voters may be explained by Ford's aggressive campaigning in rural Tennessee. Furthermore, even though the state's rural voters tend to be more conservative than urban voters, there is some variation that may have offset the impact of the ad. There is a sizeable (over 100,000) and politically active, black population that makes up 30 percent of the population in rural/small town, western Tennessee counties outside of Memphis.[52] Moreover, Ford is a close ally of Congressman John Tanner, a conservative Democrat from western Tennessee's eighth congressional district, who actively campaigned for Ford. Tanner's congressional district includes 19 counties (18 out of 19 counties are rural) in western and middle Tennessee. This may have offset Corker's influence in rural eastern Tennessee.

We conducted another logistic regression, displayed in Table 3, to assess Ford's support among prospective voters the week before the election. Those who approved of the "Bimbo" ad and whites were most likely to support Bob Corker. Our only surprise was that we mistakenly believed Ford's centrism would attract independent voters who expressed greater approval of Bob Corker.

The Ford campaign, however, neutralized Corker's support among men, and he won approval from moderate voters in the week leading to the election. If this were to remain true on November 7, it would suggest that Ford's crossover appeal cut into some voters who were expected to support Republicans. On the other hand, working to Ford's disadvantage was his poor showing in the pre-election survey among those who voted in the 2002 mid-term elections. This indicates that active voters—voters who routinely participate in elections—were more receptive to Corker than Ford.

Additional insight on Ford's electability and crossover appeal was found in the exit poll survey. Unlike the pre-election survey, immigration, religiosity, and gay marriage questions were included in the exit poll. As indicated in Table 3, whites and college-educated voters were likely to vote for Corker, although there were no distinguishing results between men and women. Ford also performed poorly among married couples and single women. This may be due to attacks, such as the "Bimbo" ad, which in addition to racial priming, also attacked his bachelor status.

The larger concern is whether Ford was able to soften white resistance to his candidacy by embracing issues that were appealing to the state's conservative base. In terms of the normalizing variables (immigration, gay marriage, religiosity), he was successful at neutralizing the vote among white evangelicals. Corker won the vote among the respondents who ranked illegal immigration as an important issue in the campaign and those who voted for the constitutional ban on gay marriage. Although it is beyond the scope of this study, further research should consider whether Ford damaged his own campaign by accentuating these two issues. One

Table 3
Logistic Regression Assessing Approval and Vote for Harold Ford, Jr.

Independent Variables	Model 1 (Pre-Election Poll)	Model 2 (Exit Poll) B	
Whites	-3.93* (1.0)	-3.5* (.65)	
Men	-.07 (.20)	-.15 (.21)	
Married	____	-.87* (.32)	
Single Women	____	-.84* (.42)	
Parents	____	-.16 (.21)	
College Educated	-.15 (.23)	-.78* (.20)	
Low-Income (under $30,000)	.12 (.26)	____	
18-29 yrs. old	-.58 (.45)		
		.28 (.31)	Age* 18-29 yrs.
		.67 (.26)*	60 yrs. and over
Negative Ads	.43 (.36)	____	
Attack Ads	____	3.3* (.41)	
Both Attacked	____	-2.9* (.35)	
Ban Gay Marriage	____	-1.2* (.25)	
Immigration (Important)	____	-.69* (.22)	
Economy (Important)		.43 (.27)	
White Evangelicals	____	-.07 (.21)	

Table 3 (cont.)

East Tennessee	-.21 (.20)		
		Region*	
		.50 (.20)	Middle/West*
		-.13 (.28)	Southwest
Rural Voters	.06 (.22)		
		Locality	
		-.48 (.57)	Urban
		-.67 (.23)	Suburban
Playboy Ad	-1.45* (.32)	____	
Election Interest	.13 (.26)	____	
Vote 2002	-.75* (.31)	____	
Moderates	1.2* (.21)	____	
Gov. Phil Bredesen	____	2.3* (.22)	
Independents	-.99** (.57)	-.24 (.20)	
Pres. GW Bush	____	-3.0* (.19)	
Economy (Important)	____	.43 (.27)	
Constant	3.89* (1.1)	5.5* (.88)	
-2 Log Likelihood 603.188		-2 Log Likelihood 864.292	
Chi-Square 142.609*		Chi-Square 1660.658*	

*p <.05, ** p < .10 *p <.05, ** p < .10
Source: Model 1 uses the same pre-election poll that was used in Table 2. The model excludes variables with missing data, so the original sample size (1,001) was reduced to 538. Weights were included in the exit poll. Also, variables with missing data were excluded from the sample (2,651), but the final results are measured on 1,822 cases.

may discover that Ford inadvertently helped to mobilize anti-gay marriage voters and opponents of illegal immigration, who otherwise may have stayed home, and this enthusiasm spilled over and benefited the Republican Party. At least in regards to gay marriage, the Republican Party has been fairly effective at linking anti-gay/civil union, state policies with its voter mobilization efforts during high profile elections.

It is also worth mentioning that Ford's vocal opposition to gay marriage and harsh criticisms of illegal immigration were, for the most part, supported by blacks. Although national political/civil rights groups such as Rev. Jesse Jackson's Rainbow/Push Coalition, the Leadership Conference on Civil Rights, and the Congressional Black Caucus, have supported anti-discrimination legislation pertaining to the LGBT (Lesbian, Gay, Bisexual, Transgender) and immigration rights' communities, rank-and-file blacks have expressed uneven support for these issues. In fact, blacks overwhelmingly voted for Tennessee's constitutional ban on gay marriage (over 80 percent) and as much as two-thirds indicated that illegal immigration is an important issue.[53] This suggests that black candidates such as Ford can use normalizing strategies on wedge issues—even those issues that are condemned by civil rights groups—and still avoid harsh criticisms from rank-and-file blacks. This is particularly the case in the South where socially conservative, faith-based leaders and institutions play a dominant role in the daily lives of blacks.

Though Ford did not win the white evangelical vote, his religious appeals may have neutralized this group. This was a surprise considering that Tennessee is the epicenter of the Bible-Belt politics and home to the religiously conservative, Southern Baptist Convention (SBC). Ford's counterbalance of the white evangelical vote may shed light on a shifting pattern among evangelicals. Since the 2004 presidential election, evangelical organizations such as the SBC have engaged in an intra-denominational struggle over the trajectory of their organization. Some evangelical leaders have urged their organizations and networks to abandon their blind support of the Republican Party.[54] Progressive groups have also initiated conversations throughout the state to counteract the Christian Right's influence. For example, the Tennessee Alliance for Progress, a statewide social justice organization, sponsored the "Doing Justly" project. Launched in October 2006, the project entailed a series of ecumenical dialogues with religious leaders about social justice issues.

We expected economic concerns to be a driving factor behind Ford's support, considering that many Democrats campaigned on economic populist issues (i.e., trade policy, wages, job displacement, etc.) during the 2006 mid-term elections. The lack of concern among voters about the economy may reveal that Ford didn't spend enough time emphasizing this issue. Some political observers believed Ford chose to focus less attention on the economy, and the Tennessee economy in particular, because this may have inadvertently sparked criticisms of Governor Phil Bredesen, a conservative Democrat and close ally of Ford.[55] Yet Ford's campaign and the voters deserved an in-depth discussion of the economy. Tennessee experienced approximately 90 plant closings from 2001-2004 and the governor led a successful effort to downsize and cut health care benefits to over 600,000 Medicaid recipients (over 200,000 of these recipients were disenrolled from TennCare, the state's Medicaid program).[56] Unfortunately, none of these issues took center stage in the campaign and Ford gave more attention to gay marriage, religiosity, and immigration.

Age was partially significant in predicting the Senate vote. Senior citizens (above 60 years old) were most likely to vote for Ford than voters between 30-59 years of age. This paralleled a national trend in which senior citizens, mainly because of concerns about health care, the costs of prescription drugs, and social security, were more inclined to support Democrats.[57] Partisanship was an influential indicator of the Senate vote. President Bush supporters and supporters of Phil Bredesen, the state's Democratic governor, were more inclined to vote for Corker and Ford, respectively. It also appears that as the election neared, Ford won over some self-identified independent voters. Although independents supported Corker in the pre-election poll, on the day of the election, there was no statistical significance between their vote for Corker and Ford.

The only jurisdictional (region or locality) indicator that significantly influenced the election was region. Middle and western Tennessee voters, compared to those from eastern Tennessee, were more likely to vote for Corker. This was predicted by every political observer of Tennessee politics because eastern Tennessee is a conservative stronghold. Ford anticipated making inroads in eastern Tennessee counties. Indeed, his electoral outreach in eastern Tennessee counties was similar to Governor Bredesen, who won a narrow victory over Congressman Van Hilleary in the 2002 gubernatorial contest. Bredesen's victory was partially attributed to cutting into Republican strongholds in eastern Tennessee. In the same election season, Bredesen won or tied in 22 of the counties that were won by Republican senatorial candidate, Lamar Alexander, nine of which were in eastern Tennessee. In eastern Tennessee's largest county, Knox County (Knoxville), Alexander won 62 percent of the vote, but many voters split their tickets and cast their votes for Bredesen, who tied his Republican challenger. Ford, on the other hand, won only 30 of the 59 counties that threw their support behind Bredesen and only three of the counties that voted for Alexander. He won only two counties in eastern Tennessee compared to 14 counties for Bredesen, and he was soundly defeated in Knox County. Thus, it is likely that Ford did not do well enough in eastern Tennessee, and Bredesen's coattails were influential in counties that traditionally vote for or leaned to the Democrats.

We fully expected Ford to lose among rural and small town residents, yet this was not the case. But as we stated earlier, Ford made an aggressive attempt to win over rural voters, especially in western and middle Tennessee. Corker, on the other hand, did fairly well in all of the metropolitan areas (Chattanooga-Hamilton County, Knoxville-Knox County, Wilson County, Williamson County, and Rutherford County) outside of Memphis-Shelby County and Nashville-Davidson County.

It is also worth revisiting the impact of political advertisements. The exit poll asked the respondents:"Did either of these candidates for U.S. senator attack the other unfairly?"Those who believed Ford was unfairly attacked held strong feelings about the race and were much more likely to vote for Ford.Yet, Corker received an unanticipated bounce from the advertisements among those who believed that both candidates unfairly attacked each other. This last point is worth considering. If there was a backlash against the "Bimbo" ad—and it appeared that there was as exhibited with the criticisms of many national media personalities—Republicans may have offset these criticism by convincing voters that Democrats (and Ford) had also initiated negative political advertisements.

In all of the regression analyses, race is a constant theme. Despite Ford's attempts to deracialize his campaign, race served as lens through which voters made their decisions. Though Ford made explicit appeals to white voters, and perhaps convinced some of them to vote for him, he was not able to neutralize race. This indicates that even when candidates use race-neutral appeals or de-emphasize salient issues that appeal to blacks, they still find it difficult to convince voters that race doesn't matter.[58] This is because the candidates' opponents may be already pre-positioned for racial priming and more receptive to sophisticated uses of racial coding.[59]

Further evidence of racial polarity—and Ford's biracial appeal—can be examined by looking at black and white voter trends in the Senate race. We conducted ecological regressions of 1,069 precincts or voter tabulation districts (VTDs).[60] Although our analysis only covers 21 of 95 counties in the state, it includes six of the seven largest metro areas/counties (Memphis-Shelby County, Nashville-Davidson County, Knoxville-Knox County, Chattanooga-Hamilton County, Williamson County, and Clarksville-Montgomery County). The remaining counties have smaller populations and encompass small towns/rural communities.[61] The VTDs chosen for this study are disproportionately in Democratic leaning counties, since we included the two largest counties, Memphis-Shelby and Nashville-Davidson Counties. As Table 4 points out, almost 56 percent of the voters in our sample are from Democratic Party precincts and the average black population in each precinct was 24 percent. To address the selective bias, we disaggregated the large counties and conducted a second ecological regression analysis.[62]

In both regression models, one sees a tremendous amount of consolidation among blacks in support of Ford. Although racial polarization exists, Ford was able to garner 40-42 percent of the white vote in both models, which is the same number identified in the exit poll. Yet what may have worked to Ford's disadvantage, notwithstanding his ability to garner 40 percent of the white vote, was that as one moves away from Memphis and Nashville, the black population shrinks in size and the proportion of Ford's white supporters also decreases. This indicates that Ford's base of support was in traditional Democratic Party strongholds, that he probably did not garner enough support in homogenous (white) counties outside of the two central cities/counties.

Also, working to Ford's disadvantage was that voter turnout in black precincts was lower than what his campaign predicted. The campaign hoped for presidential-election turnouts (about 300,000 blacks voted for John Kerry) among blacks.[63] The campaign also targeted 65,000 blacks in Memphis who voted in presidential elections, but not in mid-term elections.[64] Yet, in a separate study of the 2006 Senate race, Franklin found that only 35 percent of the black voting age population in Memphis-Shelby

Table 4
Racial Polarity in the 2006 Tennessee Senate Race

Model I

(Per Precinct)	(Percentages)	Ford		
Total Voter Turnout	41 %			
Black Population	24 %	Blacks	94 %	(S.E. .01)
Democratic Voters	56 %	Whites	42 %	(S.E. .01)

Model II (Excludes Memphis-Shelby County and Nashville-Davidson County)

(Per Precinct)	(Percentages)	Ford		
Total Voter Turnout	40 %			
Black Population	13 %	Blacks	91 %	(S.E., .002)
Democratic Voters	48 %	Whites	40%	(S.E., .01)

Note: Gary King's EiZ package is used for these two models.

and Nashville-Davidson Counties turned out to vote.[65] This percentage, if it holds across the state, would account for only 228,000 out of the approximately 650,000 voting age blacks, thus falling short of Ford's expectations. Accordingly, if Ford's loss was partially attributed to a lower than expected black voter turnout, he may have himself to blame. His focus on the normalizing variables mentioned earlier in this study, and inattention to economic security issues, may have convinced some blacks to stay home rather than vote.

Conclusion

This study uses a two-tiered analysis (logistic and ecological regression) to assess Harold Ford's deracialization strategy. One of our objectives was to explain how racial cues or symbolic appeals that prime racial stereotypes can limit the potential effectiveness of crossover or deracialized campaigns. In particular, we looked at how a Republican National Committee advertisement ("Bimbo" ad) racialized what had essentially been a deracialized campaign by Ford. The ad was intended to convince a critical segment of the (white) electorate that Ford did not abide by the traditional norms and etiquette regulating black-white relations. The advertisement implied that black men (i.e., Ford) must exercise restraint and not encroach upon the sanctity of white women. This discussion set the tone for our examination of Ford's biracial appeal and whether the South's traditional mores regarding black-white relations, religion, immigration, and gay marriage impeded his ability to win over whites, moderates, and even some conservatives. We argued that Ford focused on a host of traditional, non-racial issues such as religiosity and gay marriage, as well as accentuated illegal immigration as an important campaign issue, in order to distance himself from liberal policy positions that are perceived to be supportive by black candidates. We referred to this as the normalizing effect. We believe that in a hotly contested campaign, conservatives will make a concentrated effort to link black candidates with a broad range of liberal policy issues, such as immigration and gay marriage. The reason for this has a lot to do with the nature of southern politics. For better or worse, black candidates and elected officials, even moderate ones, are often looked at by different constituent groups of the liberal-progressive axis to advance various causes.

The normalizing effect was only partially effective. Ford neutralized the white evangelical vote, but those who felt strongly about illegal immigration as well as opponents of gay marriage, were more likely to vote for Ford's opponent, Bob Corker. Ford also neutralized support in some rural communities, although much of this can be attributed to his aggressive campaigning in these areas, and the influence of Congressman John Tanner, Ford's ally, in some western and middle Tennessee counties. Ford, however, was less successful in convincing voters from eastern Tennessee to support his campaign. His campaign also failed to capture single women, married voters, and college-educated voters.

As stated earlier, despite Ford's better than predicted performance among white voters, race was still a deciding factor in the election. Whites were more supportive of the"Bimbo"advertisement, and in the pre-election and exit polls, race was a significant factor. Ford, however, fell short of a presidential-election-year turnout in the black community.

Notes

1. Mingo Scott, *The Negro in Tennessee Politics and Governmental Affairs, 1865-1965: "The Hundred Years Story"* (Nashville, Tennessee: Rich Print. Company, 1964, c1965); James B. Jones, *Knoxville's African American Community, 1860-1920* (Nashville, Tennessee: Tennessee Historical Commission, 1989), 38-44.
2. Terry Tomziac and Mario Perez-Riley, "Effects of *Baker v. Carr* on the Distribution of Influence in the Tennessee General Assembly: An Application of Linkage Policy," in *The Volunteer State: Readings in Tennessee Politics*, eds. Dorothy F. Olshfski and T. Simpson, III, (Knoxville: Tennessee Political Science Association, 1985), 95-113.
3. Sekou Franklin, "Black Political Agency in Tennessee from Reconstruction to the Twenty-First Century," in Wornie Reed, eds. *African Americans in Tennessee* (forthcoming).
4. This included a front-cover expose in *Newsweek*, sympathetic commentaries from the conservative *Washington Times* and Fox's Brit Hume, and even a pre-election interview on HBO's *Real Time with Bill Maher*. See Jonathan Darman, "The Path to Power," *Newsweek*, October 30, 2006, available at http://www.msnbc.msn.com/id/15366095/site/newsweek/. Also, Harold Ford, Jr.'s campaign website listed all of his favorable media coverage, available at http://www.haroldfordjr.com/index.php?option=com_content&task=view&id=157.
5. Sekou Franklin, "Style, Substance, and Situational Deracialization: Racial Polarization and the Tennessee Senate Race," Paper presentation for the National Conference of Black Political Scientists' Annual Conference, March 21-25, 2007.
6. Jackson Baker, "Is Harold Ford Really a New Generation of Democrat—or Is He Just Another Ford?" (Political Notes) *Nashville Scene*, October 21, 2006, available at http://www.nashvillescene.com/Stories/News/Political_Notes/2006/10/12/Family_Matters/index.shtml; and Roger Abramson, "Prince Harold: The Sky Could Be the Limit for Harold Ford,

Jr. Conventional Wisdom Be Damned," *The Nashville Scene*, March 18, 2004, available at http://www.nashvillescene.com/Stories/News/2004/03/18/Prince_Harold/index.shtml.

7. It is unclear whether this was the official name of the ad. However, most political commentators referred to it as the "Bimbo" ad. Some referred to it as the "Playboy" ad or the "Call me" ad.

8. For more discussion of how the use of racial cues can limit deracialized campaigns, see Sharon Wright Austin and Richard T. Middleton, IV, "The Limitations of the Deracialization Concept in the 2001 Los Angeles Mayoral Election," *Political Research Quarterly* 2004; 57 (2) (June 2004): 283-293, and Timothy B. Krebs and David B. Holian, "Competitive Positioning, Deracialization, and Attack Speech: A Study of Negative Campaigning in the 2001 Los Angeles Mayoral," *American Politics Research* 2007; 35; 123.

9. Franklin, "Style, Substance, and Situational Deracialization."

10. Ibid.

11. No Author, "Put Party Affiliation in Check; Vote Early," *Chattanooga Times Free Press* (November 1, 2006): B8.

12. Andy Sher, "Corker Calls for RNC to Pull Ad," *Chattanooga Times Free Press* (October 21, 2006): B1.

13. Austin and Middleton, "The Limitations of the Deracialization Concept in the 2001 Los Angeles Mayoral Election."

14. See for example, David R. Goldfield, *Black, White, and Southern: Race Relations and Southern Culture, 1940 to the Present* (Baton Rouge: Louisiana State University Press, 1990); Brattain, Michelle, "Miscegenation and Competing Definitions of Race in Twentieth-Century Louisiana," *Journal of Southern History* vol. 71 (August 2005): 62-658; William J. Harris, "Etiquette, Lynching, and Racial Boundaries in Southern History: A Mississippi Example," *The American Historical Review* vol. 100, no. 2 (April 1995): 387-410; James F. Davis, *Who is Black: One Nation's Definition* (University Park, PA: Pennsylvania State University Press, 1991).

15. David R. Goldfield, *Black, White, and Southern: Race Relations and Southern Culture, 1940 to the Present* (Baton Rouge: Louisiana State University, 1990), 2.

16. Gail Bederman, *Manliness and Civilization: A Cultural History of Gender and Race in the United States, 1880—1917* (Chicago, IL: Univ. of Chicago Press, 1995), 3.

17. Martha Hodes, *White Women, Black Men: Illicit Sex in the Nineteenth-Century South.* (New Haven, CT: Yale University Press, 1997).

18. Christine B. Hickman, "The Devil and the One Drop Rule: Racial Categories, African Americans, and the U.S. Census," *Michigan Law Review* vol. 95, no. 5. (Mar., 1997), 1161, 1173.

19. Ibid., 1178.

20. Trina Jones, "Shades of Brown: The Law of Skin Color," *Duke Law Journal* vol. 49, no. 6 (April 2000): 1487, 1501, note 41.

21. Paul Finkelman, "The Crime of Color," 67 *Tul. L. Rev.* (June 1993): 2063, 2110.

22. See William J. Harris, "Etiquette, Lynching, and Racial Boundaries in Southern History: A Mississippi Example," *The American Historical Review* vol. 100, no. 2 (Apr., 1995): 387-410.

23. Davis, *Who is Black*, 64.

24. Charles V. Hamilton, "Deracialization: Examination of a Political Strategy." *First World* 1977 (March/April): 3-5.

25. Huey Perry, ed., *Race, Politics, and Governance in the United States* (Gainesville, Florida: University Press of Florida, 1997).

26. Timothy B. Krebs and David B. Holian, "Competitive Positioning, Deracialization, and Attack Speech: A Study of Negative Campaigning in the 2001 Los Angeles Mayoral Election," *American Politics Research* 2007; 35; 123.

27. Ibid., 142.

28. Ibid.

29. Baodong Liu, "Deracialization and Urban Racial Contexts," *Urban Affairs Review* vol. 38, no. 4 (2003): 572.

30. Ibid.

31. Austin and Middleton, "The Limitations of the Deracialization Concept in the 2001 Los Angeles Mayoral Election," 283, 291.

32. Karen Tumulty and Perry Bacon, Jr., "Why Harold Ford Has a Shot," *Time Magazine*, August 6, 2006, available at http://www.time.com/time/magazine/article/0,9171,1223381,00.html.

33. Erik Schelzig,"Faith Continues to be Prominent Issue in Tennessee Senate Race,"*Political News* (AP Wire) (November 4, 2006).

34. See "Black Point Man for the Right," *The Black Commentator* no. 120, January 6, 2005, available at http://www.blackcommentator.com/120/120_cover_harold_ford_pf.html; Jackson Baker,"Is Harold Ford Really a New Generation of Democrat—or Is He Just Another Ford?" (Political Notes) *Nashville Scene*, October 21, 2006, available at http://www.nashvillescene.com/Stories/News/Political_Notes/2006/10/12/Family_Matters/index.shtml; and Roger Abramson, "Prince Harold: The Sky Could Be the Limit for Harold Ford, Jr. Conventional Wisdom Be Damned,"*The Nashville Scene*, March 18, 2004, available at http://www.nashvillescene.com/Stories/News/2004/03/18/Prince_Harold/index.shtml.

35. Stephen Ansolabehere and Shanto Iyengar, *Going Negative: How Political Ads Shrink and Polarize the Electorate* (New York: Free Press, 1995); Stephen Ansolabehere, et al.,"Does Attack Advertising Demobilize the Electorate?" *American Political Science Review* 1994: 88: 829-838; Richard R. Lau, et al.,"The Effects of Negative Political Advertisements: A Meta-Analytical Assessment," *The American Political Science Review* vol. 93, no. 4. (December 1999): 851-875.

36. Steven E. Finkel and John Geer,"A Spot Check: Doubt on the Demobilizing Effect of Attack Advertising,"*American Journal of Political Science* vol. 42, no. 2 (1998): 573-595; Kim F. Kahn and Patrick J. Kenney,"Do Negative Campaigns Mobilize or Suppress Turnout? Clarifying the Relationship between Negativity and Participation,"*The American Political Science Review* vol. 93, No. 4. (Dec., 1999): 878; Paul Freedman and Ken Goldstein, "Measuring Media Exposure and the Effects of Negative Campaign Ads," *American Journal of Political Science* vol. 43, no. 4 (October 1999): 1189-1208; Ken Goldestein and Paul Freedman,"Campaign Advertising and Voter Turnout: New Evidence for a Stimulation Effect," *The Journal of Politics* vol. 64, no. 3. (August 2002): 721-740; John Geer, *In Defense of Negativity: Attack Advertising in Presidential Campaigns.* (Chicago, Illinois: University of Chicago Press, 2006).

37. Craig Leonard Brians and Martin P. Wattenberg, "Campaign Issue Knowledge and Salience: Comparing Reception from TV Commercials, TV News and Newspapers," *American Journal of Political Science* vol. 40, no. 1 (Feb., 1996): 172-193.

38. Tali Mendelberg, *The Race Card: Campaign Strategy, Implicit Messages, and the Norms of Equality* (Princeton, NJ: Princeton University Press, 2001); Nicholas A. Valentino, Vincent L. Hutchings, and Ismail K. White,"Cues That Matter: How Political Ads Prime Racial Attitudes during Campaigns,"*The American Political Science Review*, Vol. 96, No. 1. (Mar., 2002), pp. 75-90.

39. Andy Sher,"Attack Ads Dominate Corker-Ford Contest," *Chattanooga Times Free Press* (October 5, 2006): A1.

40. Sher,"Corker Calls for RNC to Pull Ad."

41. Steve Inskeep,"In the News and on the Air: Call Me!" (Morning E-Dition), National Public Radio, October 26, 2006, available at http://www.npr.org/templates/story/story.php?storyId=6386670&sc=emaf.

42. David Espo,"GOP Consultant Cuts Ties with Wal-Mart, (*The Associated Press*) *The Washington Post*, October 27, 2006, available at http://www.washingtonpost.com/wp-dyn/content/article/2006/10/27/AR2006102701340.html.

43. Mendelberg, *The Race Card*, 2001.

44. All reference categories rely upon "simple" contrasts in the SPSS statistical program.

45. With the exception of the simple contrasts, the independent variables in the three logistic regressions are all coded as dummy variables.

46. Gary King, *A Solution to the Ecological Inference Problem* (Princeton, NJ: Princeton University Press, 1997).

47. Kent Redding and David R. James,"Estimating Levels and Modeling Determinants of Black and White Voter Turnout in the South, 1880 to 1912,"*Historical Methods* 34, 4 (Fall 2001): 141-159.

48. MSNBC's Patrick Buchanan said "the RNC ad isn't 'racist' because Ford "likes Playboy bunnies. Almost all of them are white,"October 27, 2006, available at http://mediamatters.org/items/200610270015.

49. Panel Presentation by Seanna Brandmeir (President of the Tennessee Young Democrats), "Election 2008," Tennessee Alliance for Progress' Compass IV Conference, Nashville, Tennessee, April 14, 2007.

50. For example, Daniel Stevens found that individuals with less sophistication about campaigns, and politics in general, may inaccurately process the intent behind negative attack ads. See Stevens, "Separate and Unequal Effects: Information, Political Sophistication and Negative Advertising in American Elections," *Political Research Quarterly* vol. 58, No. 3. (Sep., 2005): 423.

51. Mendelberg, *The Race Card*; Valentino, Hutchings, and White, "Cues That Matter."

52. Nate Hobbs, "Activist Lifts Voice for Rural Blacks in W. Tenn.," *The Commercial Appeal* (January 17 1994): 1A.

53. The National Election Pool exit poll of the 2006 Senate race in Tennessee.

54. E.J. Dionne, "A Shift Among the Evangelicals," *The Washington Post* June 16, 2006, http://www.washingtonpost.com/wp-dyn/content/article/2006/06/15/AR2006061501790_pf.html; Michael Erard, "Don't Stop Believing: Renegade Bloggers Besiege the Southern Baptist Convention," *The Texas Observer*, July 13, 2007, http://www.texasobserver.org/article.php?aid=2547.

55. Sekou Franklin (co-author) thanks his student, Ben Neal, for special insight on this subject. Mr. Neal is a student activist with the Democratic Party and works in Congressman Bart Gordon's office Murfreesboro, Tennessee.

56. Data for plant closures were obtained by Sekou Franklin (co-author) from the Tennessee AFL-CIO, which has identified plant closures for the state's worker investment areas. For information on Medicaid cuts, see "TennCare Once Was Model for Public Health Care, But Now Is Cautionary Tale. Over 1,000 HIV Patients Left With No Coverage," *AIDS Alert* vol. 21, no. 1 (January 2005): 4-5.

57. See the Pew Research Center for People and the Press survey conducted from November 1-4, 2006, p. 8.

58. Charles L. Prysby, "The 1990 U.S. Senate Election in North Carolina," in Perry, ed. *Race, Governance, and Politics in the United States* (Gainesville, FL: University of Florida Press, 1996), 30-43.

59. Valentino, Hutchings, and White, "Cues That Matter."

60. Tennessee's voter tabulation districts are officially called "pseudo" districts. These districts do not provide exact counts of the voting age population. Moreover, Tennessee has experienced a population boom in recent years, and some central city neighborhoods in Nashville-Davidson County, Memphis, and Chattanooga have experienced gentrification since data for the VTDs were collected.

61. Anderson, Meigs, and Sullivan Counties represent eastern Tennessee. Although Sullivan County is majority white and is considered a racially homogenous district, it has a black representative (Nathan Vaughn) in the state legislature. Representing the western portion of the state are Hardeman, Haywood, Tipton, and Madison. These areas, excluding Dyer, have the largest concentration of rural blacks and fairly active voter mobilization coalition called the Rural West Tennessee African American Affairs Council. Bedford, Giles, Maury, and Robertson represent middle Tennessee.

62. David Waters, "Ford Country?; These Rural West Tennessee Near Always Lead to the Winner," *The Commercial Appeal* (October 31, 2006): A1.

63. See the comments by Michael Powell, Ford's campaign consultant. Andy Sher, "Ford Looks to High Black Turnout in U.S. Senate Race," *Chattanooga Times Free Press* (November 4, 2006): B2.

64. Erik Schelzig, "Ford Tries to Energize Black Vote in West Tennessee," *The Associated Press State & Local Wire* (October 30, 2006).

65. Franklin also uses Gary King's ecological regression analysis to measure black voter turnout. See Sekou Franklin, "Style, Substance, and Situational Deracialization: Harold Ford, Jr.'s Governance and Electoral Strategy," Working Paper, 2007.

Beyond the Boundaries, Volume 12; pp. 123-138

The Early Electoral Contests of Senator Barack Obama: A Longitudinal Analysis

Hanes Walton, Jr.
University of Michigan

Robert C. Starks
Northeastern Illinois University

On November 2, 2004, the state of Illinois once again made political history by sending the second of two most recent African Americans to the United States Senate. When Senator Barack Obama arrived, Illinois matched Mississippi as the only two states in the Union to have sent two African Americans to the Senate. Mississippi sent two African Americans in the Reconstruction Era, 1868-1880, while Illinois has sent two during the twentieth and twenty-first centuries. Louisiana and Massachusetts are the only other states to have sent an African American to the Senate (one each).

However, what is unique and different about Illinois is that it has sent one African American female and one African American male and both came in the period, 1992-2004. Until 1913, U.S. senators were elected by state legislatures. With the ratification of the 17th Amendment to the Constitution on April 8, 1913, candidates for the Senate had to run statewide and be elected by the popular vote of the people in each state.[1]

Besides, Illinois, only Massachusetts has popularly elected an African American to this body, Senator Edward Brooke in 1966 and 1972.[2] Again, the difference here is that both of Illinois' African American senators have been Democrats, while all of the others, including Senator Brooke, have been Republicans.[3] In fact, four of the six that have been sent to the Senate were Republicans. Hence, Illinois and only Illinois have sent the two African American Democrats.[4]

The uniqueness here is not simply the state of Illinois. The candidate is also unique. He is an African American with a Kenyan father and a white mother from Kansas.[5] He is unique not only because of his racial background, but also in terms of his electoral career. Unlike all of the other previously elected African American senators, Senator Obama comes out of the Illinois State Senate, whereas his predecessors, Senator Moseley-Braun, came out of the Illinois State House and Cook County Recorder of Deeds Offices and Senator Brooke who was a two-term elected attorney general from Massachusetts, Senator Obama had been elected for his third term to the State Senate representing the 13th Senate District from the city of Chicago. Thus, it is his electoral contests in this district and others that is the subject and focus of this chapter.

Data and Methodology

Just prior graduating from college in 1983, Senator Obama writes in his autobiography that he "decided to become a community organizer."[6] So, "I wrote to every civil rights organization I could think of, to any black elected official in the country with a progressive agenda, to neighborhood councils and tenant rights groups. When only one wrote back... I decided to find more conventional work for a year."[7] And after the passage of some time, "a consulting house to multinational corporations agreed to hire me as research assistant."[8] However, within a few months he turned in his resignation at the consulting firm and began looking in earnest for an organizing job. Once again offers were slow to come in but the college graduate got a job offer from a prominent civil rights organization in New York City.[9] During the job interview, the director of the organization offered him a job, "which involved organizing conferences on drugs, unemployment, housing" and working with the Republican Cabinet secretary at the Department of Housing and Urban Development in Washington, DC. The young college graduate declined the job because he "needed a job closer to the streets."[10]

While waiting on other organizing job offers to surface, Obama "spent three months working for a Ralph Nader offshoot up in Harlem. Then a week passing out flyers for an assemblyman's race in Brooklyn (the candidate lost and Barack never got paid).[11] Eventually, a call came from the head of the Calumet Community Religious Conference (CCRC), an organization of more than twenty suburban churches in Chicago, that Marty Kaufman would be in New York the following week to interview Obama.[12] Wanting to hire a trainee for their new city organizing drive, the job was offered on the spot, and Obama within a week moved to Chicago.

Arriving in Chicago during the historic election of African American mayor Harold Washington in 1983, he would leave his community organizing position a year after Washington's reelection and death, in 1988 to attend Harvard law School. Obama's father had attended the graduate school there in 1963 upon his graduation from the University of Hawaii.[13]

When Obama graduated in 1991, he went back to Chicago and by 1992 he "directed Illinois Project Vote, which registered 150,090 new voters." Thus, here were the beginnings, initially a community organizer in the South Side of Chicago and then a statewide voter registration organizer and activist.

Then it happened."When a seat in the state legislature opened up in 1996, some friends persuaded me to run for office, and I won," wrote Obama. Table 1 offers a comprehensive and systematic portrait of the different electoral contests that Senator Obama was involved in prior to his winning his senate seat. Overall, Senator Obama has run in five primary elections, four general elections, for a total of nine elections. Of these nine elections, he won eight of them and lost one.

As to the offices, he has run in six elections for the Illinois State Senate winning all of them, one election for a congressional seat in the House of Representatives, which he lost, and two elections for the United States Senate, both of which he won. As to his congressional race, he ran for it while he was in the Illinois State Senate due to the fact that election laws in Illinois do not prohibit one from holding one elected position and simultaneously running for another. In that race he took on an eight-year incumbent.

Table 2 indicates the number of opponents that Senator Obama faced in his primary and general elections during his entire electoral career. There were no opponents in his state senate primaries, three opponents in his congressional House of Representative race and seven opponents in his United States Senate race. All total, he has had some ten opponents in his primary races.

In his general election contests, Senator Obama faced opponents in two of his three state senate races. Only in his last general election contest, 2002,

Table 1
The Categories and Types of Elections Contested by Barack Obama: 1996–2004

Year	Primary Elections	Number Elections	Total	Results
State Senate Races				
1996	X	X	2	Won
1998	X	X	1	Won
2002	X	X	0	Won
U.S. Congressional Race				
2000	X	-	3	Lost
U.S. Senate Races				
2004	X	X	20	Won
Grand Total	5	4	26	8 Wins/1 Lost

Source: Adapted from the State Board of Elections, Official Vote, Primary Election General Primary March 17, 1992–2004 and Official Vote General Election, November 3, 1992–2004.

Table 2
The Number of Opponents Faced by Barack Obama in
Primary and General Elections: 1996–2004

Year	Number of Primary Election Opponents	Number of General Election Opponents	Total
State Senate Races			
1996	0	2	2
1998	0	1	1
2002	0	0	0
U.S. Congressional Race			
2000	3	NA	3
U.S. Senate Races			
2004	7	13	20
Grand Total	10	16	26

Source: Adapted from the State Board of Elections, Official Vote, Primary Election General Primary March 17, 1992–2004 and Official Vote General Election, November 3, 1992–2004.

did he not have any opponents. As for his congressional general election, he lost in the primary election and therefore did not proceed to that general election. His three opponents in this race appeared in the primary. However, in the Senate races, both at the primary and general election ones he had more opposition than in all of his other contests combined. Seven opponents in the primary and a whopping thirteen in the general election. In fact, in these two races, he had twenty opponents compared to only six in all of his other contests.

Therefore, the data for this study will be the election return data for all nine of his elections and similar data for all of his opponents in these elections. This official data will permit the study to develop a comprehensive portrait of the electoral trends, patterns and tendencies in his support. In addition, it will be able to follow the nature and scope of his electoral coalitions through these nine elections.

At this point, a word has to be said about the methodology, which is used to assess and evaluate the electoral trends, patterns, and tendencies as well as the coalitions over time. Both descriptive and probability statistics will be employed to produce empirical analyses of these nine elections, so that both a description of these electoral contests can be had as well as an explanation about how the victories and loses were attained. And from our findings, this case study hopes to generate several testable propositions to be used in other studies that hopefully will emerge in the future. Such empirical insights will go a long ways in helping students and scholars to understand African American Senate elections given the current dearth of academic and scholarly information on this aspect of African American politics.[14]

The Political Context: Voter Turnout in Illinois

Chicago has always been a successful city for the rise and growth of African American politicos. Political Scientists Harold Gosnell writes: "as far back as 1876, when the colored people comprised only 1 percent of the total population of the city, one of them, John W. E. Thomas, was sent as their representative to the capitol at Springfield by the Republican voters of the Second Senatorial District of Chicago."[15] After making this remark, Gosnell continues with the observation that "Representative Thomas was not reelected until 1882, but after that date there has never been a session of the Illinois General Assembly, which has lacked a colored representative."[16]

After the arrival of these state legislators came the first African American congressman from the state, in 1928. This was not only a major political breakthrough, but it also shocked the nation, and particularly the South, simply because the last African American in Congress (who just happened to be from the South) was eliminated by the region-wide disenfranchisement in 1901.[17] This African American congressman, Oscar DePriest, was a Republican. Two years into the New Deal, in 1934, African American voters in the South Side of Chicago replaced him with a Democrat, Arthur W. Mitchell, and this election greatly disturbed the southern white party elites.[18] But the rise of African American politicos did not stop there.

In 1983, African Americans and their electoral coalition allies elected an African American mayor, Harold Washington.[19] Four years later they reelected him, but he died shortly thereafter. The next major political breakthrough was the election of an African American female to the United States Senate in 1992, followed by Senator Obama's election in 2004. Thus, it can simply be said that up to this point no other state or city has matched the political achievements of this state and in the city of Chicago.

Besides having a politically active African American population and strategic acting politicians, the political landscape in Illinois is unique in that electoral power in the state is highly concentrated and located predominately in a single county. Political scientists in studying this unusual electoral phenomenon have written: "With the decline of the rural population, it is no surprise that the voter-rich areas in Illinois are clustered mainly in the state's northeast corner. Both parties must begin any serious political campaign by focusing on this small geographic area where the vast majority of people live."[20] They continue by noting, "Democrats have the same kind of advantage in Illinois that they have in New York. Fifty percent of the statewide Democratic vote for president typically originated from Cook County (especially Chicago)."[21]

Having made these insights about the geographic concentration of Illinois's population and voting electorate, they focus upon Chicago and add:
"Chicago remains the Democratic stronghold that it has been for decades.
Its population has become more diverse as upwardly mobile whites have
fled and blacks and Hispanics have moved in... African Americans and
Latinos are now core Democratic constituencies.... White ethnics control
fewer of the city's wards, and white politicians are dependent upon the
nonwhite vote to an extent never before seen in history."Thus, Chicago and
the African American electorate are central to a political party's victory in
both statewide and national elections.

Beyond Cook County but including it, Table 3 lists the counties that form
the electoral bases for each of the major parties in the state, as well as the
total percentage of the party vote that is derived from these ten counties.
Thus, while Illinois is essential a competitive two-party state, voter turnout
can help to ensure victory for either of the parties in statewide and national
elections. From the table it is clear that the Democratic Party has an electoral edge over the Republicans in the densely populated areas of the state.

Figure 1 furnishes us with the degree of voter turnout for the entire state
over time. Not only is turnout greater in general elections that in primary
elections, other extant data reveals that Democrats in the time period in
Figure 1 had turned out in larger numbers than Republicans, giving the
party the advantage that it now has in Illinois politics. This type of turnout
clearly laid the electoral foundation for the state senate and U.S. Senate
victories that Senator Obama achieved in his elections. He never had to
worry about turnout in his state senate primary elections because he never
had any primary opposition. He did face opposition in his House of Rep-

Table 3
Illinois's Top Ten Strongest Counties for Republicans and Democrats in the
1988–2000 Presidential Contests

Rank	Democratic	Republican
1	Cook (Chicago)	Cook (Chicago)
2	DuPage (Wheaton)	DuPage (Wheaton)
3	Lake (Waukegan)	Lake (Waukegan)
4	St. Clair (East St. Louis)	Will (Joliet)
5	Madison (Granite Cite-Alton)	Kane (Elgin)
6	Will (Joliet)	McHenry (Crystal Lake)
7	Winnebago (Rockford)	Sangamon (Springfield)
8	Rock Island (Rock Island)	Winnebago (Rockford)
9	Peoria (Peoria)	Madison (Granite City-Alton)
10	Kane (Elgin)	McLean (Bloomington)
Percentage of Total Vote	73.5	66.1

Source: James Gimpel and Jason Schuknecht Patchwork Nation: Sectionalism and Political
Change in America Politics (Ann Arbor: University of Michigan Press, 2003), p. 355.

Figure 1
Voter Turnout in the Primary and General Elections in Illinois: 1982-2004

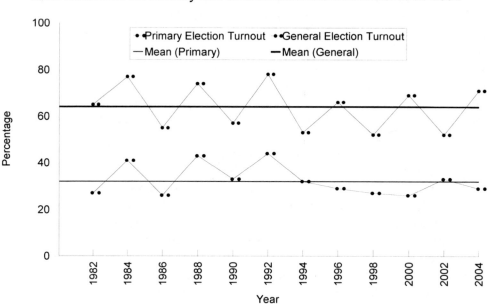

Source: *Adapted from the State Board of Elections*, Official Vote, Primary Election, General Primary March 17, 1992-2004 and Official Vote, General Election, November 3, 1992-2004.

resentatives race and U.S. Senate races, but even then he chose to run in presidential years, 2000 and 2004, when turnout was always higher than in mid-term election years.

The State Senate Electoral Contests of Barack Obama: 1996, 1998, and 2002

In 1996, the long-term incumbent in the 13th State Senate District, Alice Palmer, asked attorney and voter registration activist Barack Obama to run for her seat. Not only did he agree, he entered the Democratic state primary on March 17, 1996. No one qualified to run against him. With no opponents in the state senate primaries, he won each time the Democratic Party's nomination.

Primary opposition might not have surfaced, but he did face general election opponents in two of his three general election contests. Yet, in each of those elections, he captured a mean percentage of 85.7 percent. In his last state senate general election in 2002 he had no opponents.

Table 4 provides both the votes and the percentages, which Obama received in each of his primary and general election contests in the 13th State Senate District in Illinois. Although he received 100 percent of the primary vote each time, his total primary votes did not change much. For the first two elections they remained about the same C the mean vote was 16,536 C but in 2002 his vote total nearly double reaching a high of 30,938 votes.

However, there is a degree of similarity in the total vote count for Obama between the primary and general election. Although his general election vote total is three times as high as his primary vote total, the difference here is that the general election vote total is quite stable over all three elections. The range of his vote total runs from a high of 48,717 in this third election in 2002 to a low of 45,486 in his second election in 1998. Surprisingly, his middle level vote total of 48,592 votes came in his initial general election in 1996. But that year, he faced two opponents a Republican and a third-party candidate. By the time of his second state senate election, he only faced a Republican candidate. Thus, Obama means general election vote was 47,498.3 votes, while the mean vote for his Republican opposition was 6,494 votes.

Overall, with no primary opposition and the opposition in the general election garnering only a mean vote of 9.5 percent, Obama state senate contests were essentially a Democratic affair. The African American vote for African American Republican candidates in the South Side of Chicago has been a minuscule vote because this electorate has been aligned with the Democratic Party since 1934. Hence, winning the vote of African American Democrats nearly ensures victory at least at the ward, precinct, state, legislative and senatorial and some congressional districts levels.[22] All that Obama needed in these state senate electoral contests was a good turnout to win.

The Congressional Electoral Contest of Barack Obama: 2000

In 1998 when Obama was reelected to the Illinois Senate, he was elected to a four-year term. But two years into the four-year term, Obama decided to run for the 1st Congressional District seat held by long-time incumbent Bobby Rush of the Black Panther Party notoriety. This seat had been held by numerous political notables in the Windy City such as William Dawson, Ralph Metcalfe, Bennett Stewart, Harold Washington, and Charles Hayes.[23] Congressman Rush had initially won the seat in 1992 and had won reelection three times before the 2000 elections. Literally Rush had been in Congress some eight years. Thus, unlike his state senate elections where he faced no opposition in the Democratic primaries, this time Obama would face a seasoned incumbent as well as two other major challengers.

Shown in Table 5 are the results for the four candidates in the 2000 Illinois First Congressional District race. Under Illinois's election laws, a candidate may hold an elected office and run for another one at the same time. However, even with two successful electoral contests behind him, State Senator Obama suffered his first election defeat. The four-term incumbent Congressman Rush soundly defeated this newcomer by capturing almost two-thirds (62.5 percent) of the total vote cast. State Senator Obama came

Table 4

The Votes and Percentages in the 13th Illinois State Senate District for Candidate Barack Obama: 1996–2002

Year	Candidate	Primary Election Vote	Primary Election Percentage	Candidate	General Election Vote	General Election Percentage
1996	B. Obama	16,279	100	B. Obama	48,592	82.2
				D. Whitehead	7,461	12.6
				R. Peyton	3,091	5.2
					59,144	100.1
1998	B. Obama	16,792	100	B. Obama	45,486	89.2
				Y.B. YattuDah	5,526	10.8
					51,012	100.0
2002	B. Obama	30,938	100	B. Obama	48,717	100.0

Source: *Adapted from State Board of Elections*, Official Vote Primary Elections General Primary, March 17, 1996–2002 and Official Vote General Elections, November, 1996–2002.

in second with less than one-third (29.2 percent) of the vote cast. The rest of the opposition in the 2000 race captured less than a tenth (8.4 percent) of the vote. In fact, even if the Obama vote is combined with that of the other two challengers, it would still be significantly less than the vote that the incumbent received.

Although this was a presidential election year when turnout is highest, and that Obama's mean primary vote up to this point was 16,536 and that he increased it by 10,885 it was still less than half of the incumbent Congressman Rush's vote. The incumbent beat Obama by 31,351 votes. In fact, had Illinois been a state with a runoff primary and it is not, Obama would have still lost the primary simply because the incumbent won a clear-cut majority. Thus, the very best that can be said of State Senator Obama performance is that he significantly increased his electoral base in the city of Chicago and his political exposure. He increased his name recognition among the Cook County Democratic electorate. And this increase base of support shows up two years later when he runs for reelection to his state senate seat when he captures some 30,938 votes. This was 14,402 votes beyond his primary mean and 3,517 votes beyond his congressional primary totals. In sum, State Senator Obama foray into a congressional election contest and his subsequent State Senate reelection proved that he was able to attract a larger electoral group of supporters in a relative short period of time.

The U.S. Senatorial Contests of Barack Obama: 2004

Four years after his first attempt to represent the people of Illinois in Congress and two years after his reelection to the State Senate, Obama announced for the open U.S. Senate seat in the state. Prior to his announcement, an African American female Carol Moseley-Braun had won a U.S. Senate seat in 1992 but lost it in her reelection bid in 1998,[24] the same year that Obama won his first reelection to the State Senate. Thus, six years after an African American U.S. senator had lost her seat, another African American was making a bid for it.

Former Senator Moseley-Braun was now an announced candidate for the Democratic Party's nomination for president. She made the announcement shortly after New York civil rights activist Al Sharpton had announced that he was running for the Democratic Party's nomination for president.[25] Despite these unique contextual features surrounding this senatorial primary, there was the matter of the open seat election itself, which would attract numerous candidates. This is usually the case when no incumbent is involved.

Therefore what one sees in Table 6 in the Democratic primary is a total of some eight different candidates that attracts about 1.2 million voters to the polls. Besides State Senator Obama, this open-seat race also attracted another African American candidate, Joyce Washington that had just come

Table 5
The Vote and Percentage in the 1st Congressional District
Democratic Primary: 2000

Year	Candidate	Primary Election Vote	Primary Election Percentage
2000	Bobby Rush	58,772	62.5
	Barack Obama	27,421	29.2
	Donne E. Trother	6,590	7.0
	George C. Roby	1,296	1.4
	Total	94,079	100.1

Source: *Adapted from State Board of Elections,* Official Vote, Primary Election General Primary, March 27, 2000.

off in 2002 a race for the lieutenant governorship. Said race had proven to this candidate that she could build a statewide electoral coalition even if she had never held elective office before.

Yet in spite of this unique electoral context, State Senator Obama won the Democratic primary going away. He captured a majority of the vote, 52.8 percent and this was double his second-place opponent, Hayes who won only 23.7 percent of the total vote cast. The other African American in the race, Washington, won only one percent of the total vote cast.

In terms of votes, State Senator Obama captured more than 600,000 votes of the 1,242,996 total votes cast. To this date, this was Obama's best primary showing in his entire electoral career.[26] Having won his election, Obama would go on to represent the Democratic Party in the November 2, general election.

But before the general election occurred, the Republican party nominee, Jack Ryan, became involved in a sex scandal with his movie star wife, Jeri Ryan, and withdrew from the Senate race. In order not to let this seat go unchallenged, the Republican party at this late date asked a number of other well known personalities in the state to accept the party's nomination, but all refused. Then, the party went out of state and asked two-time African American Senate candidate from Maryland and two-time Republican presidential candidate Alan Keyes to come to Illinois and run against Democratic party nominee Obama.[27] He accepted while vigorously denying that he was a carpetbagger.

Once again Table 6 shows that in this general election contest, Obama captured nearly three-fourths (70 percent) of the total vote cast, while Keyes won less than one-third (27.15 percent) of the total vote. The other five candidates won less than three percent (2.9 percent) of the total vote. Clearly, Obama seriously defeated the carpetbagger from Maryland, who had only a token electoral base in the state from his previous participation in

Table 6
The Vote and Percentage in the 2004 Illinois U.S. Senate Race for
Candidate Barack Obama: Primary and General Elections

Year	Candidate	Votes	%
	Primary Election		
	B. Obama	655,923	52.8
	D. Haynes	294,717	23.7
	M.B. Hull	134,453	10.8
	M. Pappas	74,987	6.0
2004	G. Chico	53,433	4.3
	N. Skinna	16,098	1.3
	J. Washington	13,375	1.1
	E.J. Hunt	10	0.0
	Total	1,242,996	100.0
	General Election		
	B. Obama	3,597,456	70.0
	A. Keyes	1,390,690	27.1
	A. Franzer	81,164	1.6
	J. Kohn	69,253	1.4
	M. Kuhnke	2,268	0.04
	S. Doody	339	0.0
	Others	350	0.0
	Total	5,141,520	100.1

Source: Adapted from the State Board of Elections, Official Vote Primary Election General Primary, March 11, 2004, p. 8 and Official Vote General Election November 3, 2004, p. 17.

the Republican presidential primaries in the state. While this performance was greater than both of his previous runs as demonstrated in Table 7 it surely was not enough to be competitive and/or defeat the hometown boy. It was an embarrassing defeat for Keyes and an immediately step up for Senator-elect Obama who was now being touted as a national candidate as a possible future vice-presidential nominee.[28] The best that the data in Table 7 indicates about Keyes is that the voters in Illinois were much more willing to vote for him for senator than for president. In fact, they were a lot more willing.

Table 7
The Vote and Percentage for Alan Keyes's Presidential and Senatorial Races in Illinois: 1996–2004

Year	Vote	Percentage	Office
1996	30,052	3.7	President
2000	66,066	9.0	President
2004	1,390,690	27.1	Senate

Source: Adapted from Richard Scammon, Alice McGillivray and Rhodes Cook (eds.) *America Votes 22*, (Washington, D.C.: Congressional Quarterly, 1996) p. 58; Richard Scammon, Alice McGillivray and Rhodes Cook (eds.) *America Votes 24* (Washington, D.C.: Congressional Quarterly, 2000), p. 37 and 42; and Illinois State Board of Elections, *Official Vote, Primary Election, General Primary* (March 16, 2004), pp. 1 and 8.

Table 8
The Vote and Percentage for African American Presidential and Senatorial Candidates in Illinois's Primary Election: 2004

Office	Candidate	Vote	Percentage
Senate	B. Obama	655,923	5.8
President	C. Moseley-Braun	53,249	4.4
President	A. Sharpton	36,123	3.0
Senate	J. Washington	13,375	1.1

Source: Illinois State Board of Education, *Official Vote Primary Election, General Primary, March 16, 2004*, p. 8 and Illinois State Board of Election, *Official Vote*, General Election, November 2, 2004, p. 17.

Table 9
Comparison of the Democratic and Republican Vote and Percentage for the Presidential and Senatorial Candidates in Illinois: 2004

Office	Candidate	Vote	Percentage
Democratic Party			
Senator	B. Obama	3,597,456	69.97
President	J. Kerry	2,891,550	58.82
	Differences	+705,906	+15.15
Republican Party			
President	G. Bush	2,345,946	44.48
Senator	A. Keyes	1,390,690	27.05
	Differences	-995,256	-17.43

Source: Adapted from Illinois State Board of Elections: Official Vote, General Election November 2, 2004, pp. 1–28.

Conclusions: Testable Propositions from a Case-Study

Figure 2 provides a longitudinal look at the level of voter support for Obama in both his primary and general elections in Illinois over his electoral career. This figure starts off with the primary vote for African American incumbent State Senator Alice Palmer in 1992 before she gave up her seat to Obama and shows his percentage where he had no opposition in the primaries with the years of 2000 and 2004 where he did have opposition in the primaries. The mean primary vote for Obama stands at 77.5 percent.

Again the starting percentage is that for incumbent Palmer but drops as soon as Obama began his general election contest. Of the four general election contests, Obama has had opposition in three of them and his mean general election vote is 88.2 percent. This indicates that of the two categories across time, Obama has performed better in the general elections than in the primaries and this is due essentially to his loss in the 2000 congressional primary. His vote percentage in this election was by far and away significantly below his primary mean.

When comparing his performance in the 2004 election to that of the African American presidential candidates, Moseley-Braun and Al Sharpton, and senatorial candidate Joyce Washington as seen in Table 8, it appears that the state's electorate liked Obama far better than they liked all of the other African American candidates combined. In fact, these candidates barely garnered any support from the electorate, including the African American electorate. They failed to increase the turnout in the state, much less any serious electoral coalition. Simply put, they made quite a poor showing. In the case of former Senator Moseley-Braun, this could be credited to the fact that she withdrew from the race even before the Iowa Caucus and the New Hampshire presidential primary took place. Thus, those individuals who voted for her were voters who simply wanted to remain loyal to her in spite of the fact that she was no longer running. And even though she had withdrawn, she still got more votes than the Reverend Al Sharpton.

Therefore, in the final analysis, it was not so much the uniqueness of the political context as much as it was the political accident that emerged before the general election in which the main Republican nominee had to quit the race and a carpetbagger without roots in the state became the major party challenger. This last-minute replacement had no time to build a successful electoral coalition in the state that could rival that of Obama. Hence, he went down to a great defeat.

Moreover, when one compares Obama's senate victory with the presidential outcome in the state the sheer size and magnitude of his victory can be put into perspective. Table 9 permits us to see the relationship between Obama electoral support and that for the Democratic and Republican presidential candidates in the 2004 election. Obama ran significantly ahead of his own party's presidential ticket of John Kerry and John Edwards. He captured some 705,906 more votes than the ticket, which was some 15.2 percentage

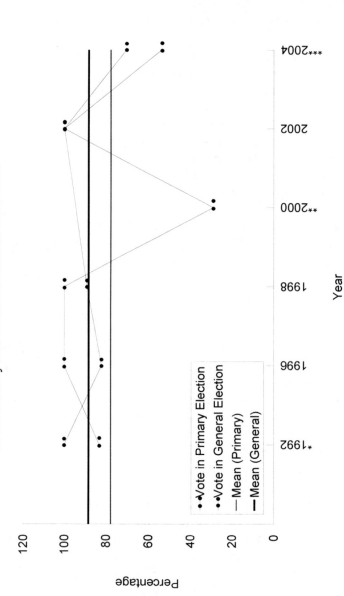
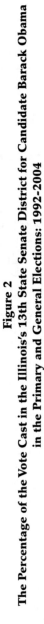

Figure 2
The Percentage of the Vote Cast in the Illinois's 13th State Senate District for Candidate Barack Obama in the Primary and General Elections: 1992-2004

Source: Adapted from the State Board of Elections, Official Vote, Primary Election, General Primary March 17, 1992-2004 and Official Vote, General Election, November 3, 1992-2004.

* = Candidate is the incumbent African American Alice J. Palmer.

** = Year that State Senator Obama ran for the House of Representative Seat, in Congressional District.

*** = Year that State Senator Obama just ran for the United States Senate Seat.

points greater and at the county level Obama beat Kerry in every county of the state as he did with all of his senatorial opponents. In addition, although the incumbent President Bush ran ahead of his senatorial candidate Alan Keyes, Obama outpolled the incumbent Republican president by nearly 1.3 million votes. This almost equaled the total number of votes that Keyes received in the election. Thus, both Obama and Kerry outpolled both Bush and Keyes.

Overall, the Obama 2004 electoral performance was exceptional in mobilizing the state's electorate behind him and as such it generates a series of testable hypotheses for the further study of African American senate elections. In Table 10 was derived from Obama's successful senate elections certain hypothesis about the: (1) Illinois's population and its concentration, (2) the state electorate, especially the dominance of the African American electorate in the state's largest county, Cook County, (3) the qualifications and biracial campaign of the African American candidate, (4) a weak and/ or scandal-laden opposition candidate, and finally (5) substantial crossover voting in the election in behalf of the African American candidate. All of these independent variables can be tested for their influence and impact in shaping the final outcome of the election. Findings from these categories of testable hypotheses will go a long way in generating an empirical theory about the nature and scope of African American senate elections.

Table 10
The Testable Propositions Empirically Deduced from the
Barack Obama Senate Elections

Number	Hypotheses
1	White crossover voting is essential for victory in African–American Senate elections
2	High African–American voter registration is essential in victorious African–American Senate elections
3	High voter turnout is essential in victorious African–American Senate elections
4	African–American Senate candidates need to run to help attain victory in African–American Senate elections
5	Scandals that eliminate the main Republican candidate helps to secure victory in African–American Senate elections
6	The political experiences of the African–American Senate candidate is germane
7	Concentration of state electorates in a few counties around Chicago provide the African–American Senate candidate with a balance-of-power position in African–American Senate election

Although these testable propositions were generated from aggregate election return data, thereby giving us an empirical portrait at the group level, these findings can surely be tested in the future with other aggregate data and can also be used in an exploratory manner with individual level data. In fact, given the cross-level nature of the proposed future research, it is essential that these future researchers understand and keep in mind that these group-level findings might not hold up at the individual level.[29] With this caveat taken in consideration, the empirical study and rending of African American senate elections can begin in earnest. Here is one of the first steps.

Notes

1. Karen O. Connor and Larry J. Sabato, *American Government: Continuity and Change* 2006 Edition, (New York: Longman, 2006), pp. 88-89. Alan Abramowitz and Jeffrey Segal, *Senate Elections* (Ann Arbor: University of Michigan Press, 1992), pp. 12-26.
2. John Becker and Eugene Heaton, Jr., "The Election of Senator Edward W. Brooke," *Public Opinion Quarterly* Vol. 31 (Fall, 2967), pp. 346-358.
3. Katherine Tate, "African American Female Senatorial Candidates: Twin Assets of Double Liabilities?" in Hanes Walton, Jr., *African American Power and Politics: The Political Contextual Variable* (New York: Columbia University Press, 1997), pp. 264-281.
4. Roger K. Oden, "The Election of Carol Moseley Braun in the U.S. Senate Race in Illinois," in Huey L. Perry, (ed.) *Race, Politics, and Governance in the United States* (Gainesville: University of Florida Press, 1996), pp. 47-64.
5. Barack Obama, *Dreams from My Father: A Story of Race and Inheritance* (New York: Three Rivers Press; Barack Obama, *The Audacity of Hope* (New York: Crown Publishers, 2006); and see also Mary Mitchell, "Memoir of a 21ˢᵗ Century History Maker," *Black Issues Book Review* Vol. 7 (January-February, 2005), ;o. 18-21.
6. *Ibid.*, p. 133.
7. *Ibid.*, p. 135.
8. *Ibid.*
9. *Ibid.*
10. *Ibid.*, p. 139.
11. *Ibid.*
12. *Ibid.*, p. 140 and 150.
13. *Ibid.*, pp. 287-289. See also, Michael Preston, "The Election of Harold Washington: An Examination of the SES Model in the 1983 Chicago Mayoral Election," in Michael Preston, Lenneal Henderson, Jr., and Paul Puryear (eds.), *The New Black Politics: The Search for Political Power* 2ⁿᵈ Edition (New York: Longman, 1987), pp. 139-171.
14. At this writing thee are no comprehensive and systematic studies of African American Senators. For them most recent work on a single Senator and his family, Lawrence Otis Graham, *The Senator and the Socialite* (New York: HarperCollins, 2006). At best one can only find such studies of African Americans in the House of Representatives. See Katherine Tate, *Faces in the Mirror: African Americans and Their Representatives in the U.S. Congress* (Princeton: Princeton University Press, 2003) and her article, "African American Female Senatorial Candidates: Twin Assets or Double Liabilities," in Walton, op. Cit. William Clay, *Just Permanent Interest: Black Americans in Congress, 1870-1991* (New York: Amistad Press, 1992); LaVerene Gill, *African American Women in Congress: Forming and Transforming History* (New Jersey: Rutgers University Press, 1997). And Sheila F. Harmon-Martin, "Black Women in Politics: A Research Note," in Hanes Walton, Jr., (ed.), *Black Politics and Black Political Behavior* (Westport, Connecticut: Praeger, 1994), pp. 209-218.
15. Harold Gosnell, *Negro Politicians: The Rise of Negro Politics in Chicago* (Chicago: University of Chicago Press, 1966), pp. 65-66.
16. *Ibid.*, p. 66. See Also Lee McGriggs, *Black Legislative Politics in Illinois: A Theoretical and Structural Analysis* (Washington, DC: University Press of America, 1977).

17. Gosnell, op. cit., pp. 163-195.
18. Dennis S. Nordin, *The New Deal's Black Congressman: A Life of Arthur Wergs Mitchell* (Columbia: University of Missouri Press, 1997).
19. Dianne Pinderhughes, *Race and Ethnicity in Chicago Politics: A Reexamination of Pluralist Theory* (Urbana: University of Illinois Press, 1987). See also Paul Kleppner, *Chicago Divided: The Making of a Black Mayor* (DeKalb, Illinois: Northern Illinois University Press, 1985); William Grimshaw, *Bitter Fruit: Black Politics and the Chicago Machine 1931-1991* (Chicago: University of Chicago Press, 1992), and Henry Young, *The Black Church and the Harold Washington Story* (Bristol, Indiana: Wyndham Hall Press, 1988).
20. James Gimpel and Jason Schuknecht, *Patchwork Nation: Sectionalism and Political Change in American Politics* (Ann Arbor: University of Michigan Press, 2003), p. 353.
21. *Ibid.*
22. See Hanes Walton, Jr., "Black Presidential Participation and the Critical Election Theory," in Lorenzo Morris (ed.), *The Social and Political Implications of the 1984 Jesse Jackson Presidential Campaign* (New York: Praeger, 1990), pp. 49-64. And his "Remaking African American Public Opinion: The Role and Function of the African American Conservatives," in Gayle T. Tate & Lewis Randolph (ed.), *Dimensions of Black Conservatism in the United States: Made in America* (New York: Palgrave, 2002), p. 147, Figure 8.1 which compares the Republican vote in Chicago's African American congressional district with those of New York. It went from a high of nearly 50 percent to about 15 percent.
23. Tate, *Black Faces in the Mirror*, pp. 183-195. See Robert Singh, *The Congressional Black Caucus: Racial Politics in the U.S. Congress* (Thousand Oaks, California: Sage Publications, 1998), Table 2.2, pp. 31-32. See also Robert C. Smith, "The Black Congressional Delegation," *Western Political Quarterly* Vol. 34 (1981), pp. 203-221; and Shirley Washington, *Outstanding African Americans of Congress* (Washington, DC: United States Capitol Historical Society, 1998), pp. 73-78.
24. Barbara Mikulski, et al., *Nine and Counting: The Women of the Senate* (New York: Perennial Books, 2001), p. 236.
25. Hanes Walton, Jr. and Robert C. Smith, *American Politics and the African American Quest for Universal Freedom* 3rd Edition (New York: Longman, 2006), pp. 133-139.
26. Kenneth Weeks, "Favorite Son," *Black Enterprise* Vol. 35 (October, 2004), pp. 88-97.
27. Hanes Walton, Jr. and Lester Spence, "African-American Presidential Convention and Nomination Politics: Alan Keyes in the 1996 Republican Presidential Primaries and Convention," *National Political Science Review* Vol. 7 (1999), pp. 188-209.
28. Christopher Benson, "Barack & Michelle Obama: Begin Their Storied Journey," *Savoy Magazine* Vol. 1 (February, 2005), pp. 61-69, 103106.
29. Christopher Achen and W. Phillips Shively, *Cross-Level Inference* (Chicago: University of Chicago Press, 1995).

Black Politics in a Time of Transition, Volume 13; pp. 3-22

Black Power in Black Presidential Bids from Jackson to Obama

Katherine Tate

Introduction

The world took notice of the November 4, 2008 election of Illinois Senator Barack Obama as America's first Black president. Many believe that Obama's success was based on his ability to mount a deracialized campaign for president. A deracialized campaign is one that avoids racial issues and specific appeals to Black voters (McCormick and Jones 1993). Nor did his Republican challenger, Senator John McCain, seek to exploit racial divisions in this race through race code politics, as past Republican presidential candidates have done since Richard Nixon (Mendelberg 2001). Obama's successful bid for the presidency and his deracialized approach, however, have raised new questions in African American politics. Can Black presidential bids still be used as vehicles to advance the political agenda of Black Americans? Can racial inequalities in the United States be reduced without explicit pressure on government from Black leaders to address the economic and social plight of African Americans? How will the policy interests of the Black community fare under the leadership of a new crop of Black politicians winning elections in majority-White jurisdictions?

In this article, I analyze Blacks' support for recent Black presidential bids. Following Jesse Jackson's historic 1984 and 1988 bids, the Reverend Al Sharpton and former U.S. Senator Carol Moseley Braun ran for president in 2004. Sharpton and Moseley Braun did less well electorally with Black voters for several reasons. First, over the twenty-year period, Blacks became better integrated within the Democratic Party, reducing their suspicion that their votes were taken for granted. Second, surveys show that Black concern about racial problems in the United States fell in the 1990s. Obama's candidacy benefited from these changes. Black voters are rejecting a Black power approach of organizing and uniting Black votes in favor of a coalitional approach. I discuss the implications of an end of a Black power approach in Black electoral politics in the article's conclusion.

Black Power Approaches in Black Politics

What exactly is Black politics? The term lacks an agreed-upon definition; broadly, it represents a description of the political efforts of Black Americans to advance the collective interest of their group. In their effort to analyze Black politics with better theoretical precision, scholars have adopted a number of different analytic frames and approaches (Barker, Jones, and Tate 1999; McClain and Stewart 2009). Some scholars have sought to expose the ideological tensions in Black politics, describing its phases of accommodationism, nationalism, and protest (Cruse 1967; Holden 1973). Others have put Black politics in historical frames, arguing that the Black political struggle has been defined by its movements, the first developing during Reconstruction following the Civil War, and a second one, emerging in the aftermath of World War II (Marable 2007). Marable (2009) writes also about defining or critical moments in Black politics, such as the 2005 Hurricane Katrina crisis during the Bush administration.

Similarly, others contend that there was a protest phase and a post-protest, electoral phase following passage of the 1965 Voting Rights Act (Preston 1987; Smith 1981; Tate 1994). Most recently, Gillespie (2010) contends that within the post-civil rights stage of Black politics, there are three phases reflecting the changing ambitions of Black political leaders, as well as the rise of a new generation unconnected to the Black civil rights past. Pluralist theories, following Robert Dahl's claim (1961), that the mobilization of Blacks will automatically lead to their political integration and advancement have been largely rejected. Browning, Marshall, and Tabb (1984) argue that minorities in the United States had to protest and mobilize in advance of having the ability to form political coalitions with liberal Whites. Other critics of pluralism contend that the history and legal status of Blacks are fundamentally different from those of European and other immigrant groups in this country (Hero 1992; Pinderhughes 1987). Furthermore, alternative frameworks have been introduced, including the internal colonialism model, which depicts Blacks as colonized people (Barker, Jones, and Tate 1999; McClain and Stewart 2009).

While there is no agreement over which frame best fits Black politics, the one chosen affects the conclusions drawn about the current status of Blacks and prospects for future social and political change. Furthermore, these different frameworks and models have two important overlapping features. First, the historical frame is often adopted because analysts seek to analyze Black politics through an understanding of the changing nature of external conditions on the Black experience. For example, the ideological currents of American courts, either liberalizing or reactionary, have been important influences in African American politics. The Supreme Court ruling that unexpectedly abolished the White primary in *Smith v. Allwright* (1944) played a role in President Truman's decision to push for the civil rights of Blacks. The Cold War also played a role in Truman's behavior.

This focus on the political environment is akin to the notion of the *political opportunity structure*. This concept was developed in the social movement field to explain why collective action arises in some instances and not others (Tarrow 1998). Doug McAdam (1999) employs the "political opportunity structure" in his analysis of the rise and decline of the Black civil rights movement. Political opportunity structure, McAdam contends, refers to the vulnerability of the existing social system to challenge and change. The political opportunity structure helps to explain the strategic choices Blacks have made. For example, Blacks have more commonly made use of noninstitutionalized means of protest to influence the political process in light of an unresponsive federal government and hostile legal system.

Secondly, models and frameworks of Black politics also seek to explain Black political actions through an investigation of the social, economic, and political position of Blacks. Here, scholars investigate the political resources of minority groups, their ideologies, geographic concentration, rates of registration, levels of group identity, cohesion and feelings of political efficacy (McClain and Stewart 2009). The massive relocation of Blacks from the South to the North starting in World War I was an important catalyst in Black politics. The change in the Black political leadership structure following the 1965 Voting Rights Act is also an important development in Black politics (Reed 1986). These frameworks, therefore, focus on different components of *internal group status*. Scholars have found that Blacks base a number of their policy positions on their shared interests (Dawson 1994; Gurin, Hatchett, and Jackson 1989; Tate 1994). Despite their group orientation toward politics, Blacks are not politically homogeneous (Dawson 2001). Fredrick C. Harris (2009) writes about the rise of political pragmatism in the Black electorate. Ronald W. Walters (2003) points to the reemergence of Black conservatives during the 1980s. These changes have produced some strong conclusions. Robert C. Smith (2009) contends that the reduction of "system-challenging behavior" among Black leaders has led to a new period of accommodationism. Black leaders, he contends, no longer seek to change "system values or upset system elites" (2009, 24; see also Smith 1996).

The two components, *political opportunity structure* and *internal group status*, are used in this paper to explain changing Black support for Black power strategies. Changes in the political opportunity structure were importantly linked to the rise of the Black power movement. While most claim the Black power movement originated when Black activists first used a "Black power" chant for a civil rights march in 1966, it had roots in Malcolm X's rise in the Nation of Islam (Joseph 2006). The Black power movement was controversial. First, African Americans had only recently rejected the label "Negro" in favor of "Black." Second, it clearly did not endorse interracial cooperation, which was the prominent goal and approach of Dr. King's Southern Christian Leadership Conference SCLC. In fact Black Power suggested a rejection of interracial cooperation.

The demand for Black power grew out of Atlanta Student Non-violent Coordinating Committee SNCC activists who began to see that Whites would not support Black candidates, and they needed to mobilize Blacks on the basis of a new consciousness that could start a new movement. The internal status of Blacks had powerfully changed with the passage of the 1965 Voting Rights Act. The Black Power approach was based on political disillusionment. SNCC leader Stokely Carmichael was a reluctant advocate of Black power. At that 1966 movement event, he stated, "This is the twenty-seventh time I have been arrested. I ain't going to jail no more. Blacks had been demanding freedom for six years, and had gotten nothing. What we gonna start saying now is 'Black power'" (*Eyes on the Prize* 2006). Early Black activists in the South felt disillusionment with the Democratic Party. The Mississippi Freedom Democratic Party (MFDP), a biracial civil rights group, was formed to challenge the all-White primary delegation in Mississippi to the Democratic Party's 1964 national convention. A compromise was reached that the party let the all-White delegation from Mississippi keep their seats, while MFDP was offered two at-large seats and promised future party rules that would prevent the seating of groups that discriminated against minority groups. The National Association for the Advancement of Colored People NAACP and Martin Luther King welcomed the compromise, as did most political observers and activists outside of MFDP. MFDP activists, however, through Fannie Lou Hamer, denounced the compromise and walked out. The state of Mississippi continued to send all-White delegations (they would not be seated) to the Democratic Party's national conventions until 1976, when something was worked out to build biracial support for Georgia Governor Jimmy Carter's presidential bid (Parker 1990).

In 1967, Stokely Carmichael (later, Kwame Ture) and Political Scientist, Charles V. Hamilton, published *Black Power*. In it they argued that the White Power Structure was organized to keep African Americans powerless and subordinate in American society, and that Blacks could only overcome this system of oppression through a Black Power strategy. The White Power Structure operated in three spheres. Economically, Blacks resided in a vicious poverty cycle. Racially segregated, high costs were imposed upon them for living in urban ghettos. Educational opportunities there were limited. Politically, Whites created a system to maintain their monopoly on power. The White power structure also co-opted Black leaders. Black leaders could not advance their real interests until they picked their own leaders. Socially and psychologically, Blacks were fed messages of their inferiority, causing self-loathing, alienation, and despair. At the same time, these messages reinforced Whites' attitudes of racial superiority. Thus, Blacks needed to form a new group consciousness. Furthermore, Blacks needed their own independent political organizations. Coalitions with Whites were rejected because White racial interests were incompatible with Black interests. Also lacking the power and resources that Whites had, Blacks were not the political equals of Whites, and could not codirect their organizations. Finally, a Black power strategy required new civil rights objectives. In a Black power approach, integration would no longer be explicitly the objective, but social justice would be. Blacks would seek to be treated with equal respect as well as having equal worth in society.

President Nixon's reelection and the 1972 National Black Political Convention in Gary, Indiana, are seen as the end of the Black power movement. Membership in the Black Panther Party declined by the mid-1970s, and the prominent spokespersons for Black power, Amiri Baraka and Stokely Carmichael, became less visible (Joseph 2006). McAdam (1999) also points out that there was repression of Black power groups through law enforcement and taxing agencies. Racial integration, while firmly resisted by Whites, would see two liberal court decisions affirming busing as a constitutional remedy for racial segregation in schools in 1971 and another decision in 1978, *Bakke*, affirming, if just barely, the constitutional legitimacy of affirmative action. While the movement of Black power leaders, indigenous groups, and grassroots backers faded, the strategy itself never became discredited. It would return during the 1980s as a way to pressure government to address issues that Blacks were most concerned with: their continued exclusion from proportional forms of political power and their economic and social marginalization as a group.

Jesse Jackson's 1984 and 1988 Presidential Bids

In 1983, the Reverend Jesse Jackson declared his intention to seek the Democratic Party's nomination for president, surprising many political analysts who felt that Jackson's time had definitely not come. Many Black Democrats pledged their support to another Democratic contender, Vice President Walter Mondale, instead. Press and public expectations for Jackson were low. Jackson campaigned with a budget approximately one-third that of other major presidential contenders. Jackson's campaigns were modeled after Ronald W. Walters' (1988) Black presidential campaign strategy, which incorporated a Black power approach. In spite of Blacks' minority status as voters, Blacks could leverage greater influence over the Democratic Party and over a Democratic president through a Black presidential bid. Although the Black vote is not usually large enough to play a determinative role in the outcome of presidential races, it can guarantee a Democratic loss if Blacks choose to vote for an independent party or candidate or to abstain and stay home. Furthermore, a successful Black campaign would be able to deny the Black vote to any of the other candidates and thereby pose a threat to the nomination for the front-runner. Walters contended that Black presidential candidacies could also assist in the institutionalization of Black politics. Not only would campaigns by Black leaders help organize the Black vote every four years, but a Black presidential contender could issue policy statements that would become part of the party's policy platform at its national conventions. Jackson won about 18 percent of the Democratic primary vote in 1984. Most of his support came from Black Democrats, 77 percent of whom voted for him over Mondale in 1984 (Morris and Williams 1989; Preston 1989).

As a leveraging strategy, Jackson ended both campaigns with few concessions from the Democratic Party. All of the minority planks proposed by the Jackson camp were overwhelmingly defeated by the Mondale–Hart forces at the 1984 convention (Barker 1989, 156). A critical problem for the Jackson camp was the delegate selection system. The 1984 system allocated delegates only to those candidates able to achieve a 20 percent threshold of votes in each congressional district. Moreover, one-seventh of the delegates at the 1984 convention were "super delegates" elected officials and party leaders who were selected by the party and not elected by the rank-and-file membership. This penalized minority and urban voters who were more likely to be concentrated in a few congressional districts, and in fact, although Jackson won 18.3 percent of the total primary vote, he ended up with only 10 percent of the convention delegates (Morris and Williams 1989, 243). The Mondale team hired Blacks for the campaign, and Jackson was able to deliver a convention floor address at prime time. In 1988, Jackson did better, having negotiated with the Dukakis forces in advance of the convention on several policies contained in the party's platform. Furthermore, in 1988, Ronald H. Brown, an African American, was selected as the Democratic Party's national chairman. His selection was seen as a move by the party to appease Black Democrats in the aftermath of Jackson's two presidential bids.

Jackson's supporters were not happy with the party in 1984. In fact, according to one political scientist who was a Jackson delegate at that convention, the Jackson delegates experienced disillusionment. "Mondale people wanted to show their control of the convention, particularly to show how badly he could beat Jackson … Along with many other Jackson delegates, I personally resented deeply this kind of treatment" (Barker 1989, 156). Jackson delegates felt that the party's treatment of their candidate at the convention was an indication of the party's attitudes toward Black Democrats in general. In 1988, Jackson supporters felt even more strongly that Jackson should have been given the opportunity to be the vice-presidential candidate on the party's ticket. The statistical evidence, however, shows no drop-off in support for the Democratic Party in response to the 1984 or 1988 nominating contests. Over the four-year period, there was a slight increase in the percentage of Blacks who labeled themselves "strong" Democrats based on the 1984–1988 National Black Election Study (Tate 1992).

As a Black power strategy, Jackson's presidential bids were essentially reformist, not radical, a point Cruse (1967) makes in his general criticism of Black power. Jackson did not run as a third-party candidate or form a national Black political party. The 1984 National Black Election Study found only 28 percent of Blacks supported the idea of a Black third party (Tate

1994). Jesse Jackson's political role in the party ultimately helped end the rebellion of Black Democrats. Jackson did not run in 1992, and he gave Clinton a rather indifferent endorsement on the convention stage in 1992. Yet, Jackson strongly endorsed Clinton for reelection at the 1996 Democratic convention even after Clinton had signed a conservative welfare reform law. Jackson's 1996 convention speech differed radically from his past three speeches insofar as there was little of his own political agenda in it. The theme of his speech was party unity.

The reasons why Jackson moved to this firm embrace of the Democratic Party are complex. In 1996, it was evident that Bill Clinton remained popular among most Black Democrats, and thus a challenge by Jackson would have been enormously difficult. The fact of the matter is that most Blacks may not have supported a third presidential bid by Jesse Jackson in 1996. While over 80 percent in 1984 thought it had been a *good idea* for Jackson to have run for president, 65 percent in the1996 National Black Election Study thought it would have been a *bad idea* if Jackson had run in 1996. For comparison purposes, Blacks were asked if it would have been a good idea or bad idea for Black Republican Colin Powell to have run for his party's presidential nomination. Most Blacks, 56 percent, thought it would have been a bad idea as well. Jackson's popularity among Blacks, however, remained as strong in 1996 as it was in 1984. Both Jackson and Powell received highly positive ratings, well in the 70s on a scale from 0 to 100, in the 1996 National Black Election Study.

Al Sharpton's 2004 Bid

The very fact that Jackson had embraced the Democratic Party's nominees at each successive presidential election since 1996 was made into an issue by Al Sharpton. In his memoir, Sharpton asked whether Jackson remained committed to an activist agenda, writing, "I began to question the direction that commitment was taking in the late 1990s. Jesse Jackson had developed a closeness to Bill Clinton. And I felt his relationship with Clinton and the White House was getting in the way of his work as an activist"(Sharpton and Hunter 2002, 197). The role of a civil rights/human rights activist, Sharpton argues, is distinct from that a Washington insider, which he felt Jackson had become during the 1990s. He illustrated this claim by pointing to Dr. Martin Luther King, who, writes Sharpton, "as close as he was to Lyndon Johnson, came out vocally against the war in Vietnam. He never took a presidential appointment. He challenged the system"(Sharpton and Hunter 2002, 197). The biblical reference he used to illustrate this point is the story of David. "David, the warrior who slew Goliath, was not the same man as King David. You have a right to be king. But if you're king, you cannot also be the warrior fighting against the powers that be. And as king, you must also respect those who are still the warriors. But you don't try to do both" (Sharpton and Hunter 2002, 202). Sharpton notes in *Al on*

America that there was distance between Jackson and himself, crediting his alliance with and support for Black nationalists as reasons. The other reasons, writes Sharpton, are not clear: "We would talk off and on, but it was clear to me that we weren't as tight as we used to be" (Sharpton and Hunter 2002, 194). Jackson visited Sharpton in the hospital after Sharpton had been stabbed in 1991, but when Sharpton ran for the U.S. Senate in 1992, Jackson supported Robert Abrams instead. Jackson also disagreed with some of Sharpton's Burger King boycott in New York.

During his campaign, Sharpton told reporters that he would not necessarily defer to the eventual Democratic nominee and pledge his support as Jackson had. He explained that he was not seeking the White power structure's support in his role as a civil rights and community rights activist. He writes: "The goal of the average black—particularly a prominent black—is to be accepted by the white power structure and by white people. And I don't give a damn if they ever accept me. I have set my own standards for what's important to me. A white supremacist is not comfortable with someone who says, 'I don't really care if you ever accept me or not; I don't care if you ever embrace me or not. I am what I am and that's enough for me.' A supremacist must always feel that you submit to him, which is why, while I respect and admire Rev. Jackson, I psychologically could not deal with his conceding or deferring to the White House." Sharpton's message was that he was running for justice. He stated: "I don't want a job; I want justice!"

Sharpton's promise that he would never compromise in his pursuit of justice was evident in the 2001 New York mayoral race. Sharpton, after strong efforts were made on the part of David Dinkins, Hillary Clinton, and Charles Rangel for Sharpton's endorsement for the mayoral candidates they were backing, chose the independent path of endorsing Latino candidate Fernando Ferrer. Following Sharpton's endorsement, liberal Democratic candidate Mark Green announced on television: "I never asked Sharpton for his endorsement." Green's efforts to distance himself from Sharpton were picked up on the press. Green won the election through a run-off against Ferrer. Even while Ferrer endorsed Green in the race against Republican Michael Bloomberg, Sharpton refused. Many Democratic officials pressed Sharpton for an endorsement, but Sharpton justified his refusal, writing: "How can I give a guy who lied about even asking me for my support?" Then Sharpton went to the press and announced that he was not going to endorse Green. In his book, *Al on America*, Sharpton admitted that he fully expected Green to win. He expected to be a critic of the Green administration, in the same fashion that he waged war against the Guiliani and Koch administrations. Instead, Bloomberg won. Sharpton writes, "To this day, I felt that the Democratic Party had to be taught a lesson and still has to be taught one nationally. We did not get the right to vote from the Democrats or the Republicans. Our grandparents went out there and faced dog bites, jail cells, and some died. And before I take that vote and give it to somebody who doesn't respect me, I would rather sit up until hell freezes over" (Sharpton and Hunter 2002, 176).

There is a closer resemblance to Black power in Sharpton's approach to coalitional politics than is evident in Jackson's approach. First, Sharpton's language evokes Black power themes. There are Sharpton's references to the "White power structure" and White supremacists. Secondly, there is the rejection of the belief that Black liberation would come through ordinary political processes. He, like Jackson, believes that there is a need for outside agitation and for defiance in Black politics today, and for a social movement protest vehicle that would be superimposed over ordinary, routine politics. Thirdly, there is the threat of political and social disorder made plain by Ture and Hamilton in their 1967 book, *Black Power*, that if White society does not provide racial justice, Blacks will rebel. The authors write: "It is crystal clear to us—and it must become so with the white society—that *there can be no social order without social justice*. White people must be made to understand that they must stop messing with black people, or the blacks *will* fight back" (1967, 53).

Sharpton's political speeches reveal a posture of continued defiance. Jackson remained a candidate in his 1984 and 1988 bids long after many political commentators and figures felt that he should have dropped out. The civil rights movement directed by Dr. King preached nonviolent, noncompliance with the laws, while Black power advocates contend that Blacks must necessarily strike back. Sharpton's message does not imply a "strike back" strategy, but it does envision nonvoting by Blacks as an act of civil disobedience.

Finally, the notion that Blacks must define themselves for the purposes of racial autonomy and pride, is far more evident in Sharpton's campaign than in Jackson's campaigns. Should Sharpton have cut his hair, changed his wardrobe, and curtailed the blunt language often found in his speeches in order to conform better to the norms and standards of running for president? For Sharpton, such moves would involve giving up his identity as a Black man. Ture and Hamilton write, "The racial and cultural personality of the black community must be preserved and that community must win its freedom while preserving its cultural integrity" (1992, 55).

Did a Black power approach work for Sharpton in 2004? Black nationalism principles garner a minority share of support in the Black community. Michael Dawson argues that nationalism is best understood as a skeptical response to liberal ideologies, which if embraced fully, "lure blacks and others to not only accede to their own oppression, but kill and die in the service of its maintenance" (2001, 87). The political strategies that flow from a Black nationalist perspective, however, range from a complete rejection of political alliances with Whites to purposeful and short-term alliances with Whites. Sharpton's bid was not to imagine that he would win or even be invited to share the ticket with the eventual nominee, but to organize Black Democrats and use that organization to wrest concessions from their political party and its eventual nominee. America, after all, was too racist to elect a Black man for president, and Sharpton was not going to engage in a charade suggesting that America would elect him. He was going to remain true to himself and invite himself to the party, without altering his identity to fit White society's expectations. It was classic Sharpton, then, to accept his ten-minute speech limitation and then remain on the platform for twenty minutes, unapologetically at the Democratic National Convention. African Americans are afforded less than their fair share in many ways, and Sharpton took what he considered to be fair.

Moseley Braun's Campaign for President

In stark contrast to Sharpton, Carol Moseley Braun ran a campaign strikingly devoid of Black Power, utilizing the strategy that she would transcend race, focus on gender, and win feminist votes. While there is new scholarship on critiquing the "masculinist posturing that pervaded Black Power," (Ward 2006; see also Spring 2006), few, if any, have frankly discussed the barriers that Black women face in organizing the Black community through race-specific appeals in their campaigns. Other Blacks had run for president on third-party tickets, but Shirley Chisholm, the New York House representative, was the first Black to run for the Democratic party's top post. Critics of her 1972 bid thought it was "premature," implying that the political advancement of Black women would have to take place after the advancement of Black men. Chisholm was a founding member of the Congressional Black Caucus (CBC). However, because of the inherent problems in organizing a Black power approach as a female, Chisholm ran a "rainbow" oriented campaign in 1972, aiming to unite the young, women, the poor, and minorities in her anti-Vietnam War platform.

In her speech to Iowans announcing her plans to run for president, Moseley Braun did not wrestle with the contradictions of America as a liberal democracy and its legacy of failures to African Americans. Nor did she speak to the inherit premise of America as a land of opportunity, even for oppressed Blacks, as Barack Obama did, as a speaker at the 2004 event. Obama emphasized how he managed to transcend the difficulties of being part-Black and being raised by his grandparents after his father left the family for a Harvard Law School education. He expressed the confidence of Black liberals that America will ultimately wake up, recognize its sins, and redeem itself, and thus, they support the institutional framework of a liberal democratic state.

Moseley Braun stopped short of embracing a "radical egalitarianism" (Dawson 2001) in which she provided a policy agenda to bring Blacks and minorities to full equality with Whites. On the issues, she was proaffirmative action, and unequivocally so. Like Sharpton, she made the case for affirmative action based on her experiences not only as an African

American, but as a female striving for, as she wrote, "the blessings of liberty." She pointed to an "old boys' network," and a decline in minority and female-owned businesses as a sign that unequal opportunities were linked directly to the unequal status of Blacks and women in America. She separately listed "women's issues" as a core component of her policy agenda on her campaign website (http://www.carolforpresident.com). Moseley Braun also emphasized the "bread and butter" issues that all the Democrats run on, which made her campaign less a direct focus on America's disadvantaged and unwanted, than Jackson's was. She favored a "balanced budget," which put her closer to the more conservative Democrats than the liberal-progressive ones. At the same time, she was in favor of a universal health care system, which then put her on the progressive end. Perhaps the most conservative element of her campaign, however, was her position on the Iraq war, which was to support the troops and not "cut and run." Again, she presented her position on the war clearly at the Democratic debate held on September 4, 2003: "I hope that it will allow us, within the tradition of U.S. command and control over our own forces, allow us to extricate ourselves with honor but continue a viable war on terrorism that gets bin Laden and his pals and all the people who would do harm to the American people" (see http://www.carolforpresident.com). Although she presented herself as a consistent critic of the Bush administration's war policy and of the Patriot Act, she did not join the other Democrats, notably Howard Dean, Al Sharpton, and Dennis Kucinich, who took clear anti-war positions during the primary contest, and in particular Bush's unilateral stance in the war. Whereas Kucinich proposed to turn the war over to the United Nations, Sharpton and Dean favored a multilateral position. Here, Moseley Braun stood with John Edwards and John Kerry (perhaps because all three had served in the U.S. Senate) favoring a U.S. presence with more a multilateral effort in rebuilding Iraq.

The only rebuke of America she provided in her campaign was that it had fallen short of equality for women. Thus, Moseley Braun's strategy reflected a feminist approach, but in a conventional form that focused on the domination of (White) males, unlike the Black feminist ideologies that involved rebukes of Black males as well as White feminists for their oppression of Black females (Dawson 2001). The special dilemmas, for example, that the confirmation hearings of Clarence Thomas to the Supreme Court in 1992 and President Bill Clinton's "Monica Gate" scandal presented that led majorities of Blacks and some White feminists to rally behind these two men, left only radical Black feminists to present the logical critiques of their rampant sexism. Dawson (2001) writes, while historically Black feminists have been found in "nationalist, communist, and liberal formations," they still largely exist in the academic community alone. Viable political coalitions are difficult for them to form as society does not want to recognize gender exclusion as well as racism inherent in Black–White liberal and Black nationalist organizations. Thus, Moseley Braun was not in the category of a Black feminist, but structured her campaign as a conventional liberal feminist.

Braun entered the national political scene when she ran for the U.S. Senate in 1992 in the gender-charged context of Black conservative Clarence Thomas' confirmation to the U.S. Supreme Court. Many women voters were given special cause to cast an anti-incumbency vote in 1992, given their disgust over the all-male Senate Judiciary Committee's mishandling of the Clarence Thomas-Anita Hill controversy. Until information was leaked to the press, the Senate's all-male judiciary committee had failed to act on the charge made by law professor Anita F. Hill that the conservative nominee to the Supreme Court, Clarence Thomas, had sexually harassed her while he headed the Equal Employment Opportunity Commission. A record number of women ran for the U.S. Senate in 1992, including Carol Moseley Braun. She was able to beat incumbent Illinois Democratic Senator, Alan Dixon, who had voted to confirm Thomas, in the primary. Prior to Moseley Braun's election, no Blacks and only two women were serving in the U.S. Senate. Exit polls revealed that Moseley Braun received 40 percent of the women's vote against 35 percent of men's votes in her 1992 bid for the U.S. Senate in the primary election against Al Dixon. However, she received 62 percent of the vote from White suburban women who felt that Thomas should not have been confirmed, but at that time, a large majority of Americans thought Thomas should have been confirmed (Tate 1997). Moseley Braun's support among African Americans was very solid. She took 85 percent of the Black vote, according to exit polls.

Moseley Braun would lose, six years later, to her Republican challenger. The 1998 reelection race was hampered by new scandals that evoked gender and racial stereotypes. First, there were allegations that she abused her privilege as Senator to take political junkets with her legislative aide. This same individual was a cad who allegedly sexually harassed her staff. She was also investigated for campaign finance abuses, but never charged.

The Quest for Votes in the Sharpton and Moseley Braun Campaigns

Carol Moseley Braun withdrew just before the Iowa caucuses, and she ended up with no delegates. Al Sharpton won 27 delegates, doing slightly better than Dennis Kucinich, but significantly less well than Jackson who won 384 in 1984 and 1,218 in 1988 (see Table 1). The question is why in 2004 did Sharpton and Braun fare strikingly less well than Jackson did? In primary states that Jackson won in 1988, such as Louisiana, and states that Jackson did well in such as Ohio, Sharpton was not on the ballot. In the District of Columbia, where Jackson took 80 percent of the primary vote in 1988, Sharpton won only 20 percent of the vote. In South Carolina, Sharpton won 10 percent of the vote. In other southern states, such as Georgia, Sharpton's vote totals were too low to earn him delegates.

Table 1
Jackson's and Sharpton's Primary Vote and Delegates at Democratic Convention, by State in 1984, 1988, and 2004

State	Jackson (1984)		Jackson (1988)		Sharpton (2004)	
	Votes	Delegates	Votes	Delegates	Votes	Delegates
Alabama	19.6	9	43.6[a]	28		
Arizona					0	0
Arkansas[c]			17.1	n.a.		
California	18.4	30	35.2	122	2.0	0
Connecticut	12.0	1	28.3	16	3.0	0
Delaware					6.0	1
District of Columbia	67.3[a]	13	80.0[a]	18	20	4
Florida	12.2	1	20.0	35	3.0	0
Georgia	21.0	17	39.8a	42	6.0	0
Idaho	5.7	2	15.7[d]	3		
Illinois	21.0	7	32.3	57		
Indiana	13.7	0	22.5	18		
Kentucky			15.6	n.a.		
Louisiana	42.9[a]	24	35.5[a]	33		
Maryland	25.5	17	28.7	25	4.0	0
Massachusetts	5.0	3	18.7	19	1.0	0
Mississippi[c]			44.4[a]	26	5.0	0
Missouri[c]			20.2	n.a.	3.0	0
Montana[c]			22.1	n.a.		
Nebraska	9.1	1	25.7	8		
New Hampshire	5.3	0	7.8	0	0	0
New Jersey	23.6	9	32.7	19		
New Mexico	11.9	1	28.1	8		
New York	25.6	51	37.1	97	8	11
North Carolina	25.4	15	33.0	35		
North Dakota			15.1[f]	3		
Ohio	16.4	10	27.4	46		
Oklahoma[c]			13.3	n.a.	1.0	0
Oregon	9.3	1	38.1	18		
Pennsylvania	16.0	18	27.3	23		
Rhode Island	8.7	0	15.2	3		
South Carolina[d]					10.0	1
South Dakota	5.2	0	5.4	1		
Tennessee	25.3	15	20.7	20	2	0
Texas[c, d]			24.5	n.a.	4	2
Vermont	7.8	3	25.7	9		
Virginia[c]			45.1[a]	42	3	0
West Virginia	6.7	0	13.5	0		
Wisconsin	9.9	5	28.2	25	2	0
Puerto Rico	0	0	29.0[a]	8		
Total	18.3	384[b]	29.0	1,218[b]	n.a.	27

Source: Congressional Quarterly Inc.
[a] Winner
[b] Includes delegates he won through state caucuses as well as primaries.
[c] Held caucus in 1984.
[d] Held a caucus as well as a primary in 1988.
[e] Held caucuses in 1984 and 1988.
[f] Based on write-in votes.

The key factor that accounts for failures of Sharpton and Moseley Braun to attract Black voters in their presidential bid is the "political opportunity structure." Analytically, an improved political opportunity structure implies a decrease in the power disparity between the group seeking power and the majority in power, and also implies that the cost of keeping the insurgent group in its place has increased (McAdam 1999). The political environment, the political–legal environment, and the organizational strength of insurgent groups are important components of the political opportunity structure that impact minority groups in advanced, industrial democracies. Jackson's bids in the 1980s were pursued in a racially hostile environment for Blacks. President Ronald Reagan had received the lowest presidential approval ratings for a Republican president among Black voters ever recorded, and surveys also revealed that a majority of Blacks felt in 1984 that the Democratic Party took the Black vote "for granted" (Tate 1994). While President George Bush's evaluations from Black Americans remained equally low, survey work revealed that Blacks felt closer to the Democratic Party ideologically than they did in the 1980s.

The political–legal environment was strikingly different in 2004 than in 1984. In 1984, Jackson campaigned against the party's delegate selection rules. Jackson campaigned on the basis of "one person, one vote" principle, in which delegates are allocated proportionately. However, the Democratic Party rules are more complicated than the Republican party delegate selection rules which favor a "winner-take-all" system. In 1976, the Democrats banned the winner-take-all primary system. However, there is a threshold rule, in which candidates typically must win at least 15 percent of a congressional district in a primary to win a share of that state's delegates. In 1984, the Democrats also reserved nearly 20 percent of their delegate seats for high-level party and elected officials known as "Super Delegates" (Cook 2000). Following the 1988 primary contest, the Jackson camp lobbied successfully to force the Democratic Party to change its party rules reducing sharply the number of super delegates as well as banning the "bonus-allocation" of delegates that a few states used to boost the number of delegates awarded to the frontrunners. The fuss that Jackson made over the party rules was a part of the racial disharmony that helped elevate the significance of Black Democrats casting a Jackson vote. The lawsuit over the spoiled machine ballots in Florida that cost Democrat, Al Gore, the presidency could have been elevated into a campaign for Al Sharpton. In the context of a terrorist attack on Americans on September 11, 2001, and wars in Afghanistan and Iraq, the Patriot Act, and gay rights, voting rights abuses aimed at Black and elderly citizens were lost as a campaign issue in the same manner that civil rights issues were buried as a result of the Vietnam war protest movement and the Watergate scandal. It was only in Sharpton's convention floor address that he skillfully addressed the manner in which Black votes were not counted and the Republicans stole the 2000 election. Had Sharpton used this campaign issue during the primary contest, he might have picked up more votes in the manner that Jackson used the elitist party rules against minority candidates.

It should be pointed out that the Democratic Party skillfully neutralized the appeal of Sharpton or Moseley Braun's candidacies by accommodating more than they had when Jackson ran in 1984. In 1984, there were committees organized to determine how much airtime Jackson would get at the 1984 national convention. While there may have been similar negotiations for Sharpton and Moseley Braun, it was not evident to the public, nor picked up on by the media. There was less to actually contest for the Black presidential contenders in 2004 than for Jackson in 1984 and 1988. The easy inclusion of these two contenders by the Democratic Party debates and at its national convention was not the case for Jackson in 1984. Whether the easy inclusion of Moseley Braun and Sharpton was due to the fact that polls revealed that they would not generate significant support or because race relations had improved within the party is not clear. Jackson himself had also opened the door for Black presidential contenders by becoming less radical, and pledging his support to the party's nominees (Barker, Jones, and Tate 1999). This was not the case in 1984, when Jackson gave a tepid endorsement to former Vice President Walter Mondale in his convention address, refusing, in fact, to mention Mondale by name. By the time President Bill Clinton ran for reelection in 1996, Jackson was seen as one of the party's national leaders and no longer a rebellious thorn in its side.

While the aspect of a highly salient racial environment undercut Moseley Braun's and Sharpton's bids, it was the absence of a highly salient gender environment for Moseley Braun that also cost her potential votes. In 1992, she ran in the "Year of the Woman," when the controversial confirmation of Black conservative Clarence Thomas to the Supreme Court was used to mobilize female voters to support women like Moseley Braun running for the U.S. Senate. In 2004, again, the international environment of terrorism, war, and the domestic issue of gay rights were more salient than abortion rights and feminist causes as issues that Moseley Braun could have campaigned on to mobilize the feminist vote.

A second element in this analysis of Black support for Black presidential contenders in 2004 is the internal political structure of African Americans. Jackson's bids were strongly supported by the Black church. While Moseley Braun and Sharpton, an ordained minister, made frequent visits to Black churches, their campaigns did not turn into the grassroots movement we saw in the Jackson bids. Again, the appeal of Jackson in the context of a new push to elect the nation's first Black mayors and representatives to the U.S. Congress was absent in 2004. There are many reasons for the failure of the Sharpton–Moseley bids to be linked to the group empowerment efforts of Blacks. First, Black rates of participation had increased since 1984. Since the 1980s, the gap between Blacks and Whites in voter participation had continued to shrink. In 1968, Whites led Blacks in registering and in voting by 9 and 12 percentage points. The 1984 presidential race lead had a much narrower racial gap than previous elections. By 2000, the racial gap between them was about 2 percentage points. When one separates out Latinos from Whites, however, the racial gap in voter turnout in presidential elections is larger. Data from the Census Bureau's Current Population Surveys show that since 1996, increasing numbers of Blacks are voting in presidential elections. While Blacks accounted for about 8 percent of the presidential vote in 1968 this number grew to almost 11 percent in both the 2000 and 2004 elections. In 2008, the highest number ever recorded of Blacks went to the polls, indicating that the candidacy of a Black (Obama) had an important positive effect on Black rates of participation. But the issue of mobilizing Blacks which had been important in 1984 has now become less important as slightly more Blacks have begun to participate in presidential elections. Second, the number of Black elected officials in Washington and nationally has increased dramatically since 1984 as well. The number of Black elected officials has skyrocketed from an estimated 1,500 in 1970 to over 10,000 by 2008 (see http://www.jointcenter.org).

The Democratic Party appointed an African American, Ron Brown, to head its national organization in 1989. President Clinton in 1992 appointed a number of African Americans to his administration as well. While Blacks remain overwhelmingly Democratic in their party affiliations, their attitudes toward the party remain mixed. In 1983, 44 percent of Blacks said that "most Democrats are sincerely committed to helping Blacks get ahead," but a matching percentage also felt that "most Democrats don't really care much about Black people" (Tate 1994). In 2006, an Associated Press/AOL/Ipsos Public Affairs Poll reported through the Roper Center found that while 51 percent of Blacks felt that "the leaders of the Democratic Party work hard to ensure the continued support of the Black community," 41 percent still felt that the leaders of the party take the "Black vote for granted." In the same poll, however, 71 percent of the Black respondents felt that the Democratic Party was really trying to "reach out to Black voters" in the election. Only 24 percent said no, that the party was not trying hard to win Black support. Still Black skepticism toward the Democratic Party persists, suggesting that Black candidates can recruit support if Blacks feel slighted by White candidates running for the party's nomination.

An important change has been an ideological one among Blacks. Racial issues have become less salient, and Blacks have also become more politically moderate during the 1990s. A large majority (67 percent) of Blacks supported Clinton's welfare reform law in 1996 that imposed a five-year life time limit for welfare benefits for families in poverty. In 1984 nearly half of the Blacks polled felt that spending on food stamps should be increased, while only 10 percent thought it should be decreased. The 1996 National Black Election Study found that twelve years later, however, that near-majority was cut down to 28 percent, while a nearly matching proportion thought that funds for this program should be cut. Furthermore, in 1996 a large plurality (40 percent) of Blacks ranked crime first and unemployment and discrimination as second and third, respectively. In 1984 only 17 percent had placed crime above the other two problems; crime, in fact, came in third for half of the sample. Black opposition to federal assistance for minorities and Blacks shot up during this period as well, from 6 percent in 1970 to 26 percent in 1988. While the source of this new Black conservatism is debated, Tate (2010) contends that Black political leaders are no longer pushing racial issues as aggressively as they once did and now rely on Democratic Party leadership. As a consequence, the Black electorate is now more moderate, and a Black power strategy emphasizing a racial agenda has less support in the Black community.

Obama's 2008 Candidacy

Barack Obama was first elected to the Illinois State Senate in 1996. His first efforts to appeal to Black voters as a "universal candidate" failed in 2000 when he tried to unseat Black Democrat Bobby Rush from his House seat in a primary challenge (Frasure 2010). Rush was by self-description a radical Black politician, boasting in his congressional biography that he was a cofounder of Chicago's Black Panther Party. Lorrie Frasure describes Obama's emphasis on his race to resemble a form of Jekyll and Hyde. He would downplay race and then quickly take offense if others criticized him for not being Black enough. Black voters, she contends, saw Obama's moderation on racial issues as an asset when he ran for the U.S. Senate in 2004. In 2008, Frasure (2010) thinks Black voters again were strategic, switching to him when he was perceived to be a viable presidential candidate as polls showed that Blacks initially had favored Hillary Clinton over Obama. Explaining, therefore, the mixed findings of a Black empowerment effect on turnout, Christopher Stout (2010) reports that Black turnout increases when viable, statewide candidacies of Blacks are examined. Thus, this research indicates Black bloc voting and turnout increases when Black candidates can demonstrate their strong viability. Fredrick Harris contends that this turning away from the government's responsibility to helping minorities and the poor has helped to elect the nation's first Black president (2009, 71).

But a key transformation since the 1980s has also been witnessed in the political behavior of White Democrats as well. White Democrats have established better records of credibility with Black voters. President Clinton had cultivated a better working relationship with Black House Democrats than had President Carter. Furthermore, Clinton had appointed more Blacks to his administration than Carter. Thus, when New York Senator Hillary Clinton ran, she benefited from the strong relationship Black Democrats had in Washington with her husband, Bill. Other White politicians have been able to run effective campaigns against other African American candidates, notably Steve Cohen, who won in the district that an African American father and son, the Fords, had represented since 1974. Cohen was elected in 2006, and again in 2008. The majority Black city of New Orleans elected its first White mayor since 1978 in its 2009 municipal elections. In Atlanta, also a majority-Black city, in 2009, a White candidate very narrowly lost her bid for mayor after having made it to a run-off election. Artur Davis, however, in his primary bid to become Alabama's first Black governor, lost to a White candidate in 2010. Davis' defeat illustrates the new climate for Black politicians today. Davis had cast some conservative votes as a U.S. House legislator, including twice voting against Obama's health care reform legislation, reducing his support among Black voters. It is now clear that Black politicians, even those with exceptional vitae, cannot take the Black vote for granted.

Conclusion: Black Power in the Age of Obama

That Sharpton and Moseley Braun were unable to mobilize Black Democrats in 2004 says much about the political environment in 2004. It was an environment in which Blacks felt that they did not have to "vote Black" in order to pressure the Democratic Party to be more responsive to their communities' needs. With President George W. Bush's popularity ratings as low as Ronald Reagan's in the Black community, most Blacks were going to vote Democratic. Nevertheless, the Democratic field of White candidates still appealed to African American voters. The Democratic national party leadership's easy reception of Sharpton and Moseley Braun helped enormously. Jackson literally had to knock the doors down to gain access to debate candidates and address the party at its national conventions in 1984 and 1988. That created drama and publicized the marginal status of Black Democrats during those years. In 2004, the absence of a rebuff of Black presidential candidates diminished the need for Blacks to register a protest vote.

Sharpton received support from Blacks who wanted to challenge the Democratic Party. Both Black presidential candidates, however, perhaps could have attracted more Black votes had they pitched their candidacies more toward Black interests, such as voting rights protection and the extension of the 1965 Voting Rights Act in 2007. However, in addition to elevating the salience of Black interests in their campaigns, both Sharpton and Moseley Braun would have needed Black organizational support, something both lacked. Jackson profited enormously from the Black churches that took up the call to mobilize Black voters. The Nation of Islam's Louis Farrakhan also took interest in the Jackson campaigns, as a key element in energizing the base of Black voters.

While I argue that the environment and internal politics were key factors, other work suggests that the nature of Black politics changed so that a Black power candidacy in the presidential election is no longer necessary or relevant to most Black voters today. After all, Barack Obama's candidacy in 2008 did not attempt a Black presidential strategy of recruiting and mobilizing Black voters in order to influence the national party's public policy agenda and the party's eventual nominee. Most tellingly, Obama resigned from his Black church as the Reverend Jeremiah Wright entered into a racialized discourse regarding the United States' basic character in its treatment of Black citizens. However, Blacks generally respond favorably to viable Black bids (Stout 2010).

The literature suggests the end of a Black presidential strategic power approach as well. First, Orey's and Ricks' (2007) survey of Black elected officials finds that a majority characterized their campaign styles as "deracialized." In the U.S. House of Representatives there are Black politicians who, David T. Canon (1999) contends, have political styles which range from the politics of difference to the politics of commonality. Canon writes that most CBC House members sit in the "middle half of the spectrum. While they reject separatism, all members of the CBC ...also reject the notion that racism and discrimination are no longer problems in our society" (1999, 47). Thus, while Obama sought to keep racial concerns from dominating his presidential bid, other Black candidates may invite these issues as prominent parts of their campaigns because it represents an inherited style. Canon finds that new majority Black districts have elected Blacks who strive to balance the interests of their Black and White constituents, while old majority Black districts possess those who see racial relations as more hopelessly conflicted. Nevertheless, Orey and Ricks (2007) have found that younger Black elected officials are more likely to run race-specific campaigns than older Black politicians.

Two features of Black politics remain which suggest that it is premature to argue that Black presidential bid-type candidates will fade from the American political scene in the post-Obama United States. First, Black candidates can find themselves in campaigns that become racialized contrary to their aims in ways that hurt their bids for White support (Mendelberg 2001). Bill Clinton's efforts to inject race into the 2008 nominating contest between his wife and Obama failed. Harold Ford Jr.'s 2008 senate bid was racialized by his opponent, however, with an ad airing a young White woman winking at the Black candidate and asking him to call her. The illicit interracial sex angle implied by this derailed a basic political showdown between two candidates strictly on the merits of the issues. Playing the race card against Black candidates will persist and severely handicap the national bids of Black candidates. The propensity of White challengers to tap into racial divisiveness to hurt the bids of their Black rivals indicates that some environments remain unreceptive to Black candidates. This can become a sore point for Black Democrats, especially if Democratic rivals play the race card in primary challenges by Blacks, to win majority-White districts.

Secondly, race remains an important component of Black politics as one-quarter of African Americans live below the poverty line, and many Black communities confront a number of urgent social and economic problems. In the end, even as Blacks helped to elect a Black president in 2008, their interests remain linked to a government that is progressive and egalitarian as well as purposively engaged in combating racial inequality in America. Black radicals will remain receptive to a Black-oriented bid for the White House. Thus, together, the propensity of White candidates to inject race in bids to undercut White support for Black candidates, as well as the degree to which Blacks remain radical, point to the future of Black power presidential contenders. The current period of progress and inclusion for African Americans has not eradicated racial tensions in America. Not only may Whites object to political leadership by Blacks, but Blacks may still find the need to challenge society and government through race-conscious campaigning. Thus, this post-civil rights period in African American politics does not represent the final end of a Black power approach in Black politics. We have entered into a new phase of post-civil rights Black politics, but the strategic needs of the Black community remain largely the same.

References

Barker, Lucius J. 1989. *Our time has come*. Urbana and Chicago: University of Illinois Press.

Barker, Lucius J., Mack H. Jones, and Katherine Tate. 1999. *African Americans and the American political system*. 4th ed. Englewood Cliffs, NJ: Prentice Hall.

Browning, Rufus P., Dale Rogers Marshall, and David H. Tabb. 1984. *Protest is not enough*. Los Angeles and Berkeley: University of California Press.

Canon, David T. 1999. *Race, redistricting, and representation: The unintended consequences of Black majority districts*. Chicago, IL: University of Chicago Press.

Cook, Rhodes. 2000. *United States presidential primary elections, 1968–1996*. Washington, DC: Congressional Quarterly Press.

Cruse, Harold. 1967. *The crisis of the Negro intellectual*. New York: Morrow.

Dahl, Robert. 1961. *Who governs? Democracy and power in an American city*. New Haven, CT: Yale University Press.

Dawson, Michael C. 1994. *Behind the mule: Race and class in African-American politics*. Princeton, NJ: Princeton University Press.

———. 2001 *Black visions: The roots of contemporary African American political ideologies*. Chicago, IL: University of Chicago Press.

Eyes on the Prize. 2006. *Eyes on the prize: America's civil rights movement, our time has come* [videorecording]. Alexandria, VA: Blackside, Henry Hampton, Producer-PBS video.

Frasure, Lorrie. 2010. The burden of Jekyll and Hyde: Barack Obama, racial identity, and Black political behavior. In *Whose Black politics? Cases in post-racial Black leadership*, ed. Andra Gillespie, 133–54. New York: Routledge.

Gillespie, Andra. 2010. Meet the new class: Theorizing young Black leadership in a 'Postracial' era. In *Whose Black politics? Cases in post-racial Black leadership*, ed. Andra Gillespie, 9–42. New York: Routledge.

Gurin, Patricia, Shirley Hatchett, and James S. Jackson. 1989. *Hope and independence: Blacks' response to electoral and party politics*. New York: Russell Sage Foundation.

Harris, Fredrick. 2009. Toward a pragmatic Black politics. In *Barack Obama and African American empowerment*, ed. Manning Marable and Kristen Clarke, 65–72. New York: Palgrave MacMillan.

Hero, Rodney. 1992. *Latinos and the U.S. political system: Two-tiered pluralism*. Philadelphia, PA: Temple University Press.

Holden, Matthew. 1973. *The politics of the Black 'Nation.'* New York, NY: Chandler Pub.

Joseph, Peniel E. 2006. *Waiting 'til the midnight hour: A narrative history of Black power in America*. New York: Henry Holt.

Marable, Manning. 2007. *Race, reform, and rebellion: The second reconstruction and beyond in Black America, 1945–2006*. 3rd ed. Jackson, MS: University Press of Mississippi.

———. 2009. Racializing Obama: The enigma of postblack politics and leadership. In *Barack Obama and African American empowerment*, ed. Manning Marable and Kristen Clarke, 1–12. New York: Palgrave MacMillan.

McAdam, Doug. 1999. *Political process and the development of Black insurgency, 1930–1970.* 2nd ed. Chicago, IL: University of Chicago Press.

McClain, Paula, and Joseph Stewart Jr. 2009. *Can we all get along? Racial and ethnic minorities in American politics.* 5th ed. Boulder, CO: Westview Press.

McCormick, Joseph II, and Charles E. Jones. 1993. The conceptualization of deracialization: thinking through the dilemma. In *Dilemmas of Black politics*, ed. Georgia A. Persons, 66–84. New York: Harper Collins College Publishers.

Mendelberg, Tali. 2001. *The race card, campaign strategy, implicit messages, and the norm of equality.* Princeton, NJ: Princeton University Press.

Morris, Lorenzo, and Linda F. Williams. 1989. The coalition at the end of the rainbow: The 1984 Jackson campaign. In *Jesse Jackson's 1984 presidential campaign*, ed. L. J. Barker and R. W. Walters, 227–48. Urbana and Chicago: University of Illinois Press.

Orey, Bryon D'Andra, and Boris E. Ricks. 2007. A systematic analysis of the deracialization concept. *National Political Science Review* 11: 325–34.

Parker, Frank R. 1990. *Black votes count.* Chapel Hill, NC: University of North Carolina Press.

Pinderhughes, Dianne. 1987. *Race and ethnicity in Chicago politics.* Urbana and Chicago: University of Illinois Press.

Preston, Michael B. 1987. The election of Harold Washington: An examination of the SES model in the 1983 Chicago Mayoral Election. In *The new Black politics*, ed. Michael B. Preston, Lenneal J. Henderson, Jr., and Paul L. Puryear, 2nd ed, 139–71. New York: Longman Press.

———. 1989. The 1984 presidential primary: Who voted for Jesse Jackson and why? In *Jesse Jackson's 1984 Presidential Campaign*, ed. Lucius Barker and Ronald Walters, 129–46. Urbana and Chicago: University of Illinois Press.

Reed, Adolph Jr. 1986. *The Jesse Jackson phenomenon.* New Haven, CT: Yale University Press.

Sharpton, Al, and Karen Hunter. 2002. *Al on America.* New York: Kensington Publishing.

Smith, Robert C. 1981. Black power and the transformation from protest to politics. *Political Science Quarterly* 96, no. 3: 431–43.

———. 1996. *We have no leaders: African-Americans in the post civil rights era.* Albany, NY: State University of New York Press.

———. 2009. System values and African American leadership. In *Barack Obama and African American empowerment*, ed. Manning Marable and Kristen Clarke, 15–24. New York: Palgrave MacMillan.

Stout, Christopher. 2010. Black empowerment in the age of Obama. Unpublished Ph.D. diss., University of California, Irvine.

Tarrow, Sidney. 1998. *Power in movement: Social movements and contentious politics.* New York: Cambridge University Press.

Tate, Katherine. 1992. The impact of Jesse Jackson's presidential bids on Blacks' relationship with the Democratic party. *National Political Science Review* 3: 184–97

———. 1994. *From protest to politics, the new Black voters in American elections.* Cambridge, MA: Harvard University Press and the Russell Sage Foundation.

———. 1997. African American female senatorial candidates: Twin assets or double liabilities? In *African American power and politics*, ed. Hanes Walton, Jr, 264–81. New York, NY: Columbia University Press.

———. 2010. *What's going on? Political incorporation and the transformation of Black public opinion.* Washington, DC: Georgetown University Press.

Ture, Kwame (Stokely Carmichael), and Charles V. Hamilton. 1992. [1967]. *Black power.* New York: Vintage Books.

Ward, Stephen. 2006. The third world women's alliance: Black feminist radicalism and Black power politics. In *The Black power movement, rethinking the civil rights-Black power era*, ed. Peniel E. Joseph. New York: Routledge.

Walters, Ronald W. 1988. *Black presidential politics in America: A strategic approach.* Albany, NY: State University of New York Press.

———. 2003. *White nationalism, Black interests: Conservative public policy and the Black community.* Detroit: Wayne State University Press.

Black Politics in a Time of Transition, Volume 13; pp. 23-40

"But, I Voted for Obama": Melodrama and Post-Civil Rights, Postfeminist Ideology in Grey's Anatomy, Crash, and Barack Obama's 2008 Presidential Campaign*

Nikol Alexander-Floyd

Since the tumultuous social movements of the 1960s and 1970s have profoundly changed the political and social landscape in many regards, members of the general public have become increasingly hard-pressed to conceptualize the subtler, yet profound ways in which inequality structures society and politics. Indeed, confronted with ubiquitous signs of formal equality or multiculturalism, social activism regarding racism and sexism, appears to be a vestige of a former era that was once necessary, but is now obsolete. This perspective, informed by what I prefer to call post-Civil Rights, postfeminist ideology, has gained greater currency not only in popular culture, but throughout political discourse, evidenced by discussions amidst the 2008 presidential campaign about "the end of race," shattering the glass ceiling, and the arrival of a "post-racial, post-gender" future.

Although scholars have assessed the work of academic and/or political figures, such as Katie Roiphe or Naomi Wolf, associated with certain forms of postfeminism, most analysis of postfeminism has centered on popular culture, particularly in terms of how postfeminism operates via television and film (McRobbie 2007; Modleski 1991; Projansky 2001; Tasker and Negra 2007). Most of this important body of scholarship, however, pays insufficient attention both to questions of race (Modleski 1991; Spring 2007; Tasker and Negra 2007) and the insinuation of postfeminist, post-Civil Rights ideology into the realm of formal politics, such as elections.[1] In this work, I address these two neglected dimensions of postfeminist, post-Civil Rights ideology by presenting a Black feminist analysis that takes into account the gender, race, and class dynamics of post-Civil Rights, postfeminist ideology, particularly as they impact Black women and Black feminist politics. Integrating insights from political science, women's and gender studies, Black Studies, cultural studies, and media studies, I explore the range and scope of postfeminist, post-Civil Rights ideology in three narrative sites encountered in popular culture and electoral politics: *Grey's Anatomy*, a popular, gender diverse, multiracial television series written by Shonda Rhimes, an African American female; *Crash*, an academy award-winning movie celebrated for its treatment of race; and Barack Obama's 2008 presidential campaign. My aim is not to conflate the realms of mass-mediated culture and formal politics, but, rather, to uncover the invisible parameters of these hegemonic ideologies that distort our understandings to the extent that we can no longer claim that inequality exists. Accordingly, I see television and movies as political in that they constitute a "system" of classed and gendered "racialization" (Littlefield 2008) through which hegemonic ideologies are refracted and produced and that influence the same "public" that is subject to and participates in formal politics (Condit 1989). Although scholars have examined the connection between popular culture and politics, broadly speaking, this work extends such scholarship by examining popular culture and formal elections. Indeed, given the increasingly intersecting terrains of popular culture and elections, this will prove to be an especially important methodology in the future.

This focus enables several critical interventions in the analysis of post-feminist, post-Civil Rights ideology. First, in terms of the absence of a critique of race, one can argue that the dominant definition of post feminism operates through appropriating but ultimately undermining the very logics of feminism and that it has been implicitly based on White, middle-class female experiences. In this essay I would like to suggest that by bringing the "margin to center" (hooks 1984), that is, by situating postfeminism within the context of post-Civil Rights ideology, we can locate the development of these postfeminist ideologies to an earlier point of origin. In this way, we can complicate and clarify our understanding of them as mutually constitutive phenomena. Second, the merging of these two discourses becomes evident, as I will argue below, in their common use of melodrama as a privileged representational vehicle for reproducing racist and sexist ideologies. Finally, as I will demonstrate, the juxtaposition of popular cultural forms and campaign discourse helps to bridge the gap between the perceived theory/practice divide in feminism by showing how feminist theorizing illuminates our understanding of formal politics.

In developing my analysis, I first provide an overview of common approaches to defining postfeminism and its central tenets, and outline how a post-Civil Rights approach can introduce a broader spectrum of concerns with regards to understanding melodrama as the narrative frame of choice in many popular forms of post-Civil Rights, postfeminist discourse. Next, placing these three narrative sites, *Grey's Anatomy*, *Crash*, and the Obama 2008 presidential campaign, in intertextual conversation, I explore several themes, grounded in a melodrama metanarrative frame, namely, a focus on individualistic interpretations of inequality, rehabilitation of the family and wounded masculinity, and racial and gender redemption centered in "fantasies of miscegenation" (Courtney 2005). I pay particular attention throughout to the implications of these themes for Black women and Black feminist politics. I argue that they render moot any ongoing critique of normative or hegemonic ideologies and short circuit exploration of Black women's lived realities and political agendas that could be socially and politically transformative. Instead, they provided an ideologically conservative narrative—that of assimilation.

"Post"-Ing Social Movements in Culture and Politics

For scholars such as Negra, McRobbie, and Tasker, postfeminist ideology extends beyond a simple notion of "backlash" in which feminist principles are directly attacked (McRobbie 2007, 28; Tasker and Negra 2007, 1–2), to actually trumpet the success of feminism. As feminist cultural studies critic, Angela McRobbie, (2007, 28) deftly observes, "…postfeminism positively draws on and invokes feminism as that which can be taken into account, to suggest that equality is achieved, in order to…emphasize that it is no longer needed, that it is a spent force." Further, postfeminism, according to McRobbie, evinces several dominant narrative tropes, one of the most important being a clash between generations, where feminist ideology is figured as belonging in the past, something necessary for an older generation of White women. The goals of social justice having been achieved, social equality is something that is now presumed to be the taken-for-granted operating logic for a younger generation. In this context, according to McRobbie (2007, 34–36), youth culture is fixated on a liberated "individualization" that feeds a range of self-regulating practices, drawing attention away from social structure and group politics, and toward an "atomized" (Hsu 2006) understanding of social and political harm.

Against this backdrop of the dominant understanding of postfeminism, how does postfeminism express itself within the context of Black politics? Kimberly Springer insightfully explains that, "As part of a racialized discourse, one must grapple with postfeminism's place in the post-civil-rights era" (Springer 2007, 253). Importantly, the term "post-Civil Rights" admits of several related meanings, including: (1) a demarcation of historical time, that is, an "era," which begins with the passage of the 1964 Civil Rights Act, signaling the end of *de jure* segregation; (2) a politics of opposition to civil rights initiatives, such as voting rights enforcement, during this same swath of historical time; and (3) more increasingly, a school of thought, which suggests that we are living in or at least teetering toward a "post-racial" society. For our purposes here, it is necessary to clarify that post-Civil Rights politics encompasses direct opposition or "backlash," but opposition that, like postfeminist opposition, often trades on and affirms certain liberal notions of formal equality. Moreover, also as with postfeminism, post-Civil Rights politics, as a concomitant strategy, appropriates the language of Civil Rights social movements, such as an emphasis on "equality" or "equal opportunity," read through a frame that suggests that equality has been achieved or is now threatened not by racism, but by forms of antiracist politics gone amok.

Notably missing from dominant readings of postfeminism and post-Civil Rights politics is an understanding of how sexist and racist forces following the social movements of the mid-twentieth century most impacted Black women. As Springer correctly notes, "The social counterpart to institutional post-civil-rights racism [such as assaults on affirmative action] was the welfare queen"(Springer 2007, 253). Likewise, the Black matriarch/Welfare Queen has also been a significant element of postfeminist politics for Black women, one that, in recent decades, played a major role in transforming U.S. public policy and bolstering conservative dominance.

The image of the Black matriarch was made notorious by the 1965 Moynihan Report. For Moynihan, the key problem was that Black families were matriarchal, that is, dominated by Black women who headed single-parent households, in a society that valued patriarchal families. Because of Black matriarchy, he averred, Black families suffered socially, economically, and politically. This Report had several critical outcomes in terms of, among other things, attitudes about social activism, the resistance to feminism, and the promotion of middle-class respectability and traditional gender roles. First, as others have detailed extensively (see, e.g., Jordan-Zachery 2001), for the broader culture, this report facilitated and legitimated political retrenchment that fingered the microinstitution of the family, not the macroinstitutional structures controlled by the state, as the source of Black people's dilemmas. The notion of Black cultural pathology promoted by the Report would serve as the narrative framework that would be used to define "the sign of Blackness"(Gray 1995) within the current era and that would pose the largest challenge to the Civil Rights and Black Power Movements' emphasis on structural change. Second, in line with this thinking, Black women have been problematically caricatured as "strong," regardless of their socioeconomic standing: poor women are in control of families and middle-class, upwardly mobile women are able to succeed, despite the realities of racism. From this vantage point, feminism is not embraced and then discarded. It is said, rather, to have never been necessary. Finally, a middle class"ideology of respectability"(White 1990) centered on restoring two-parent, patriarchal homes in Black communities has been promoted as the solution to Black social and political ills. Consequently, community organizing has been geared toward"saving"the Black male and promoting acceptable forms of Black masculinity (Alexander-Floyd 2007). As the above suggests, in the case of Black politics, postfeminism can manifest itself as both an explicit"antifeminism,"as well as an advocacy of a"traditionalism" that champions a pre-feminist politics (Projansky 2001).[2]

A Black feminist analysis exposes the ways in which what we view as post-Civil Rights and postfeminist timeframes and ideologies are not only deeply enmeshed, but, indeed, co-constitutive. Post-Civil Rights ideology, for whatever else it represents, has also been elaborated through and constituted a postfeminist politics: it is formulated through the politics of not only race, but gender and class, where Black families would come to be situated for political participation and social uplift by attaining middle-class respectability via two-parent families, patterned after an idealized White middle-class family. Likewise, this focus on the family and male uplift, and its attendant focus on self-regulation, personal empowerment, and responsibility, predated the current emphasis on these elements in mainstream, White society that have been the subject of so much scholarship on postfeminism. Once we take the history and social position of Black women into account, it is the 1965 Moynihan Report with its raced-gendered individualist frame for upward mobility and assault on Black women, not the failure to pass the Equal Rights Amendment or other sociopolitical trends of the 1980s (Projansky 2001, 14–15), that marks the onset of not only a post-Civil Rights, but also a postfeminist assault on the social movements of the mid-twentieth century.

Unsurprisingly, the Moynihan Report's focus on family rehabilitation and wounded masculinity, with its emphasis on pathos and the resolution of moral crisis, finds its perfect expression in the melodramatic mode. As opposed to a genre with fixed, defining elements, melodrama can be seen as a "mode," that is a "certain fictional system for making sense of experience" (Brooks [1976] 1995, xvii). It is grounded in "pathos" and embodied in characters that are "victims" or "villains," embodying "virtue" and "virtuelessness," good and evil, respectively (Williams 2001).[3] Melodramas are also often marked by a will to return to a prior state of safety (36). As such, melodrama is an optimal medium for quelling or resolving social anxiety. Melodrama, as others have demonstrated, is the prevailing form of narrative expression in film and other forms of cultural production, and arguably in politics as well (Kelleter, Krah, and Mayer 2007; Williams 2001). Importantly, in this current cultural and political milieu, melodrama works by extricating questions of social inequality from the realm of the public, scripted as a masculine domain, and translating it into the realm of the private and individualized world of melodrama, scripted as the special preserve of the feminine (Grindstaff 1994). Indeed, as L.A. Grindstaff remarks, "Melodrama…represents social anxieties or conflicts as sexual and familial ones" and depends "on questions of visibility, representability, pretense, and masquerade" (1994, 54). As she further explains, "In film melodrama, crises of representation and identity function to break families apart, then bring them together again at the story's end employing one of a number of formulas: the hero defeats the villain, the 'villain within' is reformed, or the villain turns out to have been the hero all along" (55). With many modern melodramas, the feminist claim that the personal is political is perverted to mean that *only* the personal is political, sidelining public claims to redress sexism.

Indeed, melodrama becomes a privileged mode of post-Civil Rights, postfeminist ideology. It serves to redirect attention away from structural inequality and toward individual attitudes and actions in at least three ways: in its focus on the microinstitution of the family and reassertion of romanticized forms of White middle-class patriarchy; in its focus on self-regulation (variously labeled self-development, self-help, and/or personal responsibility), that assumes social problems are amenable to individual redress; and, in its focus on interpersonal relationships, as opposed to institutions or the state, as the site for conflict resolution, relationships that stand in for our understanding of ourselves as a national family or community. In what follows, after providing brief overviews of the three narrative sites selected for analysis, I trace the only-the-personal-is-political melodramatic frame along three thematic dimensions: definitions of inequality, calls for family restoration, and modern-day miscegenation fantasies. In each case, the deployment of Black bodies in particular and Blackness in general serves as the backdrop against which White gender, race, and class identities are elaborated.

Description of Three Narrative Sites

Since *Grey's Anatomy* (hereinafter "*GA*") first aired in 2005, it has met with critical acclaim and high viewership. Although medical TV shows are standard fare, the show boasts a particularly impressive multicultural cast. Set in "Seattle Grace," a topnotch hospital in Seattle Washington, the show centers on Meredith Grey, a surgical intern, and a coterie of her friends as they negotiate the grueling demands of a surgical internship. In addition to Meredith, there are more than four other female surgeons that play key roles on the show, including her best friend, Christina Yang, a Korean American. In keeping with traditional casting patterns, where minorities are cast in leadership roles (Entman and Rojecki 2001), there were three African Americans in supervisory positions in the initial seasons, including Dr. Webber, the chief of surgery, Preston Burke, a renowned cardiothoracic surgeon who is one of the attending surgeons responsible for instructing the interns, and Miranda Bailey, aka "Hitler," the resident who is the interns' immediate supervisor.

The Hollywood blockbuster, *Crash* (which enjoyed a second life as a television series), is generally hailed as a progressive movie that takes a daring, forthright approach to dealing with the question of racism and prejudice. The movie, which garnered three Academy Awards, including Best Motion Picture of the Year (Mack 2006), focuses in on the multiethnic environment of Los Angeles and the seemingly ubiquitous prejudice that passes virus-like between Whites and non-Whites and among various racial and ethnic communities. The film, mostly praised by critics, is shown in "diversity" seminars (Hsu 2006, 134), and is used as a teaching aid in colleges across the country.

The 2008 Obama presidential campaign was, in the words of President Barack Obama, the former junior U.S. senator from Illinois, "an improbable story." Born the child of a Black Kenyan man and White Kansan woman, Obama was reared in Indonesia and Hawaii, where he was educated in private schools. He also attended Columbia University and Harvard Law, where he served as the school's first African American named President of the prestigious Harvard Law Review (Obama [1995] 2004). After serving three terms as a state legislator and as a first-time senator, he made an historic bid for the country's highest office, galvanizing support across the country to become the first African American to be elected President.

Melodrama: Defining Inequality

The question of defining inequality in terms of interpersonal, melodramatic terms can usefully be assessed in light of two subthemes: multiculturalism marked by racial and gender diversity and rare occurrences of hostility or structural discrimination; and multiculturalism marked by ubiquitous interpersonal conflict read as homogeneous claims of social harm.

Fantasies of Multicultural Equality

The post-Civil Rights, postfeminist ideology of *GA* takes for granted that the goals of social movement activity of the 1960s and 1970s, at least at a formal equality level, have been achieved. From this perspective, there is little room for expansive definitions of gender, race, and class inequality that take into account institutional structures, ongoing processes of engendering and racialization as they intersect with market forces, or even the daily struggles that White women and racial minorities experience in workplaces, such as hospitals. On *GA*, not all of the interns, for instance, hail from economically privileged backgrounds. Still, their varied and humble beginnings, while useful in explaining some of their personality quirks and personal foibles, do not impede their upward mobility in the highly competitive field of medical surgery.

In addition to class, racism and sexism are not seen as significant problems, and are instead seen as episodic, that is, as resting in individually directed behavior by a minority of people who are wedded to anachronistic, socially repugnant worldviews. In terms of gender, two trends hold on *GA*. On the one hand, the lead female characters are surrounded by men who stand ready to have monogamous relationships, but remain hopelessly afflicted with angst about whether "having it all"—career and family—are possible for women. On the other hand, they enact a "do me" postfeminism (Projansky 2001) in which they demonstrate their "independence" by having numerous and varied sexual partners. In terms of race, it was not until season four that racism was addressed directly, even though the cast is celebrated for its diversity. In this episode, racism is cast as a freak occurrence, embodied in misguided individuals whose views are not generally supported. By this logic, racism and sexism are relegated to the past, only to occasionally surface, before being quickly doused by egalitarian moral sentiments.

Fantasies of Multicultural Conflict Resolution

Notably, despite its attempt to address questions of racism and (to a lesser extent) other forms of inequality directly, in the final analysis, *Crash* is also scripted within the political parameters of post-Civil Rights, post-feminist ideology. Instead of avoiding a discussion of racism, *Crash* seems to take it head on. The viewer is greeted with people of all racial, gender, and class backgrounds espousing prejudiced views, ostensibly to suggest a more complicated picture of racial and ethnic strife (Nunley 2007, 339–40). Importantly, however, this globalization of prejudice masks an important distinction between prejudicial attitudes and racism, the latter of which centers on not only prejudicial views of individuals, but also, rather, on institutional racism. Indeed, *Crash* "flattens out asymmetrical power relations as they intersect with white privilege" (Nunley 2007, 340), so that the viewer is invited to make no distinctions, for instance, between a Latina and Asian woman who exchange ethnic epithets after an automobile accident, on the one hand, and the White District Attorney who abuses the power of his office to coerce a Black cop into participating in a racially motivated cover-up, on the other. Moreover, like *GA*, *Crash*'s underlying assumption is that class barriers are largely assailable through hard work and attainment of middle-class respectability (Holmes 2007, 318–19). The movie showcases individuals (largely men), such as a Persian convenience store owner, a Black cop, a Black television executive, and a Latino handyman, who are striving to overcome adversity through pursuit of the American dream.

Ultimately, despite their differences, like *GA*, *Crash* trades on a multiculturalism that positions racism and other social and political harm in the realm of pathos-driven melodrama acted out on and through individuals. *Crash* rehearses the familiar understanding of inequality read through a "melodramatic vision that foregrounds individual suffering" (Hsu 2006, 146), cast in a masculinist mode. It achieves this, for instance, through its focus on reclaiming wounded White masculinity, thereby highlighting "reverse discrimination" (146) against White men. But, as Hsu explains, "As a banal product of history, urban architecture, and state institutions, racism runs on autopilot, without much need for melodramatic acts of hate, intolerance, or malice" (148). By equating prejudice with racism and melodramatic attitudes or actions as the entire scope of racial play, *Crash* undermines the Civil Rights and Black Power imperative to make not only attitudinal, but also institutional, change and obscures the more mundane elaboration of White privilege.

Like *GA* and *Crash*, the Obama campaign constructs racism and sexism as being relics of the past and equated with melodramatic individual attitudes, stripped of an understanding of asymmetrical power relations. In his now (in)famous "Philadelphia compromise" speech (Reed 2008) on race in the United States, Obama drew a clear distinction between the past, marked by virulent racism, and the present, which is marked by substantial racial progress. For Obama, although those, such as his former pastor, Jeremiah Wright, who experienced Jim Crow-style racism were understandably "angry" about racism, he faulted Wright and presumably others for not fully acknowledging U.S. racial progress. Just as importantly, in his historic speech Obama draws a parallel between the suffering of Blacks and that of disgruntled Whites who feel harmed through affirmative action (Obama 2008b). Also, in his neglect of questions of sexism as they relate to those of class and gender, he promotes postfeminist, or more directly, a post-Black feminist, politics.

What are the implications of this post-Civil Rights, postfeminist ideology for Black feminist analyses and politics? Radical Black feminist politics operates on a basic assumption that various aspects of identity are "mutually constitutive" (Harris 1999), that is, that the elaboration of identity and politics are inherently raced, gendered, and classed and that this reality must inform any social justice agenda. Post-Civil Rights, postfeminist ideology directly contradicts this basic presumption. More pointedly, because it denies the institutional and complex nature of social inequality it is not merely inattentive to, but actively works to obscure, the realities of Black women's experiences with sexism, racism, and class-based inequality. It is interesting to highlight, by way of illustration, how the reality of Black women in the medical profession is diametrically opposed to the picture of multicultural, postfeminist integration presented on *GA*. Notably, the American Medical Association, which early in 2008 issued an apology for the longstanding history of discrimination of the organization, has established a special committee to study the racial divide in medicine (American Medical Association 2008). In addition, although Blacks comprise over ten percent of the U.S. population, "in 2006, 2.2 percent of practicing physicians and medical students were African-American"; Dr. Ronald Davison, former president of the American Medical Association, notes that there are fewer Black physicians today "per capita" than in 1910 ("Medical Association Apologizes for History of Prejudice" 2008). In her study of Black female surgeons, Patricia Dawson relates the experiences of Black women as they struggle to succeed in environments rife with "gendered racism." In one case, for instance, a Black female chief resident had to be hypervigilant in executing her work and lacked administrative backing in fulfilling her supervisory role (Dawson 1999, 82). Another Black female, Marie, states that "One of the big problems [during residency] was the fact that I was a female and then that I was Black. There are stories [or humorous jokes] that go on and on about, 'Your doctor is not only Black, she's female...your doctor is not only female, she's Black.'" (98). These experiences suggest that, far from the serene, convivial environment projected on *GA* or the symmetrical experience of suffering on *Crash*, work and social environments, such as hospitals, are spheres of intense conflict—or what Pratt (1992) refers to as "contact zones"—where previously dispossessed, disenfranchised groups interact with dominant culture and institutions in situations of radical inequality. Black women in these spaces, in particular, deeply challenge the "somatic norms" (Puwar 2004) of medical and other professional environments, given that they embody the antithesis of White masculinity. Although post-Civil Rights, postfeminist ideology embedded within popular representations showcases gender, race, and class hypervisibility as markers of social progress, it renders invisible the discrimination Black women, as well as White females and racial minorities, endure.

Melodrama and the Romance of White Middle-Class Patriarchy

The "Family In Jeopardy"

Importantly, even as it sidesteps strident critiques of inequality and reformulates representations of characters that in at least some ways downplay those characters' racial identification, GA operates on an implicit (and wayward) assumption that "second wave" feminists have thrown the family in crisis, marking women's professional "ambitions" (Grindstaff 1994) as villainous pursuits. The "family in jeopardy" is part of the "core grammar" of media and cultural productions (Lipsitz 1997, 17). And, importantly, as noted above, all of the main characters, whatever their socioeconomic status or racial or ethnic background, come from troubled families. Seattle Grace and the doctors who work there are the site of a different, more stable family unit. As would-be surgeons going through a grueling internship, they all find occasion to cover for each other's failings (as when they stand together and refuse to "give up" Izzie when she essentially temporarily kills a patient, so he can be moved up on a transplant list). They all have deep-seated personality issues and are whipped into shape and essentially mothered by Bailey, the mammy/sapphire figure. The Chief of Surgery, Dr. Webber, someone with his own family issues (i.e., his wife initially wants a divorce), is the consummate father figure. This reconstitution of family stems from the romance of a "traditionalist" White middle-class vision of patriarchy, that is, the promotion of two-parent, male-headed families, based on a male breadwinner model, as the primary solution for sociopolitical ills.

Indeed, although most minorities in authority positions on TV shows do not become intimately involved with their juniors (Entman and Rojecki 2001, chap. 9), Dr. Webber takes a keen interest in his interns. This transgression of typical boundaries seen in similar TV shows is made possible, because the African American chief of surgery is also implicitly the father in chief. In one episode, for instance, when Bailey complains about Cristina getting a light reprimand after her role in hiding Burke's hand injury is exposed, the chief, Dr. Webber, intones, "look at how she has grown." Here he is referring to Cristina's moral development in pushing aside her feelings for Burke and her desire to gain surgical experience in order to "do the right thing" by exposing her own and Burke's unethical transgressions. Some might argue that such oversight is typical or that camaraderie is a natural feature among interns, but the nurturing approach bears more resemblance to familial relations as opposed to the hardnosed training expected in hospitals. To be sure, as women of color feminists have pointed out, the family has been a key source of survival for subaltern U.S. communities (Carby 1997; Davis 2000). But, the romance of a White patriarchal family model proceeds without any critique or consideration of the family and specifically its "dominator" modes of patriarchy variety (hooks 2004) as a site of exploitation and abuse of women. Their personal family crises, in effect, are resolved through the reconstitution of family in another institutional domain, thus restoring the romance of White middle-class patriarchy that is seemingly threatened in the "real" world and asserting racial harmony (here figured in the Black chief of staff) instead of insisting on a critique of the patriarchal romance.

In the Obama campaign, the family in jeopardy emerges as a key refrain both in terms of his personal biography and his political views. As he often remarks, he is the product of a single parent family. Of his father he writes: "At the time of his death, my father remained a myth to me, both more and less than a man. He had left Hawaii back in 1963, when I was only two years old, so that as a child I knew him only through the stories that my mother and grandparents told" (Obama [1995] 2004, 5). He explains his struggle to resolve the conflicted relationship he had with his father and his racial identity development. Typically set in the context of his rendition of the all too familiar Horatio Alger story, Obama implicitly suggests the association of single-parenthood and poverty, noting that his mother once received food stamps.

The reality of his circumstances as a son of privilege (being raised by a White educated mother and having access to an elite education) notwithstanding, Obama strategically used campaign rhetoric that fits within the common refrain of broken families in the United States. Notably, the whole question of father abandonment and personal responsibility were placed in the limelight in June 2008 when, during a Father's Day address at a predominantly Black church, Obama took Black fathers to task for not caring for or assuming material responsibility for their children. In this speech, Obama explains that the "most important" rock is the family, stating that "too many fathers...are missing—missing from too many lives and too many homes. They have abandoned their responsibilities, acting like boys instead of men. And the foundations of our families are weaker because of it" (Obama 2008c). This rhetoric, criticized by some in Black communities (most notably Jesse Jackson) for essentially blaming the victim, has been a prominent theme within Obama's political career. Indeed, Jackson, in his now infamous "hot mic" debacle, was so bothered by Obama's "talking down to Blacks" that he wanted to "cut his nuts out" (Hurt 2008).

Jackson is, of course, correct in his assertion that an emphasis on personal responsibility and rehabilitating the Black family through the generation of viable Black patriarchs amounts to "talking down" to or blaming Blacks. But, Jackson's comment also points to another way in which this romance of patriarchy structures not only intimate family relations, but formal politics as well. If, as Patricia Hill Collins (2006, chap. 1) explains, the patriarchal model within families indeed comes to structure other social institutions and political arrangements, then we must interrogate this significance within Black politics, particularly in light of Black feminist objectives to assert substantive equality for Black women. Indeed, what Jackson does not remark on, but is nevertheless embedded in his comments, is how the romance of patriarchy becomes embodied in two patriarchal types, namely, the Black Symbolic Father and the Super Minority. The Black Symbolic Father refers to a male figure, such as Jackson, who stands in as a spokesperson for Black communities and whose plight can be read metonymically with that of Black people as a whole. Jackson's terror is not only at the flagellation of the beleaguered Black masses, but, rather, the demise of an approach to Black politics that Jackson best represents and embodies. Jackson, who has long occupied the role of Black Symbolic Father in Black politics, is reeling from a perceived Oedipal conquest. And, utilizing a basic form of Freudian projection, he wanted to do to Obama what he felt had symbolically been done to him.

The second figure, the Super Minority, is an African American (typically male) that is presented as being stripped of stereotypical characteristics generally associated with Blackness. A regular on the small screen, Super Minorities are constructed as "purified exemplars of White cultural ideals that…[lead to the] disruption of Whites' normal mental associations" such that these characters are seen as "not really Black" (Entman and Rojecki 2001, 222); this move implicitly suggests a liminal Super Minority status as a requirement for assimilation. In the Obama campaign, this image of the Super Minority is polished to a high shine, as Obama is greeted as an exceptional minority—politicos, for instance, such as his vice president Joe Biden, comment on his "articulateness" and describe him as "clean"—who defies the associations of dysfunction and inferiority typically aligned with Blackness. Some, in fact, dubbed him Barack the Magic Negro (Ehrenstein 2007), alluding to a standard trope in cinema, in which a Black (again typically male) character who possesses "special powers" (Kempley 2003) or extraordinary abilities saves the day and facilitates self-actualization for Whites. Also noteworthy is his decidedly "deracialized" approach to formulating his political platform. As Black political scientists Joseph McCormick, Jr. and Charles E. Jones (1993) explain, deracialization has become a political "strategy" used by politicians aiming to reach beyond Black electoral bases to garner White support in election to mayoral, gubernatorial, and, now, presidential offices. More specifically, "*as an electoral strategy*" deracialization entails, "avoiding explicit reference to [Black or] race-specific issues, while at the same time emphasizing those issues that are perceived as racially transcendent, thus mobilizing a broad segment of the electorate" (76).

To be sure, there are elements of his policy proposals that will have a disproportionate impact on Black and minority communities, but, in contrast to previous generations of Black politicians that foregrounded Black misfortune and in keeping with attempts at "deracialization," Obama's campaign supplants issues of racism with a universal appeal to broader constituencies (see, e.g., Obama 2006).[4]

The point is not that Black professionals are not indeed excellent or exceptional, but that, as Entman and Rojecki affirm:

> Inflected as they are with this symbolic freighting [as symbolic figures made even more so, because they typically appear in "superior" positions work-wise], they act less as interesting, complex characters than as inverted prototypes: they incarnate the pure values of the dominant culture in a body and with a skin color usually associated with the opposite. (2001, 159)

The espousing of universalism implicitly supports Black stereotypes that affirm therapeutic modes of personal rehabilitation in lieu of structural change. Its denial of difference, moreover, forecloses social transformation into a truly multicultural society. Also, to the extent that Super Minorities are generally defaulted to male, they reinforce a male prerogative within minority communities that displace Black female subjectivity. Finally, the Super Minority often implicitly stands in as an alternative to the endangered Black male.

In this melodramatic theme of family restoration, we can see, once again, the confluence of culture and politics. Cultural representations, media representations, and formal politics all draw upon similar themes of family distress and restoration of wounded masculinity. They function in separate spheres, but in ways that reinforce and mutually influence the current political milieu. As I argue in the next section, like the emphasis on family restoration, the last theme, miscegenation, also draws on interpersonal relations, mapping onto interracial unions the fall and/or recovery of gender norms and racial healing.

Miscegenation

Miscegenation, understood as the transgressive violation of interracial sexual boundaries, has been a cornerstone of U.S. popular culture, and provides what is perhaps the starkest, and most politically charged example of melodramatic narrative scripting. Two elements of this scripting are especially important: the use of miscegenation to channel or resolve anxieties provoked through challenges to the established raced-gendered order and the redemption of Whiteness through the Black body. First, as Susan Courtney demonstrates, in fantasies of miscegenation of the modern era, such as *Guess Who's Coming to Dinner*, the price of acceptance of racial transgressions—of affirming racial integration—comes only at the expense of, and are indeed constituted through, the reassertion of the approved "dominant sexual order" (2005, 16). So, while Sydney Poitier's presence as fiancé-in-waiting for a young White female is initially unsettling, the White father's concerns give way to acceptance as he embraces Poitier as a Magical Negro figure who would unite in wedded matrimony with his daughter, and, thereby, affirm his liberal racial commitments, even amidst the reassertion of gender norms. Second, Black characters occupy what Toni Morrison (1992) has referred to as an Africanist Presence, that is, the utilization of Blackness and Black figures to effect the elaboration of White identity and racial hierarchy. Similarly, Nunley amplifies:"…whether it is the magical Negro trope…or the servant trope…not only must the white character be redeemed, [e.g. the White father in *Guess Who's Coming to Dinner*] but the redemption must also occur upon or because of the discursive terrain of the black body"(Nunley 2007, 344).[5]

In *GA*, the primary resolution of family crisis can be seen in the life of the main character, Meredith Grey, and takes shape via a fall and redemption symbolized through transgression of the Black Body via an interracial union. Meredith Grey and Derrick Sheppard have had a fiery, albeit on-again-off-again relationship, perennially hamstrung by her"obvious daddy issues"("Damage Case"2006). This unfortunate state of affairs is owing to an extramarital affair that Ellis Grey, Meredith's high-powered surgeon mother who is now afflicted with Alzheimer's, has with Dr. Webber. This liaison effectively ended Ellis Grey's relationship with her husband. Although Ellis Grey leaves her husband to be with Webber, he decides to stay with his Black wife, Adele.

Importantly, the Grey family saga can be read as an allegory that registers a cautionary tale about the impact of the mid-twentieth-century feminist movement on White middle-class women, one in which Blackness provides the symbolic parameter for elaborating White family distress. Given her age, Ellis Grey would have entered the medical profession when there were not likely many women in the profession. In her choice to have a career, she set aside traditional family life. Although Ellis Grey is a professional success, she is a distant, emotionally unavailable mother. She also effectively emasculates her husband, driving him away from the family and causing him to abandon his daughter. Her subversion of gender norms that would prohibit her from having a career is inherently racialized. Her transgression of White middle-class gender norms is figured as a transgression of racial norms, literally (in terms of sex), as well as metaphorically (in terms of her symbolic positioning). Kimberly Springer has remarked,"Even when they are not on the screen, women of color are present as the counterpart against which white women's ways of being…are defined and refined"(2007, 249), and in *GA*, Black women, read as emasculating Sapphires, are the implicit symbolic register for women who violate gender norms. Most notably, Ellis Grey, as it relates to her husband, becomes symbolically Black: as a woman who transgresses the cult of womanhood reserved for White middle-class women, she comes to assume the stereotypical characteristics of Black women who are viewed as the antithesis, and indeed provide the constitutive boundaries, of proper femininity.[6] Interestingly, although Ellis Grey is generally stern, often cruel in her verbal engagements, she is calm, happy, and emotional when with Webber, a picture of traditional femininity. As a Black man—a "real" man—he is able to tame this otherwise unyielding, tyrannical woman. In keeping with the melodramatic mode, Webber is, in the end, a villainous character. Ellis Grey, we learn in season four, is so distressed by Webber's decision not to leave his wife that she attempts to commit suicide, a pattern that Grey's daughter ineluctably follows.

Season four ends with Meredith coming to terms with her fear of emotional intimacy with Derrick Sheppard by going to therapy and realizing that she can, unlike her mother, "have it all." She tells Derrick she is ready for a family. The Black doctor's racial presence, in the final analysis, provides the backdrop through which this story of White wounded masculinity and its recovery is actualized and gender harmony restored. This miscegenation is less a rupture of gendered racism, as some would suggest, than an explicitly depoliticized interracial union that implicitly reaffirms White male–female patriachal family unions.

In the movie *Crash*, amidst an epidemic failure of masculinity, where men are unable to protect their women or otherwise affirm their manhood on the job or in the home, the story turns on an interracial rape scene that provides the impetus for masculine redemption. This central element of the plot involves the interplay between two sets of characters, namely, two White cops, Ryan, the more senior officer, and Hansen, his junior counterpart, as well as a Black, middle-class couple, Cameron and Christine. The characters first encounter each other when Ryan decides to pull Cameron and Christine over without just cause.

Ryan's emotional trigger for making this stop stems from his woundedness as a White male, a woundedness that is grounded in a family history that serves as an allegory for the broader context of Black–White U.S. racial history. His father cannot urinate because of a urinary tract infection (a condition symbolic of wounded, White masculinity) (Hsu 2006, 133; Ray 2007, 352), and is denied access to the medical clinic after hours by a Black female, because his father's condition is not an emergency. Also, Ryan's father hired Black employees for his janitorial business and was "good to them," only to be forced out of business by Blacks who received government contracts. Ryan's father stands in for a White liberal commitment to racial reform, situated in the past, that has ultimately failed him and his family; and Ryan, symbolic of the current moment, emerges as a victim of affirmative action who is outraged by its deleterious effects on him and his family, in the first instance for his father's job loss and most immediately in terms of representing the inadequacy of the health care system. Ryan's unwarranted stop, then, is motivated by his wounded White middle-class masculinity.

Ryan seeks to assuage his wounded masculinity via a sexual violation that assaults not only Christine, the Black female, but also her husband Cameron, as well. Under the guise of a weapons check, Ryan rapes Christine, assaulting her by molesting her legs, hips, breasts, and buttocks, and driving his fingers under her dress in what her character later describes as "finger f---[ing]" (Crash 2005). From here, the story takes on a mode of White masculine redemption. In a later scene, Ryan is called to a car crash in which Christine turns out to be the victim. He enters a vehicle, leaking gas and about to catch fire, in order to save her. Christine, understandably reluctant to be helped by Ryan, relents in order to save her life. As Hsuan L. Hsu observes, this scene depends on "a familiar model of white male heroic agency at the expense of the inarticulate, passive, victimized black woman..." (2006, 133).

The scene is not only one of White male redemption in which Christine embodies an Africanist presence that allows White subjectivity to emerge (which it certainly is), but one that represents an increasingly popular narrative trope: the Black woman's body as a site for racial reconciliation and redemption. As Hsu (2006, 132–33) notes, the popular movie poster used to advertise Crash shows Ryan and Christine in what, in key ways, looks like an apparent romantic "embrace." One would certainly not gather from the advertisement that Ryan is a man who perhaps as little as a day earlier rapes her. One critic remarks: "The burning-SUV rescue, with its body contortions and spilled fluids, operates as a kind of vicarious miscegenation, essentially allowing Sgt. Ryan (and, presumably, the audience) the desired and dreaded coupling that his earlier roadside finger-f--- only hinted at" (Michael Sicinski, quoted in Hsu 2006, 150). Such popular renderings are fantasies of "miscegenation," according to Carillio Rowe (2007), where miscegenation is the crucible for production of a new "imagined community" founded on understandings of Whiteness that skirt responsibility for structural change to dismantle inequality. As with other melodramatic narratives, it vindicates wounded White masculinity by showing that "the 'villain within' is reformed or the villain turns out to have been the hero all along" (Grindstaff 1994, 55).

Obama's campaign has also depended on a melodramatic miscegenation fantasy, where he comes to embody the type of miscegenation that can move the country beyond racial and other problems. Notably, his 2004 speech at the Democratic national convention, which catapulted him into the national spotlight and generated buzz about his future potential as a presidential candidate, emphasized the "one America" narrative that subsequently became his calling card. He consistently points out his bi-racial lineage and positions himself as embodying the type of one-ness he discusses in his speeches. Obama, then, symbolically and rhetorically becomes the quintessential representation of the success of miscegenation, the racial fantasy that "transgression" of interracial sex taboos can signify a deracialized, reconstituted, yet restabilized gender order. Again, the melodramatic emphasis on personal relationships as the locus for change and national restoration is key. Although Obama has stated that "unity in this country" cannot be "purchased on the cheap" (Obama 2008a), the substance of his bearing and politics offers just that: a symbolic mode of gendered racial reconciliation rooted in essentialized notions of biological racial melding via coupling. "But, I Voted for Obama" will join the chorus of other rhetorical gestures—like "But, my boyfriend is Black" and "I gave money to the NAACP"—designed to identify one's political bonafides.

Miscegenation fantasies are a raced-gendered aspect of post-Civil Rights, postfeminist melodrama that has profound implications for Black politics as a whole and Black feminists politics in particular. In *GA*, *Crash*, and the Obama campaign, Black people are objects through which Whites usher in new modes of oppressive Whiteness and seek to normalize romantic models of White patriarchal relations. These miscegenation fantasies depend, as well, on a studied avoidance of the historical and contemporary realities that surround interracial relationships, particularly those that are sexual. It ignores, for instance, the reality that White desire for Black bodies has been part of a long tradition of exploitation and abuse, of consuming and/ or exoticizing the Other. Most heinously, it contributes to the historical amnesia and political silence we have in the United States concerning the rape of Black women by predatory White men, the ongoing truth that sexual access to Black female bodies has been a hallmark of White masculinity since this country's founding. This seemingly intractable silence solidifies and is a necessary condition for a legal and political structure that positions Black women as always already violable, profane, and inhuman nonsubjects before the State. I am not saying here that the legalization of interracial relationships or the growth in interracial unions does not signal progress in terms of race and gender in the United States. I am asserting, however, that when we highlight such relationships without an understanding of their potential complex race and gender problematics and dynamics, when we use them to symbolize regressive reassertions of race and gender and to figure a redemption of White masculinity and femininity in ways that affirm new modes of racial and gender exploitation, these miscegenation fantasies work to quell our anxieties and transfix our attention on hollow, counterproductive modes of race-gender "comity" (Entman and Rojecki 2001).

Conclusion

The melodramatic mode, with its attention to exaggerated emotion and its figuration of the social and political within interpersonal relations, marked by villains and victims, proves ideal for the post-Civil Rights, postfeminist political formation that has taken shape in the United States since the mid-1960s. The above analysis of *GA*, *Crash*, and the Obama campaign signals common trends and developments within popular culture and political discourse that work to normalize simplistic definitions of equality as residing principally in formal signs of representative equality and undermine efforts at substantive institutional change. These narratives reconstitute familiar raced-gendered codes and stereotypes in ways that are palatable for new generations, rendering our vision of U.S. politics and culture into something we, as viewers and as citizens, want to hold onto, namely, a meritocratic and unified U.S. body politic, functional political institutions and social relationships, and the image of universalism. *GA, Crash*, and the Obama 2008 presidential campaign draw upon racial and gendered discourses that are meant to conserve and reproduce existing power relations, while allowing a few Super Minorities to enter the public sphere. They demonstrate, as well, the mutually constitutive reproduction of race, class, and gender ideologies within culture and politics in the post-Civil Rights, postfeminist melodramatic landscape, one to which students of Black politics and/or feminists must attend if we are to accurately grasp and, hopefully, successfully counteract their operation.

Notes

*   Editors' note: This essay is the winner of the NCOBPS best paper award for 2010.
1.   See Springer (2007), for an excellent discussion of postfeminist Black female stereotypes.
2.   Projansky argues Black women stand "next-to-but-just-outside of postfeminism" (2001, 193). This is true, if dominant, political discourse is the reference point; I recover her insights regarding varieties of postfeminism in explaining its operation in Black politics.
3.   Like Courtney (2005, 295), while I find elements of Williams' study illuminating, her analysis problematically suggests that people are necessarily bound up with racially oriented thinking as it concerns the "Tom" and "anti-Tom" frames she assesses.
4.   Deracialization is a misnomer; the term codes race as Black, leaving Whiteness as an unmarked racial category. For an examination of recent "post-racial" politics, see Gillespie (2010).
5.   For scholars such as Aimee Carillo Rowe (2007) and Hsu (2006), miscegenation fantasies utilize an Africanist Presence as a primary vehicle for channeling and narratively resolving gender and race anxieties about change in ways that rearticulate White racial hierarchy.
6.   See DuCille (1997), for a related discussion of the "browning" of Nicole Simpson.

References

Alexander-Floyd, Nikol G. 2007. *Gender, race, and nationalism in contemporary Black politics.* New York: Palgrave MacMillan.
American Medical Association. 2008. AMA apologizes for history of racial inequality and works to include and promote minority physicians (Press Release), July 10, http://www.ama-assn.org/ama/pb/category/18773.html (accessed August 15, 2008).
Brooks, Peter. [1976] 1995. *The melodramatic imagination: Balzac, Henry James, melodrama, and the mode of excess.* New Haven, CT: Yale University Press.
Carby, Hazel. 1997. White woman listen!: Black feminism and the boundaries of sisterhood. In *Black British feminism: A reader,* ed. Heidi Safia Mirza, 45–53. New York: Routledge.
Collins, Patricia Hill. 2006. *From Black power to hip hop: Racism, nationalism, and feminism.* Philadelphia, PA: Temple University Press.
Condit, Celeste. 1989. The rhetorical limits of polysemy. *Critical Studies in Mass Communication* 6: 103–22.
Courtney, Susan. 2005. *Hollywood fantasies of miscegenation: Spectacular narratives of gender and race, 1903–1967.* Princeton, NJ: Princeton University Press.

Crash. 2005. Directed by Paul Haggis. Santa Monica, CA: Lion's Gate.

Damage Case. 2006. *Grey's Anatomy.* Directed by Rob Com. New York, NY and Burbank, CA: ABC. Episode no. 24, season 2. May 7.

Davis, Angela. 2000. Reflections on the Black woman's role in the community of slaves. In *A turbulent voyage: Readings in African American studies,* ed. Floyd W. Hayes, III, 83–96. San Diego, CA: Collegiate Press.

Dawson, Patricia. 1999. *Forged by the knife: The experience of surgical residency from the perspective of a woman of color.* Seattle, WA: Open Hand Publishing.

DuCille, Anne. 1997. The unbearable darkness of being: "Fresh" thoughts on race, sex, and the Simpsons. In *Birth of a nation'hood: Gaze, script, and spectacle in the O.J. Simpson case,* ed. Toni Morrison and Claudia Brodsky Lacour, 293–338. New York: Pantheon Books.

Ehrenstein, David. 2007. Obama the 'Magic Negro.' *The Los Angeles Times,* March 19, http://www.latimes.com (accessed August 16, 2008).

Entman, Robert M., and Andrew Rojecki. 2001. *The Black image in the White mind: Media and race in America.* Chicago, IL: The University of Chicago Press.

Gillespie, Andra. 2010. *Whose Black politics?: Cases in post-racial Black leadership.* New York: Routledge.

Gray, Herman S. 1995. *Watching race: Television and the struggle for blackness.* Minneapolis: University of Minnesota Press.

Grindstaff, L. A. 1994. Double exposure, double erasure: On the frontline with Anita hill. *Cultural Critique* 27 (Spring): 29–60.

Harris, Rose. 1999. Signifying race and gender in feminist theory. Ph.D. diss., Rutgers University.

Holmes, David G. 2007. The civil rights movement according to *crash*: Complicating the pedagogy of integration. *College English* 69, no. 4: 314–20.

hooks, bell. 1984. *Feminist theory: From margin to center.* Boston, MA: South End Press.

———. 2004. *We real cool: Black men and masculinity.* New York: Routledge.

Hsu, Hsuan L. 2006. Racial privacy, the L.A. Ensemble film, and Paul Haggis's crash. *Film Criticism* 31, no. 1/2: 132–56.

Hurt, Charles. 2008. Jesse Jackson says he wants to cut Obama's 'Nuts Out'. *New York Post,* July 9, http://www.nypost.com (accessed August 16, 2008).

Jordan-Zachery, Julia. 2001. Black womanhood and social welfare policy: The influence of her image on policy making. *Sage Race Relations Abstracts* 26, no. 3: 5–24.

Kelleter, Frank, Barbara Krah, and Ruth Mayer, eds. 2007. The melodramatic mode revisited. An introduction. In *Melodrama!: The mode of excess from early America to Hollywood,* 7–17. Heidelberg: Universitatsverlag.

Kempley, Rita. 2003. Movies' 'Magic Negro' saves the day – but at the cost of his soul. *The Black Commentator,* July 3, http://www.blackcommentator.com/49/49_magic.html (accessed August 16, 2008).

Lipsitz, George. 1997. The greatest story ever sold: Marketing and the O.J. Simpson trial. In *Birth of a nation'hood: Gaze, script, and spectacle in the O.J. Simpson case,* ed. Toni Morrison and Claudia Brodsky Lacour, 3–29. New York: Pantheon Books.

Littlefield, Marci Bounds. 2008. The media as a system of racialization: Exploring images of African American women and the new racism. *American Behavioral Scientist* 51, no. 5: 675–85.

Mack, Melanie. 2006. 'Crash' breaks the mountain at academy awards. *Sentinel,* March 9–15, B4, http://proquest.umi.com (accessed May 9, 2008).

McCormick, Joseph P., II, and Charles E. Jones. 1993. The conceptualization of deracialization: Thinking through the dilemma. In *Dilemmas of Black politics: Issues of leadership and strategy,* ed. Georgia A. Persons, 66–84. New York: Harper Collins College Publishers.

McRobbie, Angela. 2007. Postfeminism and popular culture: Bridget Jones and the new gender regime. In *Interrogating postfeminism: Gender and the politics of popular culture,* ed. Yvonne Tasker and Diane Negra, 27–39. Durham, NC: Duke University Press.

"Medical Association Apologizes for History of Discrimination." 2008. Public Broadcasting Station, originally aired July 10, 2008, http://www.pbs.org (accessed August 15, 2008).

Modleski, Tania. 1991. *Feminism without women: Culture and criticism in a "Postfeminist" age.* New York: Routledge.

Morrison, Toni. 1992. *Playing in the dark: Whiteness and the literary imagination.* Cambridge, MA: Harvard University Press.

Nunley, Vorris L. 2007. SYMPOSIUM: *Crash*: Rhetorically wrecking discourses of race, tolerance, and White privilege. *College English* 69, no. 4: 335–46.

Obama, Barack. [1995] 2004. *Dreams from my father: A story of race and inheritance*. New York: Three Rivers Press.

———. 2006. *The audacity of hope: Thoughts on reclaiming the American dream*. New York: Three Rivers Press.

———. 2008a. Remarks of Senator Barack Obama: The great need of the hour, January 20, http://www.barackobama.com (accessed August 16, 2008).

———. 2008b. A more perfect union (transcript). *National Public Radio*, March 18, https://www.npr.org/templates/story/story.php?storyId=88478467 (accessed August 16, 2008).

———. 2008c. Obama's father's day remarks (transcript). *The New York Times*, June 15, http://www.nytimes.com (accessed August 16, 2008).

Pratt, Mary Louise. 1992. *Imperial eyes: Studies in travel writing and transculturation*. New York: Routledge.

Projansky, Sarah. 2001. *Watching rape: Film and television in postfeminist culture*. New York: New York University Press.

Puwar, Nirmal. 2004. *Space invaders: Race, gender, and bodies out of place*. Oxford: Berg.

Ray, Sangeeta. 2007. *Crash* or how White men save the day, again. *College English* 69, no. 4: 350–54.

Reed, Adolph L., Jr. 2008. "Obama No." *The Progressive*, May, http://www.progressive.org/mag_reed0508 (accessed August 15, 2008).

Rowe, Aimee Carrillo. 2007. Feeling in the dark: Empathy, whiteness, and miscege-nation in *Monster's ball*. *Hypatia* 22, no. 2: 122–42.

Springer, Kimberly. 2007. Divas, evil Black bitches, and bitter Black women: African American women in postfeminist and post-civil-rights popular culture. In *Interrogating postfeminism: Gender and the politics of popular culture*, ed. Yvonne Tasker and Diane Negra, 249–76. Durham, NC: Duke University.

Tasker, Yvonne, and Diane Negra, eds. 2007. *Interrogating postfeminism: Gender and the politics of popular culture*. Durham, NC: Duke University Press.

White, E. Frances. 1990. Africa on my mind: Gender, counter discourse and African-American nationalism. *Journal of Women's History* 2, no. 1: 73–97.

Williams, Linda. 2001. *Playing the race card: Melodramas of Black and White from Uncle Tom to O.J. Simpson*. Princeton, NJ: Princeton University Press.

Black Politics in a Time of Transition, Volume 13; pp. 65-78

Dr. W. E. B. Du Bois: The Intellectual Grandfather of Contemporary African American Studies

Mack H. Jones

Introduction

In my view, Dr. Du Bois was America's most outstanding and socially significant intellectual ever, Black or White. His contributions as a scholar and political activist affected and enlightened practically every segment of American life and culture. For this paper, I choose to discuss his contributions to the development of Black or African American Studies. (Throughout the paper I use the two terms interchangeably.) Although the modern Black Studies movement did not begin until the 1960s, Du Bois made the case for Black Studies in the early days of the twentieth century and actually carried out Black Studies research long before the term was coined. In reality, Du Bois was the father, or perhaps, we might say, the intellectual grandfather of modern African American Studies. To support this assertion I will first identify some of the ideological assumptions and principles of the Black Studies movement and then demonstrate how they were reflected in the scholarship and political activism of Du Bois long before they were articulated by scholars such as Nathan Hare, Maulana Karenga, Molefi Asante, and others. Indeed, Du Bois not only addressed the assumptions and principles that were to characterize the Black Studies movement of the 1960s, but he also raised and expounded on almost all of the ideas and arguments that arose during the broader Black liberation movement of the 1960s and 1970s. Arguments about integration vs. separation, nationalism vs. assimilation, socialism vs. capitalism, male chauvinism vs. feminism, etc., were all addressed by Du Bois half a century earlier. Du Bois not only addressed all of these issues, he did so with clarity and conviction unmatched by many contemporary scholars.

191

Biography

Knowing and understanding Du Bois' biography and how it was shaped by the changing times in which he lived and struggled are critical for understanding his evolution as the intellectual grandfather of modern African American Studies. Given the often repeated assertion that he was an elitist, it is easy to forget that he was not from a privileged or middle-class family. He grew up in a single parent home and never really knew his father. His mother was a frail woman, a domestic who took in ironing from White folks to make ends meet. Du Bois was born in Great Barrington, Massachusetts, a town of some five thousand people including twenty-five to fifty Black folk, in1868, only five years after the end of slavery.[1] He and his mother attended a Congregationalist church where they were the only members of color. After graduating from high school in 1884 as the only Black student in the class, Du Bois entered Fisk in 1885 and graduated in 1888 as the top student in a class of five. While at Fisk for two summers he taught elementary school in rural Tennessee, and it was there that he developed his understanding of the place of Black people in American society. After graduating from Fisk, he entered Harvard in 1888 and received the BA cum laude in 1890 and the MA from Harvard in 1891. He pursued doctoral studies in Germany from 1892 to 1894 but did not receive the doctoral degree because he lacked one year in residence. Du Bois received the doctoral degree from Harvard in 1895. From 1897 to 1910 he served at Atlanta University. He left Atlanta University in 1910 and worked for the National Association for the Advancement of Colored People NAACP where he served on the board of directors and edited the *Crisis* magazine; he resigned from the NAACP in 1934 and returned to Atlanta University as head of the sociology department. Du Bois was retired involuntarily by Atlanta University in 1944 and returned to the NAACP. In 1948, Du Bois was again dismissed from NAACP. After 1948, Du Bois continued to work with a variety of organizations opposed to war and Western imperialism. Du Bois moved to Ghana, West Africa, in 1961 and died there in 1963 while working on his final project, an encyclopedia of Africa.

Ideological Assumptions and Principles of the Black Studies Movement

Black Studies or African American Studies as an academic discipline in American education grew out of struggles of Black students of the 1960s on campuses of both historically Black and traditionally White institutions. During the 1960s students argued that mainstream or White scholarship was irrelevant for those interested in understanding and transforming the position of Blacks in American life because it grew out of the experiences of White or Euro-Americans and was grounded in the ideology of White supremacy. As a consequence, it was argued, mainstream scholarship raised questions and generated information that gave a distorted view of American society and the place of Black folk in it. To overcome this problem, advocates of Black Studies called upon Black scholars to challenge the assumptions of mainstream scholarship and develop new paradigms and frames of reference that would be grounded in the experiences of African people in the United States and around the world. These new frames of reference would ask different questions and generate information that would illuminate more clearly the nature of oppression and suggest more effective strategies for Black liberation.

Relevance, according to the proponents of Black Studies, was not merely an academic matter. Developing new paradigms and frames of reference and conducting research was only half of the responsibility. The other half involved applying this new knowledge in the struggle against racial oppression. *To know* carried with it the responsibility *to do* was the first principle of the Black Studies movement. Thus to satisfy the call for relevance, Black scholars had to be activists as well. There could be no separation between town and gown, between campus and community.

Black Studies advocates were also concerned that Eurocentric scholarship transformed Black students into vulgar careerists concerned only with personal advancement and who assumed no special responsibility for uplifting the race. Thus, relevance required that professors not only produce a scholarship more useful for transforming the conditions of Black folk, but also that professors, strive to produce students who recognized and accepted their roles in the struggle for racial advancement.

Maulana Karenga has asserted that this call for relevance led Black Studies advocates to formulate four distinct objectives:

1. Teach the Black experience in its historical and current unfolding.
2. Assemble and create a body of knowledge that would contribute to intellectual and political emancipation.
3. Create a cadre of Black intellectuals committed to community service.
4. Maintain a mutually beneficial relationship between the campus and community.

Du Bois as a Precursor of the Black Studies Paradigm

Du Bois, through his scholarship and political activism, not only satisfied these objectives, he also addressed topics that have become hot-button issues in our time, issues such as feminism and imperialism. He was the quintessential model of the African-centered professor. Let me demonstrate. I will do so by first discussing his argument for a distinct African-centered frame of reference. I will then discuss his application of that frame of reference in his works on Africa and his classic, *Black Reconstruction in America*. I will also highlight the link between his scholarship and his activism by examining his conflict with Booker T. Washington.

According to proponents of Black Studies, all efforts to know and explain the world, to explain social reality, begin necessarily with a set of prior assumptions about the nature of that reality. The assumptions that people, including scholars, have about their social reality, are derived from their societal worldview. Immersed in the compelling assumptions of the dominant world view, the argument continues, academicians in the social and cultural sciences develop conceptual frameworks and paradigms that give rise to studies that reinforce dominant ideas and power relations. Mainstream American or White Studies, according to Black Studies advocates, are grounded in the Euro-American worldview and constructed within frames of reference that serve the interests of those in power. Such studies produce a distorted Eurocentric view of social reality, a view that reinforces the global domination of European people. To be relevant, therefore, the first and critical task of Black Studies was the development of an alternative African-centered perspective that would issue from an African worldview and give rise to questions and develop responses as prescribed by the experiences of African people. Asante, Karenga, Carruthers, Stewart, and others have made valuable contributions toward the development of African-centered conceptual schemes, but they were preceded by Du Bois.

Du Bois, like all of his contemporaries, was initially trained in institutions grounded in Eurocentric perspectives. However, he was not oblivious to the disconnect between the life experiences of African Americans and the assumptions of Eurocentric scholarship. Indeed he spent his professional life actively disabusing himself of his Eurocentric educational beginnings. Some of his early works such as "Jefferson Davis as Representative of Civilization," "The Conservation of Races," *Souls of Black Folk*, "First Universal Races Congress," and "Criteria of Negro Art," all written between 1890 and 1926, reveal a growing African-focused racial consciousness. Several of the essays in *Souls*, including "Spiritual Strivings," "Of the Dawn of Freedom," "Of the Meaning of Progress," and "Of the Training of Black Men," are clearly African-centered contributions. By the time he published *Black Reconstruction in America*, in 1935, his scholarship was clearly African centered. However, as far as I have been able to ascertain, Du Bois did not address directly, at least in print, the issue of epistemology, perspective, and frames of reference. He did, however, address such issues in the context of his exegesis on the role and responsibility of the Black college. The Black college, Du Bois argued, was to give students an African-centered understanding of the world and prepare them for political action. In a 1933 address to the Fisk alumni, as I will explain below, he enunciated this epistemological stance.

The 1933 address was given in the-then still ongoing debate about the optimum education and training for Black students and the appropriate role for Black colleges. By that time, Du Bois had witnessed the largely successful efforts of White industrialists and philanthropists of the Mohonk conferences of 1890 and 1891 to make vocational training the center piece of Black education and he had suffered the consequences of challenging Booker T. Washington who became the embodiment of the Mohonk doctrine; and he had also witnessed and participated in the debate over the proper focus of "Negro Art."

Apparently, the address to the Fisk alumni was designed to make the case that Fisk should remain a full-blown university in the traditional meaning of the term. But, the address went much further than that. In it Du Bois raised fundamental epistemological questions about the role of culture and worldviews in the process of knowing and the role and responsibility of individuals and institutions that generate and teach knowledge. Essentially, Du Bois argued that all knowledge grows out of the strivings of the people involved in its creation and that, therefore, all knowledge is parochial. In his view, there is no such thing as universal understanding apart from the effort to understand the universal through the process of understanding the particulars that give rise to a certain instant in the struggle to know. From these thoughts emerge the clearest statement of the nature of, and need for, African-centered education that I have encountered in his writings.

Writing in 1933, Du Bois argued that the American Negro problem must be the center of the Negro American University. After pointing out, as an example, that the Spanish university is founded in Spain and uses the Spanish language, he says "It starts with Spanish history and makes conditions in Spain the starting point of its teaching. Its education is for Spaniards - not for them as they may or ought to be but as they are with their present problems and disadvantages and opportunities"(Weinberg 1970, 179). In the same vein, his argument continues:

> A Negro university in the United States of America begins with Negroes. It uses that variety of the English idiom which they understand; and above all, it is founded or it should be founded on a knowledge of the history of their people in Africa and in the United States, and their present condition. Without whitewashing or translating wish into fact, it begins with that; and then it asks how shall these young men and women be trained to earn a living and live a life under the circumstance in which they find themselves or with such changing of those circumstances as time and work and determination will permit. (Weinberg 1970, 179)

Du Bois' admonition that the Black university should be founded on a knowledge of the history of Africa and Blacks in America made him one of the first Afrocentric scholars if we accept that"'Afrocentric'...means essentially viewing social and human reality from an African perspective or stand point"(Karenga 1993, 35). One could argue, of course, that one could begin with Africa but that the beginning could still flow from Eurocentric assumptions, but Du Bois made it clear that he was arguing for an African-centered approach. He continued:

> ...starting with the present conditions and using the facts and the knowledge of the present situation of American Negroes, the Negro University expands toward the possession and conquest of all knowledge. It seeks from a beginning of the history of the Negro in America and in Africa to interpret all history; from a beginning of social development among Negro slaves and freedmen in America and Negro tribes and kingdoms in Africa, to interpret and understand the social development of all mankind in all ages. It seeks to teach modern science of matter and life from the surroundings and habits and aptitudes of American Negroes and thus lead up to understanding life and matter in the universe.

...it is a matter of beginnings and integrations of one group which sweep instinctive knowledge and inheritance and current reactions into a universal world of science, sociology, and art. In no other way can the American Negro College function. It cannot begin with history and lead to Negro history. It cannot start with sociology and lead to Negro sociology (Weinberg 1970, 181).

The foregoing excerpt is a clear and cogent statement of the nature of, need for, and defense of, an Afrocentric approach to knowing. Du Bois acknowledged the difficulty of developing such an enterprise because he said "... it asks that teachers teach that which they have learned in no American school and which they never will learn until we have a Negro university of the sort that I am visioning" (Weinberg 1970, 183).

When Du Bois advanced the idea that a relevant education for Black people must be African centered, he was just beginning to educate himself on the history of African peoples. In 1915 he had published a slender volume called "The Negro" which he said some time later "... gave evidence of a certain naive astonishment on my own part at the wealth of fact and material concerning the Negro peoples, the very existence of which I had myself known little despite a varied university career" (*World and Africa* 1965, vii). In 1939, an expanded version was published as *Black Folk Then and Now*. Du Bois' most complete work on the subject, *The World and Africa*, was published in 1946 and later enlarged and republished in 1965, two years after his death. In writing *The World and Africa*, Du Bois drew on an extensive inventory of previously published and unpublished manuscripts. In the foreword, he offers a running critique of the various works that he used, taking care to point out the works that disrespected or devalued the African experience. And he made clear that he imposed his own African-centered perspective on the factual information that he had gleaned from other sources.

Du Bois admitted that he might not have had the ideal academic background and training for embarking on the important task of writing an African-centered history of African peoples but inasmuch as no one else had assumed the responsibility he felt it a duty to do so. As he put it:

> With meager preparation and all too general background of learning, I have essayed a task, which, to be adequate and complete, should be based upon the research of a lifetime! But I am faced with the dilemma, that either I do this now or leave it for others who have not had the tragedy of life which I have, forcing me to face a task for which they may have small stomach and little encouragement from the world round about.
>
> If, out of my almost inevitable mistakes and inaccuracies and false conclusions, I shall have at least clearly stated my main issue - that Black Africans are men in the same sense as white European and yellow [sic] Asiatics, and that history can easily prove this-then I shall rest satisfied even under the stigma of an incomplete and, to many, inconclusive work. (Du Bois 1965, xii)

Du Bois' concern with African-centered knowledge went beyond issues of epistemology and extended to the institutionalization of an African-centered approach to knowing. For him, the Black college was the appropriate agency for generating and teaching an African-centered understanding of social reality and for using that knowledge to transform the life conditions of African people. After short stints at Wilberforce and the University of Pennsylvania, in 1897 he joined the faculty of Atlanta University, a private Black university, and remained there until 1910; he served a second tenure at Atlanta University from 1934 to 1944. Before Du Bois came to Atlanta University, two other Black colleges, Tuskegee and Hampton, had become the designated institutions for studying and devising uplift programs for the rural Black population. Du Bois was brought to Atlanta University to start a similar program focusing on urban Blacks.

To fulfill this responsibility, in 1897, Du Bois inaugurated a Black Studies research project that has yet to be matched for its scope and depth. As a centerpiece of their efforts, Tuskegee and Hampton held annual conferences. Workers, experts, and observers came to exchange ideas about the predicament and promise of rural Blacks. Atlanta University held a similar urban-focused conference in 1896, the year immediately preceding the appointment of Du Bois. Prior to his coming, according to Du Bois, the conferences were primarily meetings of inspiration directed toward social reform and propaganda for social uplift (Du Bois 1968, 214). Du Bois changed the focus of the Atlanta University Studies to systematic, scientific studies of the entire Black population. He proposed a ten-year cycle of studies of various dimensions of the problems of Black people. Basic data would be collected and updated every ten years. This would eventually yield, Du Bois thought, a comprehensive scientific description and analysis of the Black predicament which could be used continuously to inform strategies and programs for racial uplift. The focus and content of all of the studies grew out of his African-centered perspective. The sixteen works completed as parts of the Atlanta University Studies remain as examples of the research possibilities of Black Studies. A listing of the titles of some of them will reinforce this point.

Mortality Among Negroes in Cities
Social and Physical Conditions of Negroes in Cities
The Negro in Business
The College Bred Negro
The Negro Church
Notes on Negro Crime
The Negro American Family
Economic Cooperation among Negro Americans

The decision to limit the Atlanta University project to the production of scientific studies of the Black condition did not mean that Du Bois forsook the Black Studies objective of linking the production and application of knowledge to social uplift programs; nor did it mean that he was unsupportive of establishing and sustaining mutually supportive links between the campus and the community. Perhaps the best example of Du Bois' effort to link the production and application of knowledge was his proposal submitted in 1942 to the organization of Negro Land Grant Colleges for the establishment of coordinating structures through which the Black land grant college of each southern state would undertake continuous studies of the " ... facts concerning the Negroes of the State by counties, subdivision of counties, villages, towns, cities, wards, blocks, and households" (Du Bois 1968, 315). Each university would establish a division of social sciences and develop curriculums appropriate for carrying out the research. Arrangements would be made with northern colleges to carry out similar research on Blacks in the North. A national planning institute would gather and interpret this extensive body of data that, in turn, could be used by interested parties for racial advancement. Practically all institutions of the Black community including churches, lodges, sororities and fraternities, business groups, health professionals, etc., would be involved in the enterprise. The idea was based on the assumption "...that if the college is to make real and advantageous approach to its community, either its local or its general community, it must be helped by a careful, broad and continuous study of the social and economic set-up of that community" (*Autobiography* 1968, 313).

The Du Bois proposal was actually accepted by the presidents of the Black land grant colleges and the first conference of the Negro land grant colleges for coordinating a program for cooperative social studies was held in Atlanta on April 19–20, 1943.

Unfortunately, for reasons not yet clear, at least to me, Du Bois was forced to retire by the president of Atlanta University in 1944 and his ambitious effort did not survive his departure.

In addition to offering epistemological clarity on the nature and purpose of African-centered knowledge and working for the institutionalization of Black Studies, Du Bois and his scholarship were supportive of the other objectives specified by advocates of Black Studies. His research always portrayed the Black experience in its historical and current unfolding and his scholarship was always driven by his desire to contribute to the intellectual and political emancipation of Black people. His disposition toward that end was best summed up in his statement regarding "Negro" art. He avowed," I stand in utter shamelessness and say that whatever art I have for writing has been used always for propaganda for gaining the right of black folk to love and enjoy. I do not care a damn for any art that is not used for propaganda. But I do care when propaganda is confined to one side while the other is stripped and silent" (Huggins 1996, 1000).

His seminal work, *Black Reconstruction,* is a prime example of his efforts to place the Black experience in its historical context and contemporary unfolding while, at the same time, contributing to the intellectual and political emancipation of the race. Black Reconstruction was an analysis of Reconstruction from an African centered or Black perspective and it was written to refute mainstream White supremacist interpretations and to celebrate the contribution of African Americans in that turbulent period. Prior to writing *Black Reconstruction,* Du Bois and other Black scholars had challenged the racist interpretations of White historians of the era, but their challenge had received only marginal attention. In 1929, the editor of Encyclopedia Britannica had refused to publish Du Bois' article on Reconstruction because Du Bois insisted on including two sentences that informed readers that "*White historians have ascribed the faults and failures of Reconstruction to Negro ignorance and corruption. But the Negro insists that it was Negro loyalty and the Negro vote alone that restored the South to the Union, established the new Democracy, both for black and white, and instituted public schools*" (found in Lewis, 1995, ix). That shows the partisan nature of White scholarship on Reconstruction.

The publication of *Black Reconstruction* should be seen as an African-centered counterattack in a war to ascribe meaning to this pregnant historical moment and influence the future course of events as the emancipated Black nation struggled for survival. In a special note "To the Reader," Du Bois opened the book by stating categorically that *Black Reconstruction* was based on his African-centered assumptions about the equality and humanity of African people. He acknowledged that those who did not share his views would not be persuaded by his argument and that he would make no effort to change their minds. Specifically he asserted:

> It would be only fair to the reader to say frankly in advance that the attitude of any person toward this story will be distinctly influenced by his theories of the Negro race. If he believes that the Negro in America and in general is an average ordinary human being, who under given environment develops like other human beings, then he will read this story and judge it by the facts adduced. If, however he regards the Negro as a distinctly inferior creation, who can never successfully take part in modern civilization and whose emancipation and enfranchisement were gestures against nature, then he will need something more than the sort of facts that I have set down. But this latter person, I am not trying to convince. I am simply pointing out these two points of view, so obvious to Americans, and then without further ado, I am assuming the truth of the first. (Du Bois 1995)

He then proceeded to publish a seventeen chapter, 746 page volume that not only completely recast and reinterpreted the period but also included analyses and assessments of individual historians and their scholarship based upon their attitudes toward Black people. *Black Reconstruction*, in my view, remains a model of African-centered scholarship.

Each chapter of Black Reconstruction opens with an epigram that previews the substantive message of the chapter and in the process highlights the African centeredness of his approach. A brief listing of some of the epigrams will reinforce this point.

Chapter 1 the Black Worker
How Black men, coming to America in the sixteenth, seventeenth, eighteenth, and nineteenth centuries, became a central thread in the history of the United States, at once a challenge to its democracy and always an important part of its economic history and social development.

Chapter 2 the White Worker
How America became the laborer's Promised Land; and flocking here from all over the world the White workers competed with Black slaves, with new floods

of foreigners, and with growing exploitation, until they fought slavery to save democracy and then lost democracy in a new and vaster slavery.

Chapter 3 the Planter

How 7 percent of a section within a nation ruled five million White people and owned four million Black people and sought to make agriculture equal to industry through the rule of property without yielding political power or education to labor.

Chapter 5 the Coming of the Lord

How the Negro became free because the North could not win the Civil War if he remained in slavery. And how arms in his hands and the prospects of arms in a million more Black hands, brought peace and emancipation to America.

Chapter 16 Back Toward Slavery

How civil war in the South began again—indeed had never ceased; and how Black Prometheus bound to the Rock of Ages by hate, hurt, and humiliation, has his vitals eaten out as they grow yet lives and fights.

Chapter 17 the Propaganda of History

How the facts of American history have in the last half century been falsified because the nation was ashamed. The South was ashamed because it fought to perpetuate human slavery. The North was ashamed because it had to call in the Black men to save the Union, abolish slavery, and establish democracy.

In the bibliography at the end of the volume, Du Bois categorized the entries according to their position on the question of the humanity of African people. He called them out by name. For example, one group was designated as Standard-Anti-Negro authors who believe the Negro to be subhuman; another group of scholars was listed as Propaganda, authors who select and use facts and opinions in order to prove the South was right in Reconstruction, North vengeful or deceived and the Negro stupid.

Of course, based on ideological presuppositions one might challenge the conceptualization, orientation, structure, or content of *Black Reconstruction*. African centeredness, as Karenga has reminded us, is a quality of thought rooted in the interests of African people. It is an orientation, and not a dogma of authenticity through which we may struggle to know the world. Du Bois' *Black Reconstruction* is an exemplar in this regard.

Next, let me turn to two themes that are frequently addressed in contemporary Black Studies: feminism or the woman question, and the question of the role and predicament of African people in international affairs. On both of these, Du Bois presaged contemporary thinkers. On the woman question, as Lewis has pointed out, Du Bois was an acknowledged pioneer (Lewis 2000, 12). On the other hand, his personal and professional relationships with women were far short of the ideal reflected in his writings. Du Bois gave his own assessment of his relationship with women in the autobiography in the chapter entitled "My Character" (Du Bois 1968).

In his writings, Du Bois discussed and praised the contributions of women to human growth and development, argued against extant negative stereotypes, and supported women's rights, especially the right to vote.

He was especially effusive in his defense of, and praise for, Black women. His essay, "The Damnation of Women," published in 1920, was perhaps his most elegant statement on the issue. Lamenting the general problems of women, he offers a poignant statement that placed the woman question in its universal context: "All womanhood is hampered today because the world on which it is emerging is a world that tries to worship both virgins and mothers and in the end despises motherhood and despoils virgins." He goes on to show how sexism and the derivative stereotypes deny women opportunities for their full development and how, in turn, the subordination of women retards overall human growth and development. He argues that the future woman must have a life work and economic independence.

In praise of Black mothers, Du Bois notes that Africa gave the world what he called the mother-idea. It appears, he said, "...the great black race in passing up the steps of human culture gave the world, not only the Iron Age, the cultivation of soil, and the domestication of animals, but also, in peculiar emphasis, the mother-idea"(Lewis 1995, 301). After detailing the critical role played by women in different African societies and the respect accorded them, he notes how the crushing weight of slavery fell on Black women, and he links in a causal fashion the degradation of Black women with many of the problems faced by Black people in American society. Du Bois concluded that "The uplift of women is, next to the problem of the color line and the peace movement, our greatest modern cause. When, now, two of these movements - women and color combine in one, the combination has deep meaning" (Lewis 1995, 309).

On the political scene, Du Bois supported the Suffrage Movement and he took to task those in opposition, dismissing their arguments as ancient. For example, in 1915, as the editor of *Crisis* he published an essay opposing women suffrage by the noted Howard University dean, Kelly Miller. He then published his own rejoinder calling Miller's argument sheer rot. He said "It is the same sort of thing that we hear about the 'darker races' and 'lower classes.' Difference, either physical or spiritual, does not argue weakness or inferiority" he fumed.

The aggressiveness and assertiveness that Du Bois displayed in support of women was equally apparent in his devotion to Pan-Africanism.

Du Bois was a lifelong Pan-Africanist. Dating back to his first major work, Suppression of the African Slave Trade, he recognized the negative impact that Europe and North America had on the growth and development of Africa and African peoples. Beginning with the first Pan-African Conference of 1900 and continuing throughout his life, Du Bois sought to create a united front of African people, both from the Continent and the Diaspora, to resist Western imperialism. His position on the role and predicament of African people in international affairs was built on at least six major assumptions: (1) prior to the fifteenth century, African and Asian civilizations far outstripped that of Europe; (2) European imperialism dating back to the fourteenth century, particularly the slave trade, stunted the growth and development possibilities of Africa and African people; (3) the discovery of "whiteness," a modern notion dating back only to the nineteenth century, resulted from the need of Europeans to rationalize and justify their exploitation of people or color; (4) following the Second World War, Europe and North America became coequal partners in the exploitation of people of color; (5) African people in the United States and elsewhere in the Americas and on the continent share a common fate and should develop a united resistance to Western imperialism; (6) only through some form of socialism can African people become independent.

His description of the international predicament of African people changed as his understanding of imperialism evolved. Drawing on his letter to Nkrumah to mark Ghana's independence and two speeches he prepared during the last decade of his life, we can begin to reconstruct his final position on the question. One speech was prepared to be delivered at the 1957 Ghanaian independence celebration. The other was delivered in China in 1958 where he celebrated his ninety-first birthday. Parenthetically, it should be noted that Du Bois recognized that his earlier Pan-African work had been paternalistic. He confessed apologetically in his address from China that "Once I thought of you Africans as children, whom we educated Afro-Americans would lead to liberty. I was wrong. We could not even lead ourselves, much less you" (Du Bois 1968, 406).

In a letter to Kwame Nkrumah, the Ghanaian president, and the speech read by his wife to the Ghanaian independence celebration, Du Bois declared that Ghana must be the representative of Africa and exhorted Nkrumah to adopt what he referred to as Pan-African Socialism, a system that would seek to establish the welfare state in Africa. It would seek to develop a new African economy and cultural center standing between Europe and Asia taking from each that which could be helpful. It would avoid subjection to and ownership by foreign capitalist who seek to get rich from African labor and raw material. "It should try to build a socialism founded on old African communal life, rejecting the private initiative of the West..." (Du Bois 1968, 400).

Nkrumah was urged to pursue a Pan-Africanism that would seek to preserve its own past history:

> and write the present account, erasing from literature the lies and distortions about black folk which have disgraced the last centuries of European and American literature; above all the new Pan-Africa will seek the education of all its youth on the broadest possible basis without religious dogma and in all hospitable lands as well as in Africa for the end of making Africans not simply profitable workers for industry nor stool-pigeons for propaganda, but for making them modern, intelligent, responsible men of vision and character. (Du Bois 1968, 400)

Du Bois was especially concerned that the newly independent Africans would not opt for temporary advantage—automobiles, refrigerators, and Paris gowns—spending income in paying on borrowed money instead of sacrificing present comfort for economic independence. He cautioned Pan-Africanists to realize that as buyers of capital goods they were not helpless because the imperialist sellers would have to either sell or face bankruptcy. "You can wait. You can starve a while longer rather than sell your great heritage for a mess of western capitalistic pottage" (Du Bois 1968, 403).

The speech given in China in 1958 was somewhat unusual inasmuch as it was addressed to the peoples of China, Africa, and African Americans. In it he commented briefly on the history of Western exploitation of China, the continuing exploitation of African Americans, and the collusion of the White American worker and owners of capital in maintaining the system. He suggested that Africans and African Americans had been indoctrinated to believe that development is possible only through capitalist exploitation. This he said "… is a lie. It is an ancient lie spread by the church and state, spread by priest and historian, and believed in by fools and cowards, as well as by the downtrodden and the children of despair" (Du Bois 1968, 405). The Chinese, he asserted, know this but Africa and African Americans had yet to learn it.

Regarding relationships between newly independent Africa and America, including African Americans, Du Bois said that he was "…frightened by the so-called friends who are flocking to Africa. Negro Americans trying to make money from your toil, white Americans who seek by investment and high interest to bind you in serfdom to business as the Near East is bound and as South America is struggling with. For this America is tempting your leaders, bribing your young scholars, and arming your soldiers. What shall you do?" (Du Bois 1968, 406–7). He encouraged Africans to come to China and look around. To Africans he exhorted:

> China is flesh of your flesh, and blood of your blood. China is colored and knows to what a colored skin in this modern world subjects its owner. But China knows more, much more than this: she knows what to do about it. She can take the insults of the United States and still hold her head high. She can make her own machines, when America refuses to sell to her American manufactures, even though it hurts American industry, and throws her workers out of jobs. China does not need American nor British missionaries to teach her religion and scare her with tales of hell. China has been in hell too long, not to believe in a heaven of her own making. This she is doing. (Du Bois 1968, 407).

Finally let me turn to the Du Bois–Washington conflict and demonstrate how the role played by Du Bois reflected his commitment to the objectives advocated by proponents of Black Studies. Recall that advocates were implored to not only study the world through an African-centered perspective but to also to act based on what they had come to know. The conflict between Mr. Washington and Du Bois was not simply a dispute between two men. Rather the conflict was about the gravest question facing the United States at that time: what to do about, to, or for the newly freed population. Remember we are speaking of the last decade of the nineteenth and the first decade of the twentieth century. At that time, even though Reconstruction had ended, African Americans were desperately clinging to the tenuous political beachhead that they had forged during Reconstruction. A smattering of Black elected officials remained in the US Congress and in state and local governments. Blacks still owned significant parcels of land and some still had the vote. The Ku Klux Klan (KKK) and other terrorists were using violence and economic intimidation to drive Blacks off the land and out of the political arena. Given the stark imbalance of power between the two forces, Mr. Washington and others assumed the inevitability of White domination and counseled Black folk to cease agitating for political rights, give up on the idea for college education for Black youth, and settle for vocational or industrial training and concentrate on economic development.

The position assumed by Mr. Washington, however, was not unique to him, nor did it begin with him. It was the position advocated by an imposing segment of the White ruling classes, captains of industry and commerce, philanthropists, and educators—that had assumed responsibility for charting the course for the development of the African American community. With their support, Mr. Washington became the most powerful Black leader of his times. He became the gatekeeper for the Black community. A nod from him could determine the fate of individuals and institutions that depended upon government or philanthropic support, and his power was used by him and his patrons to punish those who challenged the imposed orthodoxy. It was in that context that Du Bois wrote his essay: "Of Mr. Booker T. Washington and Others."

That essay was a systematic analysis of the evolution of the Black predicament in America and of the struggle for transforming it. Du Bois places Washington and the Tuskegee machine in an insightful historical and systemic context and offers a logically consistent reason for opposing them. He argued in 1903 that over the past fifteen years, Mr. Washington had asked Black people to give up three things: (1) political power, (2) insistence on civil rights, and (3) higher education of Negro youth. The return, Du Bois insisted, had been (1) the disfranchisement of the Negro, (2) the legal creation of a distinct status of civil inferiority for the Negro, and (3) the steady withdrawal of aid from institutions of higher training for the Negro. Du Bois argued that without political power and an educated leadership class there would be no way to protect nascent Black economic development.

Du Bois concluded his argument by asserting that it was his duty and responsibility and the duty and responsibility of all who shared his view to oppose the forces represented by Mr. Washington. If they did not do so, he averred:

> ...the thinking classes of American Negroes would shirk a heavy responsibility, a responsibility to themselves, a responsibility to the struggling masses, a responsibility to the darker races of men whose future depends so largely on this American experiment. ... it is wrong to encourage a man or a people in evil-doing; it is wrong to aid and abet a national crime simply because it is unpopular not to do so.... We have no right to sit silently by while the inevitable seeds are sown for a harvest of a disaster to our children, black and white. (Du Bois 1989, 47)

Du Bois did not limit his opposition to the written word. In 1905, he started the Niagara movement to "oppose firmly present methods of strangling honest criticisms; to organize intelligent honest Negroes; and to support organs of news and public opinion."The Niagara movement eventually gave way to the National Association for the Advancement of Colored People and a new chapter in the struggle for racial equality. This was an example of African-centered scholarship and activism at its finest.

Note

1. Editors' note: The Emancipation Proclamation was signed in 1863, but slavery was not formally ended, throughout the country until after the end of the Civil War in 1865, the same year that the Thirteenth Amendment was passed.

References

Du Bois, W. E. B. 1965. *The world and Africa*. New York: International Publishers.

———. 1968. *The autobiography of W. E. B. Du Bois*. New York: International Publishers.

———. 1989. *The souls of Black folk*. New York: Penguin Books.

———. 1995 [1935]. *Black Reconstruction in America*. New York: Simon and Shuster.

———. 1999. *Darkwater*. Mineola, NY: Dover.

Huggins, Nathan, ed. 1996. *Du Bois writings*. New York: Library of America

Karenga, Maulana. 1993. *Introduction to Black studies*. 2nd ed. Los Angeles, CA: Sankore Press.

Lewis, David, ed. 1993. *W. E. B. Du Boi: Biography of a race, 1868–1919*. New York: Henry Holt.

———. 1995. *W. E. B. Du Bois: A Reader*. New York Henry Holt.

———. 2000. *W. E. B. Du Bois, the fight for equality and the American century 1919–1938*. New York: Henry Holt.

Stewart, James. 1984. The legacy of W. E. B. Du Bois for contemporary Black studies. *Journal of Negro Education* 53, no. 3: 296–311.

Weinberg, Meyer, ed. 1970. *W. E. B. Du Bois: A reader*. New York: Harper and Row.

Black Politics in a Time of Transition, Volume 13; pp. 111-114

The Politics of Ethnic Incorporation and Avoidance: The Elections and Presidencies of John F. Kennedy and Barack Obama

Robert C. Smith

Irecently completed the book-length manuscript, *The Politics of Ethnic In-corporation and Avoidance: The Elections and Presidencies of John F. Kennedy and Barack Obama.* From the time it appeared likely that Obama would become the first Black president, I knew I would write a book on his election and presidency. Beginning with my dissertation in 1976, I have devoted much of my research to describing and trying to understand the consequences of the processes of incorporation of Black leaders into the political system. Viewing these processes as a near-inevitable outcome of the civil rights movement, an abiding concern of my research for more than three decades has been that these processes also would inevitably result in the marginal-ization of the Black poor, leaving them leaderless and the processes of their full incorporation into the society stalled. The Obama "phenomenon," as it has been frequently labeled, reinforced this concern. Thus, while rejoicing in and contributing to Obama's election, I told anyone who would listen that his election and presidency could likely be good for America; good for the system but probably bad for Black people because it would likely reinforce the already powerful illusion that racism is no longer a significant barrier to the full incorporation of the African American ethnic community. Related to this illusion, Gary Wills writing of JFK's election recalls "the old story: for 'one of your own' to get elected, he must go out of his way to prove he is not *just* one of your own. The first Catholic President had to be secular to the point (as we used to say in Catholic schools) of supererogation" (1982, 61). In Obama's case "supererogation" would require him—probably more so than Kenne-dy—to lean over backwards so as not to appear to be doing anything "for his own" people.

Given this understanding, the problem became how to go about the work, theoretically and methodologically. Knowing that in the decades ahead there will be countless books on Obama, I wanted to craft a work that would be innovative and enduring. And, as with all of my work, I wished it to contribute—to the extent academic work can—to the full and complete liberation of Black people. In *We Have No Leaders*, my penultimate work on post civil rights era Black politics, I state two interrelated propositions that provide a partial theoretical grounding and a methodological point of departure for study of Obama's election and presidency.

Proposition I: In the post civil rights era virtually all of the talent and resources of the leadership of Black America has been devoted to integration into the institutions of the American society and polity. Meanwhile the core community that they would purport to lead has become increasingly segregated and isolated, and its society, economy, culture and institutions of internal uplift and governance have decayed (Smith 1996, 278).

Proposition II: Compared to the experience of other ethnic groups in the United States this situation is near unprecedented. The integration or incorporation of Irish, Jewish, Polish and Italian American leaders into the institutions of the society and polity roughly paralleled the integration of their communities as a whole (Smith 1996, 279).

These two propositions suggested a historical, comparative study of the elections and presidencies of Kennedy and Obama, the first two "ethnic"— non-White Anglo-Saxon Protestant Americans elected president. To further ground the study theoretically I decided to use Michael Hechter's theory of ethnic, cultural, economic, and political incorporation. Hechter (1975) developed his theory in research on the "Celtic fringe" in British national development; specifically to explain why Wales and Scotland were incorporated into the United Kingdom while Ireland followed the course of nationalism and independence. The explanation for these differential patterns of ethnicity is the greater extent of subordination of the Catholic Irish, and as Hechter puts it, to "the especially brutal policies perpetrated by the English and Anglo-Saxon settlers in Ireland" (1975, 270). Although developed to explain ethnic politics in the British Isles, I adapt Hechter's theory to explain the differential patterns of Catholic Irish and African American subordination and incorporation in the United States.

The actual research involved a year or so of what Wildavsky (1989, chap. 3) called "Reading with a Purpose" in the literatures on Catholic Irish and African American subordination, and the subsequent processes of full incorporation for the former and semi-incorporation of the latter. This literature is extensive and a good bit of is directly concerned with comparing the Catholic Irish and African American experiences. There is also an extensive literature on Kennedy and the 1960 election. The major weakness of the study is the relative paucity of literature on Obama, the 2008 election, and his presidency. But this is unavoidable in all studies of the phenomenon at this point. This work along with the many others in-progress will contribute to remedying this weakness. I suspect these other works will both confirm and challenge the central findings of this study.

Appendix

The Politics of Ethnic Incorporation and Avoidance: The Elections and Presidencies of John F. Kennedy and Barack Obama

List of Chapters

Introduction

Chapter 1   Understanding Ethnicity and Ethnic Incorporation In the United States

Chapter 2   Comparing the Subordination of Irish Catholics And African Americans

Chapter 3   Identity, Solidarity and Culture: Irish Catholics And African Americans

Chapter 4   Boston and Chicago and the Rise of Kennedy and Obama

Chapter 5   Ethnic Men: The Al Smith and Jesse Jackson Campaigns

Chapter 6   The Incorporation of the Catholic Irish, and the Semi-Incorporation of African Americans

Chapter 7   Kennedy and Obama: Charisma, Character and Ethnic Identity

Chapter 8   The Paradox of Religion and Race in the 1960 and 2008 Elections

Chapter 9   The Politics of Ethnic Avoidance in the Kennedy and Obama Administrations

Chapter 10   Conclusion

References

Hechter, Michael. 1975. *Internal colonialism: The Celtic fringe in British national development, 1536–1966.* Berkeley: University of California Press.

Smith, Robert C. 1996. *We have no leader: African Americans in the post Civil Rights era.* Albany: State University of New York Press.

Wildavsky, Aaron. 1989. *Craftways: On the organization of scholarly work.* New Brunswick, NJ: Transaction Publishers.

Wills, Gary. 1982. *The Kennedy imprisonment: A meditation on power.* New York: Pocket Books.

Change Is on the Way!

Georgia A. Persons

The contemporary variant of African-American politics has evolved from successive breakthroughs that were the political legacies of the Civil Rights Movement. The Civil Rights Movement mobilized Black America at the mass level, and helped to galvanize a loosely organized but sizeable biracial coalition that subsequently supported an impressive array of political breakthroughs. These included the election of Lyndon B. Johnson in 1964, the Civil Rights Acts of 1964 and 1968, and the Great Society Program of the Johnson administration. These breakthroughs were major contributors to significantly expanding the ranks of the black middle class and in securing blacks their place in the American mainstream. The Voting Rights Act was the premier policy victory to emerge from the successes of the Civil Rights Movement in terms of helping to shape and institutionalize a sizeable black political class. The Voting Rights Act of 1965 had a significantly transformative effect in that it led to an enormous expansion in the number of black elected officials nationwide, an expansion that has spanned some four decades. These developments have been manifestations of deep social change in a nation that, relatively recently, was defined by enforced racial segregation and the formalized subordination of the African American population. Whatever might be its shortcomings, contemporary black politics has been a highly successful social and political movement.

Yet, at least since the 1990s, many analysts of black politics have alternated between lamenting the failings of black politics, and pronouncing its demise. Much of the lamentations seem to have derived from disappointments with the incomplete victory of black politics in that it has not resulted in a broader transformation of the economic status of Black America—given the persistently large gap between white and black income and wealth, and given the growing economic black underclass. For many analysts, black politics has lost its defining, quasi-revolutionary zeal and has become too much a part of status-quo politics. The strategy of deracialization has been met with considerable mixed sentiments. These sentiments have vacillated between group pride in achieving an increased number of BEOs in higher-level positions, and strategic concerns about the loss of "a black agenda" that might be the legacy of this strategy. These concerns about the loss of a black agenda have not been set aside by the enormity of pride and joy in the election of Barack Obama as the first African American president of the United States. Indeed, the Obama presidency is the apotheosis of the deracialization strategy. Joining the debate about how best to evaluate the Obama presidency is beyond the scope of this project. However, one observation that is most appropriately made here is that Obama's election as president is a reflection of broad based social change in America, at the heart of which is significant change in the composition of the electorate.

There are two significant threads of change in the American electorate, both tied to ongoing demographic changes in the U. S. population at large, and both of which have implications for the future dynamics of black politics. One is that the U.S. population and subsequently the electorate are transitioning away from an historic and predominantly black-white racial dichotomy. The major change is in the direction of a more diverse, multicultural population and electorate. Indeed, the 2008 electorate was the most racially diverse in U.S. history, with each of the three largest minority groups—African Americans, Hispanics, and Asians each accounting for unprecedented shares of the 2008 presidential vote (Lopez and Taylor 2009). The most significant factor in this diversity was reflected in the fact that white Americans comprised only 76.3 percent of the 2008 presidential electorate. This sizeable percentage sounds impressive at first blush, but not when one considers that the size of the white voter base stood at 84.9 percent in the 1988 election. On a quadrennial basis, the white voter base in presidential elections has shown a small, but steadily increasing decline over the past two decades. By the 2000 presidential elections, the white percentage was down to 80.7 percent, and had decreased to 79.2 in 2004. A pattern of quadrennial increases has occurred in this same time period in the percentages of African American and Hispanic voters. The African American and Hispanic voter bases stood at 9.8 percent and 3.6 percent respectively in 1988; 11.5 percent and 5.4 percent respectively in 2000; and had reached 12.1 percent and 7.4 percent respectively in the 2008 presidential election (Lopez and Taylor). This broad based structural and demographic change in the U.S. population and electorate greatly facilitated the success of a deracialized political strategy by a black presidential candidate.

The second significant thread of change is similarly tied to broad based structural and demographic change in the U.S. population resulting in an overall increase in number of minorities in America. Minorities, mainly Hispanics, African Americans, and Asians, now comprise approximately 36 percent of the total U.S. population. Demographers found that there has occurred "an absolute decline in white young people under 18 in the past decade, and a somewhat smaller decline in black youths; and that

Hispanics, Asians and to a lesser degree multiracial children accounted for all of the net growth in the nation's under-18 population growth. William Frey concluded that this development is perhaps more telling about the nation's future—socially, economically, and politically—than any other statistic (Frey 2011a). Other key findings of demographic change from the 2010 Census include the following:

- The first decade of the twenty-first century represents a clear break from the twentieth as the U.S. transitions from a largely white/black nation experiencing robust population growth, to one that juxtaposes an aging white population, growing new minority populations, and a sharply altered geography for Blacks (Frey 2011a).
- Of the 27.3 million added to the U.S. population between 2000 and 2010, only 2.3 million were non-Hispanic whites, representing about 9 percent of the total growth. This compares with a 20 percent contribution in the 1990s, and far higher contributions in earlier decades. Hispanics accounted for well over half of all gains, while Asians made the next biggest contribution (Frey 2011a).
- The "X factor" of new minority growth looms large locally as well as nationally. Among the 49 states with growing populations, the combination of Hispanics, Asians, and members of smaller new minorities accounted for all or most of the growth in 33 of these states. These include traditional melting-pot states such as Florida, Texas, and California, as well as whiter, slow growing states such as Ohio, Pennsylvania, Iowa, and Nebraska. States in the latter category depend especially on new minority growth for their demographic survival (Frey 2011a).
- Blacks have increased their presence in the South. About 75 percent of the country's black population growth last decade took place in the South, compared with 65 percent in the 1990s (Frey 2011a).
- Hispanics now outnumber Blacks in the U.S. population and represent the largest minority group in major American cities (Frey 2011b).
- Well over half of America's cities are now majority non-white. Primary cities in 58 metropolitan areas were "majority minority" in 2010, up from 43 in 2000 (Frey 2011b).
- Minorities represent 35 percent of suburban residents. Among the 100 largest metropolitan areas, 36 feature "melting pot" suburbs where at least 35 percent of residents are non-white. The suburbs of Houston, Las Vegas, San Francisco, and Washington, D.C. became majority minority in the 2000s (Frey 2011b).
- More than half of all minority groups who live in large metropolitan areas, including Blacks, now reside in the suburbs. The share of Blacks in large metropolitan areas living in suburbs rose from 37 percent in 1990, to 44 percent in 2000, to 51 percent in 2010 (Frey 2011b).
- There was a "black flight" of sorts from big cities with high concentrations of Blacks in the past decade. The number of blacks declined in 19 of the 30 biggest cities with the largest black concentrations. The losses were steepest in the largest northern black magnets of the past, Detroit and Chicago, but also occurred in southern cities like Atlanta, Dallas, and Houston (Frey 2011a).
- Black residential segregation declined in fully 92 of the 100 largest metropolitan areas over the past decade (Frey 2011a).

These findings are perhaps the strongest portents of change in the nature of black politics that have developed since the start of the great black migration north in the late 1920s. The foundations for many black electoral successes in northern cities that were laid by that great demographic shift are now being undone by a return of Blacks to the South—which actually began around 1968, and by a major dispersion of Blacks to the suburbs. A corresponding growth of whites in central cities due to gentrification and black displacement will combine with major additions of Hispanics and other minorities to render central cities newly contested territories in a manner different from a context of longstanding black-white divisions. How these new patterns of demographic change will manifest in political and electoral change is not easy to predict. And, analysts will be better able to gauge the implications of demographic changes once more refined levels of analysis have been completed. However, some conjectures are suggested by the available demographic highlights. For example, it is likely that the "old black politics of place" will be substantially altered. We might expect that the major shift in the black population to the southern states will result in an overall diminution of black political clout. The black population in the South has always tended to be more spatially dispersed than in northern states. This has resulted in a heightened underrepresentation of the southern black population. We might also expect that a new demographic mix of African Americans, Hispanics, and other minorities in northern cities will make for a new form of coalition-based, progressive urban politics. Similarly, the growing diversity in close-in suburbs might make for an increase in minority-dominated congressional districts that are proximate to central cities in some parts of the country, perhaps resulting in increased minority representation in the U.S. Congress. And so on. A point that seems certain is that political change is on the way. Of course, the greatest consequence of the ongoing demographic change in America seems to be the growing realization that the zenith of black politics as a social and political movement turned out to have been an all too fleeting moment in history.

References

Frey, William H. 2011a. *A Pivotal Decade For America's White and Minority Populations*. Brookings Institution, Washington, D.C.: State of Metropolitan America. Number 28.

Frey, William H. 2011b. *Melting Pot Cities and Suburbs: Racial and Ethnic Change in Metro America in the 2000s*. Brookings Institution, Washington, D.C.: State of Metropolitan America. Number 31.

Lopez, Mark H. and Paul Taylor. 2009. *Dissecting the 2008 Electorate: Most Diverse in U.S. History*. Pew Research Center, Washington, D.C.: (April 30, 2009).

Epilogue
Into the Future: African American Politics in the Post-Obama Era

Georgia A. Persons

What will African American politics look like in the era following the two-term presidency of Barack Obama? Does the Obama presidency in some ways represent"a normalization"of black politics? While there are no easy answers to these questions, the raising of them serves to remind us of the quite unpredictable nature of social and political change in America of which African American politics is a part.

We are to be reminded that the legacy conception of African American politics that developed well before the civil rights movement and was carried over in the shift to electoral politics strategies was that of a politics of low resources; defined by an insurgent, black-liberationist thrust; bounded by the restrictions and opportunities of relatively small and spatially concentrated primary support bases of black voters; and limited by the persistent resistance of most white voters to supporting black candidates. Against this backdrop emerged the presumption and reality of black electoral gains as being disproportionately restricted to areas characterized by a critical mass of black voters, and the subsequent inability of black candidates to be successful in statewide electoral contests in all but a handful of cases. It was widely assumed that the aspirations of black candidates for national office were just dreams. Analysts of African American politics had arrived at a conventional wisdom that conceded a virtual cap on both the possible number of black elected officials and the level of elective office to which they could ascend.

Some deracialized political strategies seemed to offer better prospects for more black politicians to be able to break out of a dependency on a concentrated black voter base and to be successful in electoral contests in majority-white districts. However, it was widely assumed that the number of fully successful deracialized political strategies would be both small and episodic in their occurrences. It was expected that the nuanced variations across deracialized campaign strategies would provide interesting grist for researchers and journalists, but not many seasoned observers expected victories by many of the black candidates. Such was the prevailing conventional wisdom that also rested on the assumption of a mainly linear progression in blacks winning elective office—that there would be some expansion over the years of blacks winning in statewide office; then perhaps the appearance of a black candidate in the vice presidential spot on the Democratic Party presidential ticket. In short, the future of deracialization seemed to suggest a trajectory of limited change, followed by an almost certain containment as the presumed limits of deracialization were realized.

Yet, in the fall of 2006, some half dozen black candidates contended for statewide office. A full spate of black candidates pursuing statewide office was seen as evidence of something new, perhaps the emergence of a new structure of ambition in African American politics. In the fall of 2008, the prospects of Barack Obama obtaining the Democratic nomination for president provoked even greater reflection on the possibly enhanced electoral prospects for candidates pursuing deracialized strategies. As Robert Smith noted, perhaps some black politicians, Patrick Deval (Massachusetts) and Barack Obama among them, had concluded that growing portions of the white electorate in the twenty-first century were willing to vote for "an ideologically and culturally mainstream black candidate for any office" (Robert C. Smith, symposium editor, Volume 12, *National Political Science Review*).

The two complimentary strands of thought—that apparently more and more black politicians were seeing the possibility of electoral opportunity in pursuing deracialized campaigns, and that possibly a growing number of white voters were prepared to vote for mainstream black candidates— framed a critical set of questions about the future of African American politics. Some questions were immediately suggested: What would future black politics look like? Would black politics become just another variant of American politics—a general politics practiced by candidates who "happened to be black"? What would be the fate of "the Black Agenda" in the context of a fully deracialized black politics? Did the election of Barack Obama as president in 2008 and his re-election in 2012 portend a fully deracialized black politics going into the future?

Experiencing the Obama Presidency as African American Politics

The 2008 election of Barack Obama as president of the United States represented a tremendous milestone and achievement in the unfolding history of the American experience. In particular, the Obama election represented an almost indescribable special achievement for African Americans. Indeed, mere words are insufficient for explaining the range and depths of sentiments experienced by African Americans, and by many white Americans as well. While Barack Obama might have run a fully deracialized campaign for the presidency, among African Americans his victory was considered "an achievement for the race." In terms of political analyses, within the context of any range or mix of politics and strategy, the Obama election completely upstaged everything else about African American politics.

The Obama election also confounded thinking about black politics. What might black politics be now with the election of a black president? What might it mean for the activities and dynamics of black politics to have a black man in the presidency? What might come next for black politics once the Obama presidency has ended? America had elected a black president, but what exactly did that signal about the prospects for deep change for Black America? What did the twice election of Barack Obama to the presidency mean for "The Black Agenda," that both specific and unspecified set of social and economic conditions and associated policy questions that had long served to define and energize the black struggle? These are the questions that have persisted into a second Obama presidential term, and these questions will extend beyond President Obama's time in office. The twice election of Barack Obama to the presidency has possibly significantly redefined African American politics, but in ways that are not readily yet discernible.

It is very important to state the obvious in regard to the context of the times in which Barack Obama served as president. President Obama did not occupy the presidency during a time of steady-state political and economic affairs in America. Rather his first term was characterized by deep economic upheavals that had been surpassed only by the Great Depression of 1929-1934. The Great Recession of 2007-2010 not only challenged and disrupted the usual and prevailing patterns of assumptions about the distribution of economic opportunities and rewards, but also ushered in significant losses of income and wealth for millions of Americans. Disproportionately affected by these economic losses were African Americans and other minorities. Such inhospitable economic conditions as those that defined the Obama presidential years have constrained the political imagination from which far-reaching policy innovations might have sprung. The need to wind down two wars while recharging a war on terror, and a generally hostile body of GOP members of Congress further constrained the political environment within which President Obama attempted to govern. To be sure, President Obama had little opportunity to launch a robust domestic policy agenda, even if he had held a desire to do so.

President Obama clearly did not advocate any components of what might be labeled as race-specific issues. He rarely, if ever, spoke about the poor in America in a way that suggested that their particular fate was an area of policy priority. Rather, President Obama might well be remembered as a president who worked hard to restore the unraveled fortunes of America's middle class—perhaps due to his personal conviction that their restored status was central to restoring and preserving the long-term strength of the American economy.

However, African Americans and poor Americans of every race and ethnic identity stand to substantially benefit from two major Obama domestic policy priorities: expanding access to affordable health care, and improving elementary- and secondary-level public education. Indeed, one might read into these two critical policy initiatives the core thrust of what might be called the policy philosophy of deracialized politics: that black candidates should seek to build coalitions around progressive, race-neutral policies that would especially benefit more disadvantaged groups while avoiding the label of being race-specific policies. In both 2008 and 2012, candidate Obama was able to assemble a winning coalition with a race-neutral policy agenda. In both elections, Obama won majorities of the African American and Hispanic votes along with a critical component, but less than a majority, of the white vote. In many ways, the Obama presidential elections represented the apotheosis of deracialization.

Post-Obama African American Politics

While it is immensely interesting to raise the question of what will African American politics look like in a post-Obama era, there is no easy way to develop an answer to this question. It is not easy to speculate about the political posture of future black candidates for political office, nor about the general direction of progressive and leftist politics in America that might help to determine the thrust and context of a post-Obama black politics. Perhaps it is easier to contemplate the future of black politics by way of reflecting on some major aspects of the broader social and political context that define the ways in which African Americans experience life in America. Thus, post-Obama, there will still be "a Black America." The concept of Black America will continue to connote a large population group that is disproportionately disadvantaged across a broad array of social and economic indicators of well-being. Race will continue to be a factor in assigning advantage and disadvantage, for American society will not yet have evolved beyond the contradictory evolutionary phase wherein the declining significance of race is in many ways accompanied by the persistent legacy of race as a structural determinant of opportunity and achievement.

The contradictory unevenness of racial and social change in America served as a poignant canvas against which an oft-times magisterial President Obama presided. Developments such as increases in the rate of black-on-black violent crimes in the president's hometown of Chicago seemed the equivalent of the eruption of long festering sores of poverty, drugs, broken families, unemployed black males, alongside hardworking residents stuck in blighted neighborhoods—all seemingly consigned to a kind of never ending hopelessness that prevails just beyond the reach of policy remedies.

The formal bankruptcy of the city of Detroit—the largest municipal bankruptcy in the nation's history—shortly after President Obama's election to a second term and the concomitantly disproportionate entrapment of black residents and black public employees in that city were particularly brutal manifestations of the lost fortunes of some once-promising black-mayor cities of the zenith phase of the new black politics. President Obama's rescue of the American economy after the Great Recession of 2007-2010 included the bailout of the U.S. auto industry ($80 billion in federal loans to General Motors and Chrysler Group) around which Detroit had once flourished, but the auto bailout did not save the city of Detroit from bankruptcy. In a most jarring way, the black predicaments in Chicago and Detroit point to the limits of political change as it has unfolded in America.

What comes after President Obama in terms of African American politics? African American politics as we currently speak, think, and write about it developed out of and responded to a context of bi-polar racial politics that was characterized by white racial oppression. Much has changed from the early days of Marcus Garvey, Frederick Douglas, Booker T. Washington, W. E. B. Du Bois, Martin Luther King, Jr., Stokely Carmichael, Whitney Young, Dorothy Height, and other black activists whose organizing and leadership roles preceded the shift to electoral strategies. The nearly 10,000 black officials who in 2013 held elective offices are actualizing the dreams of the civil rights movement and manifesting the benefits of one of its singular policy achievements, the now challenged Voting Rights Act of 1965. A Congressional Black Caucus that has grown to a relatively robust size of forty-three members in its forty-two year existence now enjoys the dubious distinction of having its members lobbied by the full range of corporate lobbyists who seek policy favor and support on Capitol Hill.

Much has changed. Yet race and racism remain a stunting twin-problem while many of its blunt-force manifestations have lessened and evolved into a more multifaceted and systemic resistance to full black incorporation into the myriad manifestations of advancement and advantage that characterize modern American life. How do African Americans effectively develop a politics that addresses the problems associated with newer, less blatant manifestations of racism? How do we effectively develop a politics that addresses the seemingly entrenched status of the truly disadvantaged in America among whose ranks African Americans are disproportionately trapped? The answers to these questions will greatly determine what comes after President Obama in terms of defining African American Politics.

Whether the Obama presidency has redefined African American politics, or whether the Obama presidency will prove to have been "a thing apart" from African American politics is a set of questions that future analysts will no doubt debate. What does seem certain about the future is that it does not hold much promise for a return to a particularly racialized form of African American politics. America is an increasingly multicultural society, with a broad dispersion of Hispanics, Asians, and other minorities even to the smallest hamlets across the country. This means that electoral contests generally, and particularly those involving black candidates, will increasingly take place in election districts that are no longer populated along purely racial lines. This demographic change has already occurred in ways that have shifted the gravitational pull of politics in many formerly black strongholds. Another significant demographic shift is occurring with the dispersion of the African American populations out of the very dense residential concentrations that originally formed the bedrock of many black electoral successes. A more spatially dispersed African American population may well reap more social, economic, and overall quality-of-life benefits from society, but the contradictory accompaniment to these benefits might well be a diminution in the number of African American elected officials.

Into the Future: African American Politics, Scholarship, and Praxis

Just as members of the National Conference of Black Political Scientists in the past have played pivotal roles in defining the issues and structuring the terms of political debate and scholarly discourse around African American politics, it is easy to anticipate such critical involvement from future generations of black scholars and scholar-practitioners. As the year 2013 draws to a close and the final volume of this three-volume anthology is readied for press, we can look back and think in terms of at least three generations of contemporary scholars and scholar-practitioners of African American politics. This author counts herself as being a member of the third generation of black scholars of African American politics. A torch is being passed as the third generation of scholars and scholar-practitioners of African American politics increasingly moves toward retirement. In Volume II of this anthology, we wrote about the emergence of"a black political science"(as conceptualized and practiced by some black political scientists) as a distinct part of the evolutionary focus on black political struggle and, in part as a manifestation of a racially defined struggle internal to the larger discipline of political science. In reflecting on the legacy to date of the National Conference of Black Political Scientists, and in anticipating the future of African American politics, it is useful to attempt to imagine the scholarly and praxis contexts within which the continuing"black predicament"might most effectively be studied and addressed.

Heading into the future, there are some recommendations that seem critical to a viable and impactful future for individual scholars and scholar-practitioners of African American politics, and for the National Conference of Black Political Scientists as a professional association. These recommendations are offered with great humility. The National Conference of Black Political Scientists must resist the tendency to devolve into a large African American Politics caucus or study group. It must both cultivate and embrace deep foci on the varied components of the larger political science discipline that help to inform remedies to the core concerns of Black America. African American political scientists should engage in more collaborative research efforts, both as a means of increasing individual productivity and as a means of leveraging the impact of the work of African American scholars. Just as in many other scholarly disciplines, the era of "the single greatest researcher" has likely passed. More collaborative research alliances should seek to be developed across gender lines. African American political scientists must seek to embrace a more multidisciplinary approach to scholarly inquiry, thereby more effectively probing the broader issues which challenge American society and which significantly structure the black predicament. This will mean embracing inquiry across domains such as demography, technology and social change, public health, economics, public finance, public policy, and public management among others. Indeed from a more multidisciplinary perspective, the future of both the study and praxis of African American politics seems pregnant with great promise.

CPSIA information can be obtained at www.ICGtesting.com
Printed in the USA
BVOW06s0542030214

343720BV00004B/6/P